D0872246

POLITICAL LEADERS IN BLACK AFRICA

This book is dedicated to my wife Gill

Political Leaders in Black Africa

A Biographical Dictionary of the Major Politicians since Independence

AAW- 4811

John A. Wiseman

Edward Elgar

Published by
Edward Elgar Publishing Limited
Gower House
Croft Road
Aldershot
Hants GU11 3HR
England

Edward Elgar Publishing Company
Old Post Road
Brookfield
Vermont 05036
USA

British Library Cataloguing in Publication Data
Wiseman, John A.
    Political leaders in black Africa: a biographical
dictionary of the major politicians since independence.
    1. Africa. Government
    I. Title
    351.0031309226

Library of Congress Cataloguing in Publication Data
Wiseman, John A.
    Political leaders in black Africa: a biographical dictionary of
the major politicians since independence/John A. Wiseman
        p.   cm.
    Includes index.
    1. Politicians–Africa, Sub-Saharan–Biography–Dictionaries.
2. Statesmen–Africa, Sub-Saharan–Biography–Dictionaries.
3. Africa, Sub-Saharan–Biography–Dictionaries.   4. Africa, Sub
-Saharan–Politics and government–1960– –Dictionaries.   I. Title.
DT352.8.W57   1991
967.03'2'0922–dc20   91–3753
    [B]   CIP

ISBN 1 85278 047 9

Printed in Great Britain by
Billing & Sons Ltd, Worcester

Contents

Preface

In recent years there has been an increasing recognition of the fact that individual political leaders are important and cannot merely be seen as corks bobbing about on an uncontrollable sea of social and economic forces. Individuals make decisions from a range of options, each of which would allow for different decisions to be made. Whilst the choice of decision is necessarily constrained by other factors it is not predetermined. These decisions have consequences and if the individual making them is powerful and influential these consequences will make an impact on the political process and on the wider society. This is especially true in the states of black Africa where weak institutionalization has tended to produce a situation in which individual leaders, of very varying types, have exercised a degree of political influence which would be more difficult to obtain in more established systems. For good or ill the individual leaders presented in this book have played, and in many cases continue to play, a vital role in shaping the destinies of their nations.

If one were to ask any number of observers of Africa each to compose a list of those they believed to be the most important political leaders in the post-independence period it is inevitable that no two lists would be the same. No doubt a degree of overlap would occur because of the uncontestable importance of certain individuals, but beyond that there would be considerable variation resulting from personal judgement. Certainly I have found that decisions on whom to include and whom to exclude have been extraordinarily difficult in many cases. I have no doubt that some readers of this volume would be able to put forward good arguments for the inclusion of some I have excluded and for the exclusion of some who are here. Perhaps most would agree with most of the decisions and I do not think I can ask for more than that.

One of the major sets of factors in determining the number of entries for each state has been the size, complexity and importance of the state. Because Nigeria and South Africa are the most populous, the most complex and the most important states of black Africa they have the greatest number of entries. There are, however, other criteria. In some states a single leader has dominated the political system for all or most of the post-independence period to such an extent that it is difficult to see beyond him. In such cases other members of government and political elites may be rather marginalized in terms of real power and largely dependent on the patronage of the top man. In other states the situation has been quite different. Where the political system is highly pluralized it has frequently thrown up considerable numbers of important leaders, none of whom has been able to establish domination. Alternatively some political systems have exhibited a rapid turnover of political leaders who have exercised a very ephemeral domination. Because I am dealing with such a large number of very different states there is no single easy criterion for inclusion. Most leaders have or have had an important position in government, but this is not a prerequisite: if it were, all black South Africans, for example, would be excluded. Most of those included would describe themselves as politicians but I have added a small number of writers, clerics and trade unionists who might not be politicians in the narrow sense of the term but who have exercised an influence on politics. Nobody with any knowledge of post-independence Africa will be surprised to find a large number of military men included.

As most African states became independent within a few years of each other comparability for inclusion presents few problems. Where states were independent markedly earlier (for example, Ethiopia, Liberia and South Africa) or markedly later (for example, Namibia and Zimbabwe) I have still used a date of around 1960 to work from. I have taken 'black' Africa to mean the same as sub-Saharan Africa and, following conventional academic distinctions, have not included the Arab states of North Africa, although I have included Sudan and Mauritania, which enjoy an ambiguous categorization between the two groups of states. The island states of Africa (for example, Mauritius, Madagascar and Seychelles) have all been included.

One inescapable fact concerning the individuals in this volume is that the overwhelmingly majority are male, but I do not believe that this represents a sexist approach on my part. Indeed I have even operated a little positive discrimination by including women political leaders wherever it was feasible to do so. The problem is that there have been very few women political leaders in Africa and none at the very top level. Black Africa has yet to produce an Indira Gandhi, Benazir Bhutto or Margaret Thatcher and the predominance of men in this volume reflects the reality of African politics rather than the bias of the author.

A brief note on orthography is in order. It is not uncommon to find considerable variation in the spelling of African names in the literature. This is especially so in the case of Muslim Africans where transliteration of Arabic names is often involved. Where there are several alternative spellings I have chosen to use the one which is used in the official documentation of the state involved. In cases where even this source produces inconsistencies I have simply opted for what appears to be the most commonly used version.

Whilst I have made every effort to ensure that the biographical facts presented are accurate it has to be recognized that they may sometimes, but I think not too often, be more approximate than they appear. Even a basic piece of information like the date of birth of the individual may be unknown or contentious or, in some cases, a state secret. All of Africa's post-independence political leaders were born in the colonial period. It is likely, especially if they were born and raised in the rural areas, that there simply are no written records of their early life. Even if records were kept the deterioration of the archival resources in most African states, due both to climate and poverty (and, sometimes, wilful neglect), makes retrieval of information a chancy business. In an extreme case, President Ali Soilih of the Comoros Republic ordered the burning of all government records and archives in 1977.

In collecting the material for this book I decided to write to the representatives of the government of every state to be included. The results of this endeavour proved rather disappointing as only seven replied and some of those could only say that they had no information on their leaders. However I should like to thank the representatives of the governments of Chad, Gabon, Mauritius, Rwanda, Swaziland, Uganda and Zambia, some of whom were very helpful (I am at a loss to see a common link between these seven). I am grateful to my colleague Rod Hague for introducing me to that invaluable, but at times vindictive, piece of modern technology, the word processor. Edward Elgar has been an exemplary publisher to work with, providing full and useful answers to all my queries by return of post (an unknown experience for most authors). At the editing stage Julie Leppard was both sensitive and thorough and I owe her my gratitude. Finally I should like to thank my wife and children for the forbearance they have shown while I have been working on this book and for the day-to-day encouragement they provided.

I would like to conclude on a somewhat sombre note. Working through several hundred individual cases has provided constant reminders of just how hazardous and insecure a business it is to be a political leader in Africa. Although there are a small number of states which provide welcome exceptions to the general rule it is true that in a distressingly large majority of states the incidence of political killing of leaders is high. The number of times I have typed in words like 'executed', 'assassinated' or 'murdered' has brought this home to me very forcibly. In addition to this there are large numbers of leaders who have spent long periods in exile or in prison. Much of this change from high government office to firing squad or jail (and sometimes back again for the latter) appears to exhibit a surprisingly random quality. In Africa to be a political leader is to follow a very dangerous occupation. It is my hope that this feature of African politics will diminish in the future and that the natural tensions and conflicts of political life will produce less tragic consequences for those involved.

John A. Wiseman
University of Newcastle-upon-Tyne

Alphabetical List of Entries

286 Alphonse MASSAMBA-DEBAT, *Congo*
287 Robert Stanley MATANO, *Kenya*
288 Philip Parcel Goanwe MATANTE, *Botswana*
289 George Mzimvube MATANZIMA, *South Africa (Transkei)*
290 Dick Tennyson MATENJE, *Malawi*
291 Gabriel Baccus MATTHEWS, *Liberia*
292 Leon M'BA, *Gabon*
293 Serigne Abdoul Ahad M'BACKE, *Senegal*
294 Govan Archibald Mvuyelwa MBEKI, *South Africa*
295 Thabo Mvuyelwa MBEKI, *South Africa*
296 Amadou Mokhtar M'BOW, *Senegal*
297 Thomas Joseph MBOYA, *Kenya*
298 Antoine Idrissou MEATCHI, *Togo*
299 Leon MEBIAME, *Gabon*
300 MENGISTU Haile Mariam, *Ethiopia*
301 Michel MICOMBERO, *Burundi*
302 Francis Misheck MINAH, *Sierra Leone*
303 Saydi MINGAS, *Angola*
304 Idriss MISKINE, *Chad*
305 Peter Simako MMUSI, *Botswana*
306 MOBUTU Sese Seko Kuku Ngbendu Wa Za Banga, *Zaire*
307 Daniel Torotich Arap MOI, *Kenya*
308 Ntsu MOKHEHLE, *Lesotho*
309 Charles Dube MOLAPO, *Lesotho*
310 Joseph Saidu MOMOH, *Sierra Leone*
311 Eduardo Chivambo MONDLANE, *Mozambique*
312 Suresh MOORBA, *Mauritius*
313 King MOSHOESHOE the Second, *Lesotho*
314 Zephania Lekoane MOTHOPENG, *South Africa*
315 Jason Ziyaphapha MOYO, *Zimbabwe*
316 Attati MPAKATI, *Malawi*
317 Keyecwe Motsamai MPHO, *Botswana*
318 MPINGA Kasenda, *Zaire*
319 Cleopa David MSUYA, *Tanzania*
320 King MSWATI the Third, *Swaziland*
321 Robert Gabriel MUGABE, *Zimbabwe*
322 Murtala Ramat MUHAMMED, *Nigeria*
323 Solomon Tandeng MUNA, *Cameroon*
324 Nalumino MUNDIA, *Zambia*
325 Abubakar Balarabe MUSA, *Nigeria*
326 Yoweri Kaguta MUSEVENI, *Uganda*
327 Kebby Sililo Kambulu MUSOKOTWANE, *Zambia*
328 Didymus MUTASA, *Zimbabwe*
329 King MUTESA the Second, *Uganda*
330 Paulo MUWANGA, *Uganda*
331 Simon Vengai MUZENDA, *Zimbabwe*
332 Abel Tendekayi MUZOREWA, *Zimbabwe*
333 Ali Hassan MWINYI, *Tanzania*

334 Stephen NAIDOO, *South Africa*
335 Lassimiau (Raymond) NAIMBAYE, *Chad*
336 Claude NDALLA, *Congo*
337 Atanasio NDONGO Miyone, *Equatorial Guinea*
338 Agostinho Antonio NETO, *Angola*
339 Pierre NGENDANDUMWE, *Burundi*
340 Lamin NGOBEH, *Sierra Leone*
341 Marien NGOUABI, *Congo*
342 NGUZA Karl I Bond, *Zaire*
343 Babacar NIANG, *Senegal*
344 Moustapha NIASSE, *Senegal*
345 Pierre Sarr N'JIE, *The Gambia*
346 Charles NJONJO, *Kenya*
347 Enos Mzombi NKALA, *Zimbabwe*
348 Joshua Mqabuko NKOMO, *Zimbabwe*
349 Kwame Francis Nwia Kofie NKRUMAH, *Ghana*
350 Harry Mwaanga NKUMBULA, *Zambia*
351 King NTARE the Fifth (Charles NDIZEYE), *Burundi*
352 Sam Daniel NUJOMA, *Namibia*
353 Jafar Muhammed NUMEIRI, *Sudan*
354 Akwekwe Abyssinia NWAFOR-ORIZU, *Nigeria*
355 Simon Sishayi NXUMALO, *Swaziland*
356 Maurice Tapfumaneyi NYAGUMBO, *Zimbabwe*

Abbreviations and Acronyms

ACDL	Association for Constitutional Democracy in Liberia	BPC	Black People's Convention
ACP	Action Congress Party	BPP	Bechuanaland (later Botswana) People's Party
AFRC	Armed Forces Revolutionary Council	BPS	Senegalese Popular Bloc
AG	Action Group	CAF	Central African Federation
AJ-MRDN	And-Jef Revolutionary Movement for a New Democracy	CAR	Central African Republic
		CAZ	Conservative Alliance of Zimbabwe
ANC	African National Congress	CCM	Party of the Revolution
	African National Council (Zimbabwe)	CDC	Constitution Drafting Committee
ANYL	African National Youth League	CDR	Committees for the Defence of the Revolution
AP	Ashigga Party	CIA	Central Intelligence Agency
APC	All People's Congress		
AREMA	Vanguard of the Malagasy Revolution	CMRN	Military Committee of National Redress
ASP	Afro-Shirazi Party	CNIP	Ciskei National Independence Party
AWB	Afrikaner Resistance Movement	CNLGE	National Crusade for the Liberation of Equatorial Guinea
BCM	Black Consciousness Movement		
BCP	Basutoland Congress Party	CNR	National Council of the Revolution
BDA	Basotho Democratic Alliance	CONAKAT	Confederation of Associations of Katanga
BDP	Bophuthatswana Democratic Party	CONCP	Conference of Nationalist Organizations of the Portuguese Colonies
	Botswana Democratic Party	COSATU	Congress of South African Trade Unions
BDS	Democratic Bloc of Senegal	CP	Conservative Party
BFP	Basutoland Freedom Party	CPDM	Cameroon People's Democratic Movement
BIP	Botswana Independence Party	CPP	Convention People's Party
BMS	Bloc of the Senegalese Masses	CUT	Committee of Togolese Unity
BNF	Botswana National Front	DCA	Democratic Congress Alliance
BNP	Basutoland National Party	DP	Democratic Party

DTA	Democratic Turnhalle Alliance	KNDP	Kamerun National Democratic Party
FAN	Armed Forces of the North	KPU	Kenya People's Union
		KY	Kabaka Yekka
FEDECO	Federal Electoral Commission	LAP	Liberia Action Party
		LESOMA	Socialist League of Malawi
FEDSAW	Federation of South African Women		
		LLA	Lesotho Liberation Army
FESTAC	Festival of Arts and Culture	LPAI	African People's League for Independence
FNLA	National Front for the Liberation of Angola	LPP	Liberian People's Party
		LPSA	Labour Party of South Africa
FNS	National Front of Senegal		
		MAC	Casamance Autonomous Movement
FRELIMO	Front for the Liberation of Mozambique		
		MAFREMO	Malawi Freedom Movement
FROLIZI	Front for the Liberation of Zimbabwe		
		MCP	Malawi Congress Party
FRONILAT	Front for the National Liberation of Chad		Muslim Congress Party
		MDP	Popular Democratic Movement
GDB	Gabonese Democratic Bloc		
		MDV	Democratic Voltaic Movement
GDP	Gabonese Democratic Party		
		MFP	Marema-Tlou Freedom Party
GNPP	Greater Nigerian People's Party		
		MLP	Mauritius Labour Party
GPP	Gambia People's Party	MLSTP	Movement for the Liberation of Sao Tome and Principe
GUNT	Transitional National Union Government		
HNP	Herstigte Nasionale Party	MMM	Mouvement Militant Mauricien
ICFTU	International Confederation of Free Trade Unions		
		MNC	Congolese National Movement
IDASA	Institute for a Democratic Alternative for South Africa	MNR	National Movement for the Revolution
IFB	Independent Forward Bloc	MNRCS	National Movement for Cultural and Social Revolution
IMF	International Monetary Fund		
		MNSD	National Movement for a Development Society
INM	Imbokodvo National Movement		
		MOJA	Movement for Justice in Africa
IP	Independent Party		
IPGE	Popular Idea of Equatorial Guinea	MORENA	National Movement for Redress
ITT	International Telephone and Telegraph	MPD	Movement For Democracy
KADU	Kenya African Democratic Union	MPEA	Mouvement Populaire de l'Evolution Africaine
KANU	Kenya African National Union	MPLA	Popular Movement for the Liberation of Angola
KAU	Kenya African Union	MPLA-PT	MPLA Workers' Party

MPR	Popular Movement of the Revolution	NUP	National Unionist Party
MRND	Revolutionary National Movement for Development	OAU	Organization of African Unity
MSM	Mouvement Socialiste Mauricien	OPO	Ovamboland People's Organization
MUNGE	Movement for the National Unity of Equatorial Guinea	PAC	Pan-Africanist Congress
		PAI	Party for African Independence
NAC	Nyasaland African Congress	PAICV	African Party for the Independence of Cape Verde
NAL	National Association of Liberals	PAIGC	African Party for the Independence of Guinea and Cape Verde
NAP	National Alliance Party	PAL	Progressive Alliance of Liberia
NCNC	National Council of Nigeria and the Cameroons	PARMEHUTU	Party of the Movement for Hutu Emancipation
NCP	National Convention Party	PCD	Democratic Convergence Party
NDM	New Democratic Movement	PCT	Congolese Labour Party
		PDC	People's Defence Committee
NDP	National Democratic Party	PDCI	Democratic Party of the Ivory Coast
NDPL	National Democratic Party of Liberia	PDG	Democratic Party of Guinea
NLC	National Liberation Council	PDGE	Democratic Party of Equatorial Guinea
NLM	National Liberation Movement	PDS	Senegalese Democratic Party
NNDP	Nigerian National Democratic Party	PDU	United Party of Dahomey
NNLC	Ngwane National Liberatory Congress	PF	Patriotic Front
		PFP	Popular Front Party (Ghana)
NP	National Party		Progressive Federal Party (South Africa)
NPC	Northern People's Congress		
NPN	National Party of Nigeria	PLP	Party for the Liberation of the People
NPP	Nigerian People's Party		
NRA	National Resistance Army	PM	Parti Mauricien
		PMSD	Parti Mauricien Social-Démocrate
NRC	National Reformation Council (Sierra Leone) National Resistance Council (Uganda)	PMU	Police Mobile Unit
		PNDC	Provisional National Defence Council
NSO	National Security Organization	PNP	People's National Party (Ghana, Sierra Leone)
NUDO	National Unity Democratic Organization	POLISARIO	Popular Front for the Liberation of the Spanish Sahara
NUM	National Union of Mineworkers	PP	Progress Party (Ghana)

xxi

PP	Progressive Party (South Africa)	SDP	Seychelles Democratic Party
PPA	People's Progressive Alliance		Social Democratic Party (Madagascar)
PPD	Djibouti People's Party		Swaziland Democratic Party
PPM	Mauritian People's Party		
PPN	Niger Progressive Party	SLOS	Sierra Leone Organization Society
PPP	Protectorate People's Party, later People's Progressive Party (The Gambia)	SLPP	Sierra Leone People's Party
		SMC	Supreme Military Council (Ghana, Nigeria)
	Popular Progressive Party (Mauritius)	SNL	Somali National League
PPS	Senegalese Popular Party	SPLA	Sudan People's Liberation Army
PPT	Chadian Progressive Party	SPLM	Sudan People's Liberation Movement
PRC	People's Redemption Council	SPP	Swaziland Progressive Party
PRP	People's Redemption Party	SPPF	Seychelles People's Progressive Front
PRPB	Benin People's Revolutionary Party	SPUP	Seychelles People's United Party
PS	Socialist Party		
PSM	Parti Socialist Mauricien	SRC	Supreme Revolutionary Council
PSS	Senegalese Socialist Party	SRSP	Somali Revolutionary Socialist Party
PTP	Togolese Progress Party		
RDA	Democratic African Rally	SSLM	South Sudan Liberation Movement
RDC	Central African Democratic Assembly	SSU	Sudan Socialist Union
RENAMO	Mozambique National Resistance	SWAPO	South West Africa People's Organization
RF	Rhodesian (later Republican) Front	SYL	Somali Youth League
		TANU	Tanganyika African National Union
RND	National Democratic Assembly	TFL	Tanganyikan Federation of Labour
RPP	Popular Rally for Progress	TWP	True Whig Party
RPT	Rally of the Togolese People	UANC	United African National Council
SACP	South African Communist Party	UDDIA	Democratic Union for the Defence of African Interests
SADCC	Southern African Development Coordination Conference	UDF	United Democratic Front
		UDI	Unilateral Declaration of Independence
SADF	South African Defence Force	UDPM	Democratic Union of Malian People
SAP	Structural Adjustment Programme	UDPT	Democratic Union of Togolese People
SASO	South African Students' Organization	UDSP	Democratic Union for

	Social Progress
UDV	Democratic Voltaic Union
UFB	Women's Union of Burkina
UGCC	United Gold Coast Convention
UMBC	United Middle Belt Congress
UNC	Cameroon National Union
	Uganda National Congress
	United National Convention (Ghana)
UND	Democratic Union of Niger
UNESCO	United Nations Education, Scientific and Cultural Organization
UNFT	National Union of Togolese Women
UNIGOV	Union Government
UNIP	United National Independence Party
UNITA	National Union for the Total Independence of Angola
UNLA	Uganda National Liberation Army
UNLF	Uganda National Liberation Front
UP	Umma (People's) Party (Tanzania)
	United Party (The Gambia, Ghana, South Africa, Zimbabwe)
	Unity Party (Liberia)
UPA	Union of the Peoples of Angola
UPC	Uganda People's Congress
	Union of Comoran Progress
UPD	Progressive Union of Dahomey
UPLGE	Popular Union for the Liberation of Equatorial Guinea
UPM	Uganda Patriotic Movement
UPN	Unity Party of Nigeria
UPP	United People's Party (Liberia, Nigeria)
	United Progressive Party (Zambia)
UPRONA	Unity for National Progress
UPS	Senegalese Progressive Union
US	Union Soudanaise
WPE	Workers' Party of Ethiopia
ZANLA	Zimbabwe African National Liberation Army
ZANU	Zimbabwe African National Union
ZAPU	Zimbabwe African People's Union
ZDP	Zimbabwe Democratic Party
ZIPRA	Zimbabwe People's Revolutionary Army
ZNC	Zambia National Congress
ZNP	Zanzibar National Party
ZNU	Zanzibar National Union
ZUPO	Zimbabwe United People's Organization
ZUM	Zimbabwe Unity Movement

A

1 Sanni ABACHA

Nigeria

Abacha is a leading figure in the Babangida military regime in Nigeria.

Born in 1943 in Kano State into the Kanuri ethnic group, he joined the army in 1962 and received officer training in Britain. He held a number of senior military posts including director of army training. He was a major participant in the 1983 coup which ended the Second Republic and was the man who made the first announcement of the coup on the radio. In 1985 he was appointed army chief of staff by Babangida following his support for the latter in the ousting of Buhari. He is also a member of the Armed Forces Ruling Council. He retained his positions in the purge of army leadership which took place at the end of 1989.

2 Ibrahim ABATCHA

Chad

Abatcha was the founder of FROLINAT and the leader of armed opposition to the Chadian government in the 1960s.

Born in 1938, he was a militant trade unionist who was jailed by the French for a year before independence and again by President Tombalbaye after independence. From 1963 to 1965 he lived in exile in Sudan, Ghana and Egypt. In 1966 he returned to Chad and succeeded in merging the fragmented opposition groups to form FROLINAT, which began an armed struggle against the Tombalbaye dictatorship. Abatcha was the recognized political leader and field commander of the movement, but had to struggle hard to keep it together. For two years he led guerrilla attacks on the national army in eastern Chad. In March 1968 he was killed in fighting in Abeche and his death provoked a major power struggle within FROLINAT.

3 Ibrahim ABBOUD

Sudan

Abboud was the leader of the first coup in Sudan in 1958 and was prime minister until 1964.

Born in 1900, he joined the army in 1925 and later fought with the British army in North Africa in the second world war. At independence he was commander-in-chief of the armed forces and in 1958 led the first coup in Sudan. He became prime minister and President of the Supreme Council of the Armed Forces. Although he was a skilled military leader he lacked political skill and having lost much of his army support he was finally forced to resign in 1964, following a general strike. He remained in Sudan but went into retirement.

4 Ahmed ABDALLAH

Comoros

Abdallah became president of Comoros at independence in 1975, was ousted in a coup shortly afterwards and returned to power by another coup in 1978. He continued as president until 1989.

1

Born in 1919, he was a successful businessman before entering politics. He was a member of the French Senate from 1957 to 1972. As a nationalist political leader he adopted a strongly pro-independence line. In July 1975 Comoros issued a unilateral declaration of independence from France and he became the first president. One month later he was ousted in a coup led by Ali Soilih. In May 1978 he was reinstated following a mercenary-led coup. Many of the mercenaries participating were the same ones who had been involved in his original ousting. Comoros was declared an Islamic state and in 1979 any opposition to Abdallah's UPC was banned. He continued with a highly authoritarian style of rule but tried to coopt some of his old opponents into the regime. There were several unsuccessful coup attempts, led by mercenaries acting for his unreconciled opponents and defeated by mercenaries employed by Abdallah to keep him in power. In 1989 his own mercenaries turned on him and killed him in an attempt to seize power for themselves.

5   Moshood Kashimawo Olawale ABIOLA

Nigeria

Abiola is a wealthy businessman and press baron who was one of the senior Yorubas in the NPN in the Second Republic.

Born in 1937 in Abeokuta, he was educated locally before going to Glasgow University to study accountancy in 1961. Back in Nigeria he built a very successful business career, which included chairmanship of the International Telephone and Telegraph (ITT), and acquired great wealth. He founded the Concord Press, which became one of the main newspaper publishers in Nigeria. In 1978 he supported the NPN from its foundation and was regarded as one of its most important Yoruba backers. In 1982 he tried to gain the NPN nomination for the presidential election due the following year. When this attempt failed he withdrew from the party and went into political retirement.

6   Siddiq ABUBAKAR

Nigeria

Abubakar was sultan of Sokoto for 50 years, from 1938 until his death in 1988.

Born in 1903 in Sokoto on the day the British forces entered the city to bring an end to resistance to colonial rule, he became the most senior of Nigeria's traditional leaders. He succeeded his uncle, Hassan, in 1938 and as sultan was the spiritual leader of all Nigeria's muslims and the leading Islamic figure in black Africa, enjoying the title 'Sarkin Musulmi' ('Commander of the Faithful'). He was also the leading figure in the political system of the northern Nigerian emirate structure. He used his vast influence to pursue cautious reform, including the extension of education to women. He was knighted by the British following the second world war. In the pre-independence period he was a dominant figure in the Northern House of Chiefs and a minister without portfolio in the regional government. After independence he refused to become involved with party politics in spite of his enormous personal influence. He con-

2

stantly supported political and religious tolerance in a country where tolerance was often in short supply. He died from natural causes in November 1988.

7 Ignatius Kutu ACHEAMPONG

Ghana

Acheampong was military head of state in Ghana from 1972 until he was overthrown by a coup in 1978. He was executed by firing squad the following year.

Born in 1931 in Mwamase, he was educated in Ghana and worked as a teacher before joining the army in 1953. He received military training in Britain and the USA and from 1962 to 1963 was a member of the UN peace-keeping force in the Congo. Although he was not involved in the 1966 coup he was appointed chairman of the administration in the Western Region by the military government. Following the return to civilian rule in 1969 he advanced within the army and in 1971 became commander of the First Infantry Brigade. In 1972 he led the coup which overthrew the Busia regime and became head of state and chairman of the National Redemption Council.

During the early years of his rule an increase in world cocoa prices produced some buoyancy in the Ghanaian economy but later on the economy went into a steep decline which was exacerbated by the corruption and inefficiency of the regime. Acheampong was unwilling to contemplate any move towards demilitarization of the political system and instead proposed a system of Union Government (known locally as UNIGOV) in which some civilians would be brought into the government. This proved widely unpopular and provoked riots and strikes in opposition to it. Although a referendum on the issue claimed a narrow majority in favour, few believed in the authenticity of the result. In July 1978, before UNIGOV could be introduced, a coup led by Akuffo ousted Acheampong.

After a short period in detention he was released and sacked from the army. Following the Rawlings coup in June 1979 Acheampong was tried for corruption and executed by the new regime.

8 Chinua ACHEBE

Nigeria

Achebe is one of Africa's leading literary and academic figures and has played an important role in Nigerian politics.

Born in 1930 in Ogidi into the Ibo ethnic group, he graduated from the University of Ibadan and began a career in radio broadcasting. He is best known as a novelist, having published a series of major novels, from *Things Fall Apart* (1958) to *Anthills of the Savannah* (1987). During the civil war he was a strong supporter of the Biafran cause. After the war he held a number of senior academic posts at universities in Nigeria and abroad. He has been awarded a number of honorary degrees and other prizes by several different countries. In 1988 he joined the PRP, the most radical of the parties of the Second Republic, and became its deputy national president. Although he has never held senior government office, and has never indicated any desire to do so, he has played an important role as a critic of the failings of all governments in Nigeria and as a crusader for integrity in public life.

9   Ahmat ACYL

Chad

Acyl was the leader of one of the major military factions in the Chadian civil war and became foreign minister in the GUNT government in 1979.

Born in 1944, he completed his education in France before returning to Chad in 1966. In that year he was elected to the National Assembly and was an influential member of its foreign affairs committee. In 1971 he joined the revolt against the government of Tombalbaye and established his own powerful guerrilla army, known as the Volcan Force. The latter received considerable support from Libya and Acyl was regarded by his opponents as a Libyan stooge, which was only partly true. In 1979 he used his army to back Goukouni and was rewarded with the foreign affairs portfolio in the latter's coalition GUNT government. When this government was ousted by the forces of Habre, Acyl withdrew to the east of the country to continue his armed opposition. In 1982 he was killed in a bizarre accident when he inadvertently walked into the propeller blades of an aircraft he was boarding as he tried to retrieve a shoe which had fallen from his foot.

10   Tawia ADAMAFIO

Ghana

Adamafio was a leading figure within the government and the CPP in the early Nkrumah period but was later arrested and charged with plotting a coup.

A member of the Ga ethnic group, he worked as a civil servant and journalist before entering politics. Initially he opposed Nkrumah but later joined the latter's CPP and became its general secretary. He was appointed minister of presidential affairs and then minister of information and broadcasting. In the latter role he was responsible for the creation of the personality cult surrounding Nkrumah.

In 1962 he was arrested and charged with plotting a coup but was found not guilty by the courts, much to the annoyance of Nkrumah. The latter ignored the verdict and kept Adamafio in jail. Following the overthrow of Nkrumah in 1966, Adamafio was released. He stayed out of public life until he worked for the Acheampong regime in the 1970s before it was ousted. He retired to write his memoirs, which were published in 1982.

11   Robert Adeyinka ADEBAYO

Nigeria

Adebayo has been a major politician in Nigeria both within the military and as a civilian.

Born in 1928 in Ile-Ife, he was educated locally and in Lagos before joining the army in 1948. He received training in Britain and, from 1961 to 1963, was part of the UN peace-keeping force in the Congo. In 1964 he was appointed army chief of staff and in 1966 became military governor of the Western Region. Following the civil war he was responsible for the reintegration of Biafran soldiers into the Nigerian army and in 1971 was made head of the Defence Academy in Kaduna. In 1975

4

he was one of those compulsorily retired from the army. In 1978 he joined the NPN and as one of its major Yoruba leaders became national vice-chairman of what was to become the ruling party of the Second Republic. In 1989 he founded a major group of Yoruba leaders which was presented as a think-tank with no direct political ambitions.

12   Benjamin Maja Adesanya ADEKUNLE

Nigeria

Adekunle was a major military leader in the civil war and a prominent member of the post-war regime.

Born in 1937 to a Yoruba father and Bachama mother, he was educated locally before joining the army in 1958. He received officer training in Ghana and at Sandhurst in England. In 1962 he was appointed military ADC to the governor of the Eastern Region. After further training in India he became adjutant general of the army in 1965. In 1967 he was appointed brigade commander of Third Marine Commando. He was a major field leader for the federal forces during the civil war and was widely known by his nickname of 'Black Scorpion'. After the war he was appointed director of training and planning for the army and was also given the difficult job of clearing the congestion of the port in Lagos. Following the overthrow of the Gowon regime in 1975, he was retired from the army and became a businessman. During the Second Republic he joined the NPP and later defected to the ruling NPN, but he was not a leading figure in either.

13   Ako ADJEI

Ghana

Adjei was one of the main nationalist leaders in Ghana and a prominent figure in the post-independence government, serving as foreign minister.

Born in 1915 into the Ga ethnic group he was a student in London with Nkrumah. In 1948 he was one of those arrested in Ghana following the riots. He supported Nkrumah in the CPP and, for a time, was politically very close to him. From 1959 to 1962 he was foreign minister but in the latter year he was charged with planning a coup and detained. He remained in detention until the 1966 coup when he was released and retired from politics.

14   Okatakyie Akwasi Amankwa AFRIFA

Ghana

Afrifa was one of the leaders of the coup which overthrew Nkrumah and a senior figure in the ensuing military regime, in which he served as head of state.

Born in Mampong in Ashanti in 1936, he was educated locally and joined the army in 1957. He received officer training at Sandhurst and then served in the UN peace-keeping force in the Congo. In 1966 he was one of the principal leaders of the coup and became a leading figure in the ruling military group, the NLC. In 1969 he became chairman of the NLC, and hence head of state, and was instrumental in the return to civilian rule that year.

He retired from the army and was arrested in 1972 for opposing the Acheampong coup. He was released in

1973 and campaigned for a further return to civilian rule. After the overthrow of Acheampong in 1978, the process of demilitarization began and Afrifa was elected to parliament in 1979. Almost immediately the Rawlings coup took place and Afrifa was arrested and charged with corruption. After a hasty, and rather notional, trial he was executed, along with two other ex-heads of state, Acheampong and Akuffo. The execution of Afrifa can be seen as the least justified of the acts of vengeance by the Rawlings regime against previous military leaders.

15 Johnson Thomas Umunankwe AGUIYI-IRONSI

Nigeria

Ironsi was the first Nigerian military head of state in 1966, before being assassinated.

Born in 1924 into the Ibo ethnic group, he joined the army in 1942. During the Congo crisis he was the African Force commander in the UN peacekeeping operation. In 1965 he became general officer commanding of the Nigerian army. He did not participate in the January 1966 coup but became military head of state as the senior surviving officer. This caused much resentment, especially in the north of the country, as he was from the same ethnic group as those who had staged the coup and, lack of any evidence notwithstanding, many believed his position derived from an Ibo plot. Although he was a skilled military figure he had little political competence. During his short time in office he changed Nigeria from a federal state to a unitary one, which was

seen by some as further proof of an Ibo plot to dominate the country. He was assassinated in the coup of July 1966. His killing was one of the events which led to the civil war.

16 Jean AH CHUEN

Mauritius

Ah Chuen was the leading Mauritian politician from the Chinese community for several decades.

Born in 1911, he was educated locally and became a successful businessman and chairman of the Chinese Chamber of Commerce. He constantly acted as a spokesman for the minority Chinese community in Mauritius. He served on the legislative council from 1948 to 1963 and was also active in local government. In the 1967 pre-independence elections he was elected to parliament as a candidate of the PMSD. Following independence he became minister of local government. He retired from politics in 1976.

17 Ahmadu AHIDJO

Cameroon

Ahidjo was the dominant figure in Cameroonian politics for over two decades, from independence in 1960 until his voluntary retirement from the presidency in 1982.

A Fula Muslim from the north of the country, he was born in 1924. He was educated at Yaounde's Higher Primary School before becoming a radio operator in the post office. He was first elected to the Representative (later Legislative) Assembly in 1947 and by 1957 had become vice-prime minister in the pre-independence government. In 1958 he became prime minister and at independence in 1960 he was elected president. Ahidjo was a strong supporter of the unification of the former British Cameroons with the new Cameroonian republic. In 1961 a referendum was held and the southern part of British Cameroons opted for unification whilst the northern part chose to be part of Nigeria. Cameroon became a federal republic but Ahidjo remained as president of the enlarged state. He then actively supported the idea of moving from a federal state structure to that of a unitary state and finally achieved this in 1972. Although a number of the old Anglophone politicians have been unhappy with what they see as their under-representation in the major positions of power, the unification and centralization of Cameroon was undoubtedly a major achievement by Ahidjo.

Under Ahidjo the country enjoyed a relatively prosperous and stable period, but this was achieved at the cost of increasing authoritarianism and a decline in civil liberties. All opposition was crushed and Ahidjo's UNC became the only legal party. Press censorship and a high level of surveillance by the secret service became common practice. The style of rule became highly personal and paternalistic.

In 1982, Ahidjo resigned the presidency voluntarily. Rumour has it that he was convinced that his health was fading and that he had only a short time to live. He was succeeded as president by the prime minister, Paul Biya, who was Ahidjo's personally chosen successor. The ex-president remained leader of the party at first. To the surprise of many, and the annoyance of Ahidjo, Biya began to assert his new authority and in 1983 replaced his former patron as party leader. Ahidjo went into exile but was associated with a coup plot in 1983 and a coup attempt which nearly succeeded in 1984. He was tried in his absence and sentenced to death, although Biya later commuted this to life imprisonment. Ahidjo remained in exile in France and Senegal, clearly regretting his decision to let go his firm grasp on power. He died in Senegal in 1989.

18   Justin AHOMADEGBE

Benin

During a period of chronic political instability, Ahomadegbe was vice-president, prime minister and, briefly, president. He has been involved in several coups and has spent considerable periods of time in prison.

Born in 1917, he qualified as a dentist in Dakar. In the post-war period he entered politics, emerging as the dominant figure of the south-west amongst the Fon ethnic group. In 1960 he formed a tactical alliance with President Maga and became president of the National Assembly. Within months this alliance broke down and Ahomadegbe was imprisoned. In 1962 he was released and, after Maga's overthrow in 1963, he formed an alliance with President Apithy and became vice-president and prime minister. In 1965 he attempted to oust Apithy, but his failure sparked another coup and he went into exile in Togo and France, where he unsuccessfully plotted several further coups. In 1970 the military leaders invited Ahomadegbe to return and a new agreement was worked out between him and Maga and Apithy to share a rotating presidency. In May 1972, under the agreement, Ahomadegbe became president, but in November the same year he was overthrown by a further coup led by Mathieu Kerekou. He was arrested and remained in prison until 1981. He went into exile in France but returned to Benin in 1990.

Like all leaders in the pre-Kerekou period, Ahomadegbe never had more than a tenuous and ephemeral hold on political power.

19 Michel AIKPE

Benin

An army officer with a considerable popular following, Aikpe held very senior positions in several regimes before his assassination in 1975.

Born in 1942, Aikpe completed his military training in France before becoming Commander of the Parachute Commandos. His first experience of government was as a member of the Revolutionary Military Council in 1966. In 1967 he became vice-president of the Council and in 1968 minister of the interior. With the return to civilian rule in July 1968, Aikpe returned to military duties.

In October 1972 he was one of the major organizers of the coup which brought Mathieu Kerekou to power. A major figure in the new regime, Aikpe was minister of both the interior and of security. He had strong support from the left, especially from students and trade unionists and was viewed as one of the most popular figures in the regime. In 1975 he was shot by Kerekou's Presidential Guard following a roman-tic affair with the president's wife. His killing provoked massive anti-government riots in the south of the country.

20 Michael Adekunle AJASIN

Nigeria

Ajasin was a leading politician of the Second Republic and was governor of Ondo State.

Born in 1908 in Owo, he was educated locally and in Sierra Leone before going on to higher education in England. On his return he had a successful career in teaching before entering politics in 1951, when he was a founder-member of the Action Group (AG) and became its vice-president. He was also president of Egbe Omo Oduduwa, an important Yoruba cultural organization which was banned by the military in 1966. He was an opposition parliamentarian in the First Republic. With the lifting of the ban on party politics in 1978, he was a founder member of the UPN for whom he won the governorship of Ondo State in the 1979 election. He won this post again in 1983, but only after the courts had reversed the original outcome which had awarded victory to the NPN candidate in a seriously rigged election. He was arrested after the 1983 coup but was released in 1985.

21 Anani Kuma AKAKPO-AHIANYO

Togo

Akakpo-Ahianyo was a leading diplomatic and political figure and was foreign minister from 1978 to 1984.

Born in 1937 in Tsevie, he was educated locally before proceeding to Paris

8

for higher education and earning a doctorate in rural sociology. On his return to Togo in 1971 he was appointed director general of the National Institute of Scientific Research. In 1975 he became permanent secretary of rural development and also joined the central committee of the ruling RPT. In 1977 he became ambassador to China and in 1978 foreign minister. He held this position for six years before he was dropped from the cabinet in 1984.

22 Simeon AKE

Côte d'Ivoire (Ivory Coast)

Ake is a leading diplomat and politician who has been foreign minister since 1979.

Born in 1932, he graduated in law from the universities of Dakar and Grenoble. In 1959 he joined the Ivoirian diplomatic service, where he made rapid progress. In 1966 he was appointed permanent representative at the United Nations. He also served as president of the Economic and Social Council. In 1979 he was appointed foreign minister, a post he has retained ever since. He has pursued the foreign policy options favoured by the president, including dialogue with South Africa, the establishment of diplomatic relations with Israel in 1985 and the re-establishment of relations with the USSR and Cuba in 1986.

23 Richard Osuolale Abimbola AKINJIDE

Nigeria

Akinjide was a senior figure in the politics of the Second Republic.

Born in 1931 in Ibadan, he was educated locally before going to Britain where he qualified as a lawyer. On his return to Nigeria in 1959 he was elected to parliament on the NCNC ticket. He was appointed federal minister for education in 1965 but his ministerial tenure was cut short by the January 1966 coup. During the military period he returned to legal work and from 1970 to 1973 he was president of the Nigerian Bar Association, as well as serving in a number of senior university posts. In 1978 he joined the NPN and became its legal adviser. Although he failed to secure election in 1979, he became very prominent in the legal debate over the election of the president, which required the winner to have over one-quarter of the votes in two-thirds of the states, but which failed to make clear the precise meaning of what constituted two-thirds of nineteen (the then number of states). His interpretation, which favoured his party leader, was upheld by the Federal Electoral Commission and the Supreme Court. He was subsequently appointed attorney-general and minister of justice. He went into exile in Britain following the 1983 coup.

24 Samuel Ladoke AKINTOLA

Nigeria

Akintola was a major political figure in the First Republic who was assassinated in the first coup of 1966.

Born in 1910 in Ogbomosho into the Yoruba ethnic group, he worked as a journalist before going to Britain to gain a law degree. Returning to Nigeria in 1949 he became a leading figure in the Egbe Omo Oduduwa, a major Yoruba cultural–political grouping. He was an early member of the AG and became its deputy leader in 1955 under Awolowo. He was the leader of the AG group in the Federal House of Representatives and a minister in the pre-independence government. In 1959 he became premier of the Western Region. In 1962 conflict between Akintola and Awolowo led to a split within the AG and in the following year Akintola's newly-formed UPP headed a ruling coalition government in the Western Region.

Politics in the Region became dominated by conflict between the two leaders and in 1964 Akintola formed another new party, the NNDP which formed an alliance with the national ruling party, the NPC. He became the major southern ally of the dominant northern political elite. In October 1965, elections in the Western Region returned him to power but accusations of ballot rigging led to major unrest. In January 1966 he was assassinated during Nigeria's first military coup.

25   Tshafe Tezaz AKLILU HABTE-WOLD

Ethiopia

Habte-Wold held many senior government positions in Ethiopia and was prime minister from 1961 to 1974.

Born in 1912 in Addis Ababa, he was educated locally before reading law at the Sorbonne. Following the Italian invasion he went into exile with Emperor Haile Selassie, remaining close to the latter for several decades. In 1941 he returned home and was appointed vice-foreign minister, becoming foreign minister two years later. For the next two decades he dominated Ethiopia's foreign relations and was to play a key role in the establishment of the OAU in Addis Ababa in 1963. In 1957 he was appointed deputy prime minister and, in 1961, prime minister. In this role he gained a reputation as a cautious modernizer but in the unrest following the 1973 famine he was dropped from the government, in February 1974. When the coup which ousted Haile Selassie occurred later the same year he was arrested. In November he was executed by the new regime.

26   Aper AKU

Nigeria

Aku was a senior figure in the Second Republic and was governor of Benue State.

Born in 1938 in Ikobo, Benue State, he received his university education in Sierra Leone. He returned home to teach and became principal of the Federal Training Centre in Lagos in the late 1960s. He later resigned to work as a businessman. He gained a reputation as a popular crusader against corruption in Benue-Plateau State, but was jailed on corruption charges himself in 1974. This was viewed by many as a political act to silence a critic of the incumbent regime and he was released when the regime was overthrown in the 1975 coup. When the ban on political parties was lifted in 1978 he joined the NPN, which was to become the ruling party in the Second Republic. In the 1979 and 1983 elections he secured election as governor of Benue State and was very influential in swinging the state behind the NPN. He was detained after the 1983 coup but was subsequently released and died of natural causes in 1987.

27 Frederick William Kwasi AKUFFO

Ghana

Akuffo was a senior member of the military regime of Acheampong before overthrowing the latter in 1978 and replacing him as head of state. The following year he was overthrown by Rawlings and was subsequently executed.

Born in 1937 in Akuapem, he was educated locally before joining the army in 1957. He received officer training at Sandhurst and served in the UN peacekeeping force in the Congo. Although not a significant participant in the Acheampong coup of 1972, he rapidly rose to prominence in the subsequent military regime and by 1976 he was a member of the ruling SMC and chief of defence staff.

By 1978, Acheampong had become extremely unpopular and in July of that year Akuffo led a coup to oust him and replaced him as chairman of the SMC and head of state. Akuffo significantly liberalized the regime by releasing many political prisoners and planning a return to civilian rule. In June 1979, before the return to civilian rule was completed, Akuffo was ousted in the first coup by Rawlings. He was arrested, briefly tried and rapidly executed, along with Acheampong and Afrifa.

28 Edward AKUFO-ADDO

Ghana

Akufo-Addo was one of the leading political figures in Ghana's first Republic and became president in the second.

Born in Akwapim in 1906, he was educated locally before reading mathematics at Oxford University and then qualifying as a lawyer. He was a founder-member of the UGCC in 1947. In 1948 he was one of those briefly detained after anti-colonial riots. In the pre-independence elections he stood as an anti-Nkrumah candidate and continued his opposition to the latter after independence.

In 1962 he was appointed to the Supreme Court but was sacked two years later for defending the independence of the judiciary. Following the 1966 coup he was appointed chief justice of Ghana and held a variety of other important public positions including chairman of the Constitutional Commission which produced the 1969 constitution. From 1970 to 1972 he was president of the republic in the regime of prime minister Busia. His health then started to decline and he was not arrested after the 1972 coup. He lived in retirement until his death from natural causes in 1979.

29 Abel ALIER

Sudan

Alier was one of the most important southerners in the Numeiri regime from 1969 to 1985.

Born in 1933 into the Dinka ethnic group he studied law in Khartoum and London before entering politics. He was first elected to parliament in 1968 and following the 1969 Numeiri coup he was appointed to the government as minister of housing. He briefly held the supply and public works portfolios before being appointed vice-president in 1971. This appointment was designed to add more regional balance to the predominantly northern regime. In 1972, Alier represented the Sudanese government in talks with southern rebels which led to the Addis Ababa Agreement of that year and which, for a time, ended the rebellion in the south of the country. He was appointed president of the Southern Region High Executive Council, retaining his national vice-presidency. He combined these positions until 1982 when he became just the national vice-president. In 1983 he was demoted to minister of construction and public works. His government career finally came to an end when the Numeiri regime was overthrown in a coup in 1985.

30   Mohammed ALI SAMATAR

Somalia

Samatar was a senior member of the Somali regime from 1969 until it was overthrown in January 1991.

Born in 1931 in Chisimaio, he received only primary education before joining the colonial police force, but by 1956 he was its commander. At independence in 1960 he switched to the army and later received military training in Italy and the Soviet Union. He was a leading figure in the coup which brought Siad Barre to power in 1969 and has been a top ranking member of the regime ever since. He was minister of defence from 1971 to 1987 and commander-in-chief of the armed forces from 1971 to 1978. He was vice-president from 1971 to 1987, when he was moved to the newly created post of prime minister, and in 1989 he was appointed to both posts simultaneously.

He has also been vice-president of the ruling SRSP since its creation in 1976. His role for more than two decades was very much that of lieutenant to President Siad Barre: when the latter was injured in a car crash in 1986 he took over as acting head of state. He was one of the increasingly few senior government figures not to have close kinship ties with the president. His political position was inextricably linked to that of the Siad Barre regime, which was overthrown in 1991.

31   Alphonse ALLEY

Benin

Alley was army chief of staff and, briefly, president, but also served periods of imprisonment before going into exile.

Born in 1930, he fought for the French army in Indochina and Algeria before joining the Dahomey army at independence. He was involved in the coups of 1963 and 1965 and in the latter year was appointed chief of staff by President Soglo. Following the 1967 coup which ousted the latter, Alley was briefly detained, but his popularity in the army was such that the new regime chose him as president. In 1968 he returned power to civilian leaders but in 1969 was sentenced to ten years' hard labour following accusations of a coup plot. Later the same year he was released and appointed secretary-general of national defence. Following the 1972 Kerekou coup, he was sacked from the army but given a bureaucratic sinecure as commissioner for the National Oil Mills. In 1973 he was sentenced to 20 years' imprisonment for allegedly plotting against the new regime, but in 1975 a group of supporters released him from prison and he escaped to exile in France.

He was granted a government amnesty in 1984.

32   Camille ALLIALI

Côte d'Ivoire (Ivory Coast)

Alliali has been an important politician and member of the government since independence.

Born in 1926 into the Baule ethnic group, he was educated in Dakar and then graduated in law from the University of Grenoble. Following a period working as a lawyer in Paris he returned home and was vice-president of the territorial assembly from 1957 to 1959. Following independence he was appointed ambassador to France and in 1963 became deputy minister of foreign affairs. In 1966 he became minister of justice. He has been a senior member of the PDCI executive committee and, more recently, a minister of state. He is one of several politicians regarded as a possible successor to President Houphouet-Boigny.

33   Nito Baptista ALVES

Angola

Nito Alves was a senior member of the MPLA and of the post-independence government who became the centre of a faction opposed to the national leadership and was subsequently executed following an attempted coup.

From the Ovimbundu ethnic group, Alves was born in 1945 and after completing his education joined the Portuguese colonial administration. A covert member of the MPLA from 1961, he fled the capital to avoid arrest in 1966. As a guerilla fighter Alves rose through the MPLA hierarchy, becoming commander of the First Military Region in 1971 and political commissar for the Region in 1973. In 1974 he was elected to the MPLA Central Committee and became minister of the interior at independence in 1975.

Alves was a populist politician and as a great orator built a large mass base of support, especially in the slums of Luanda. For a time he was second only to President Neto in political power but his increasingly racist attacks on what he saw as the dominance of mixed-race elements within the government brought him into conflict with the president. By 1976 he was the leader of an opposition faction, known as the 'Nitistas', and was sacked from the government. In May 1977 he was expelled from the party and arrested. Later that month an attempted coup failed, but resulted in the death of several government leaders. The coup leaders released Alves from prison and proclaimed him president. When the coup collapsed Alves fled but was subsequently captured, tried in secret and executed. A mass purge of his supporters within the MPLA followed his death.

34   Abra AMEDOME

Togo

Amedome has been one of the most important female politicians in Togo.

Born in 1933 into the Ewe ethnic group, she studied pharmacy in France and worked as a pharmacist for most of the 1960s. She also developed extensive business interests and emerged as the dominant figure amongst the vitally important merchant-queens of Lome. Since 1975 she has been president of the UNFT. In 1979 she was brought into the cabinet as minister of social affairs and women's production, but was dropped at the end of 1983. She has also been an important figure in the ruling party, the RPT.

35 Atsu-Koffi AMEGA

Togo

Amega has been a major figure in the Togolese government and is currently president of the Supreme Court.

Born in 1932 in Lome, he was brought up in Congo-Brazzaville after his family moved there and later qualified as a lawyer in France. He worked as a lawyer in Brazzaville before he returned home to Togo in 1964 to become an advisor to the Supreme Court. In 1972 he joined the cabinet as minister of rural economy. The following year he began his first period as president of the Supreme Court which lasted until 1981, when he became Togo's ambassador to the United Nations. In 1984 he returned to occupy the post of foreign minister. He occupied this role until 1987, when he returned to the post of president of the Supreme Court, a post which he still holds. He has been a leading figure in the ruling party, the RPT, since its inception in 1969.

36 Idi AMIN Dada

Uganda

Amin is the most infamous of all post-independence political leaders in Africa. His time in power from 1971 to 1979 can only be described as a disaster for Uganda.

Born in 1925 in the north-west of the country into the Kakwa ethnic group,

he received little formal education and remained largely illiterate. He joined the colonial army in 1946 and later fought against the Mau Mau in Kenya. With his huge and powerful physique, he was heavyweight boxing champion of Uganda from 1951 to 1960. By the time of independence he had become an officer in the army and his close alliance with President Obote led to further rapid promotion, so that by 1966 he was commander of the armed forces. Obote used Amin to suppress his opponents, a task for which the ruthless Amin was well suited, and ignored mounting evidence of his corruption. By the end of 1970, Obote had come to fear Amin and had decided to replace him but in January 1971, with Obote abroad at a conference, Amin defended his position by seizing power in a coup.

For the next eight years Amin's rule was based almost entirely on terror and coercion. An estimated 300 000 Ugandans were killed by the forces of the regime, including most of the educated elite who had not gone into exile. With his habit of awarding himself preposterous and pompous titles, Amin was often viewed as a figure of fun abroad, but there was nothing amusing about his rule for the Ugandan population. The once prosperous Ugandan economy was reduced to a devastated shambles. The damage to the economy was exacerbated by the expulsion in 1972 of the Asian population whose assets were expropriated by Amin and his henchmen. The infrastructure of the country collapsed as any government spending not designed to keep Amin in power was abandoned.

There were several attempts to assassinate him, but all failed. He was eventually undone by his expansionist territorial ambitions. In 1978 he invaded Tanzania. The Tanzanian army counter-attacked and, linking up with dissident Ugandans, marched into Uganda. Despite armed assistance from Libya, the Amin forces disintegrated and, in April 1979, Amin went into exile, first in Libya and then in Saudi Arabia. In 1989 he turned up in neighbouring Zaire, claiming that he was going back to govern Uganda, but was soon back in Saudi Arabia. No balanced assessment of Amin's rule is possible or necessary; his influence was entirely negative.

37   Mario Pinto de ANDRADE

Angola

Andrade was a founder member of the MPLA and served periods as its president, general secretary and secretary for foreign affairs.

Born in 1928, he attended university in Lisbon and Paris, where he came into contact with other nationalist leaders. In 1956 he became a founder member of the MPLA and was its president from 1960 to 1962. In the latter year he handed the presidency of the movement to Agostinho Neto, but remained as general secretary until 1973, despite a serious clash with Neto in 1963. He was extremely active in building up the MPLA guerrilla army, whilst establishing himself as a widely published poet. In 1974 he broke with Neto to join the 'Active Revolt' opposition and was imprisoned but subsequently released. He lived in exile until his death in 1990.

38   Michael Okon Nsa ANI

Nigeria

Ani has been a leading public servant and was chairman of FEDECO, which was responsible for the 1979 elections.

Born in 1917 in Calabar, he was educated locally before going to England, where he graduated from the London School of Economics. On returning to Nigeria he joined the civil service and by the time of independence in 1960 had risen to the rank of permanent secretary. In 1967 he was appointed administrator of the areas of Biafra which had been recaptured by federal forces. He served in a number of other senior public positions but his most important posting came in 1977, when he was appointed chairman of FEDECO. This was the body which organized the 1979 elections, which ushered in the Second Republic. Ani had the most crucial and difficult job ever held by a Nigerian bureaucrat. After the elections there was unusually widespread agreement that he had performed superbly and that the elections had been the best organized and most fair in post-independence Nigeria. He was thus responsible for the successful launch of the Second Republic. The commission was dissolved the following year.

39   Joseph Arthur ANKRAH

Ghana

Ankrah was military head of state in Ghana from 1966 until 1969, when he was forced to retire.

Born in 1915 in Accra into the Ga ethnic group, he was educated locally before joining the army. During the second world war he received officer training in England. He later served with distinction with the UN peace-keeping forces in the Congo. From 1961 to 1965 he served as deputy chief of staff in the Ghanaian army, but in the latter year he was forced to retire by President Nkrumah, who feared a coup.

Although Ankrah took no part in the coup of 1966, its leaders reinstated him in the army and he became commander of the armed forces and, as chairman of the NLC, head of state. By 1969 he had lost the support of his colleagues and, following a corruption scandal, he was forced to accept retirement.

40   Gladys ANOMA

Côte d'Ivoire (Ivory Coast)

Anoma is the leading woman politician in Ivory Coast and a vice-president of the national assembly.

Born in 1930, a daughter of Joseph Anoma, a leading figure in the colonial period, she obtained a doctorate in tropical botany before entering politics. She has been a member of the political bureau of the PDCI and secretary-general of the Association of Ivoirian Women. Since 1975 she has been a vice-president of the national assembly.

41   Georges Amakue Dohue APEDO-AMAH

Togo

Apedo-Amah was a senior figure in Togolese politics from the colonial period until the late 1980s.

Born in 1914 in Aneho, he was educated locally before joining the colonial administration and becoming secretary to the French high commissioner in Lome. In 1946 he joined the PTP, becoming a leading figure in it. He served in Grunitzky's pre-independence government as minister of finance but, when the latter was defeated by Olympio in the pre-independence elections, Apedo-Amah left to work in France. When Grunitzky was restored to power by a coup in 1963 he returned to Togo to serve as foreign minister until the regime was ousted in yet another coup in 1967. This time he went into exile in Côte d'Ivoire but returned in 1973 to become ambassador to Nigeria. In 1980 he was elected president of the legislature, a post he held until his retirement in 1987. He was regarded as an efficient if somewhat conservative figure.

42   Sourou-Migan APITHY

Benin

A major politician of the independence period, Apithy was president from 1963 to 1965. An agreement under which he would have been president from 1974 to 1976 was forestalled by a coup.

Born in 1913, he trained as an accountant and was a member of the French National Assembly from 1946 to 1958. A leading member of several political parties in the 1950s, he was prime minister of Dahomey's provisional government in 1958–9, just prior to independence, but lost this position to his rival Maga. At independence he was appointed minister of finance in Maga's cabinet and, later, vice-president. In 1963 he left the country to become ambassador to France but following Maga's overthrow the same year he returned as president. He was overthrown by a coup in 1965 and went into exile. In 1970 he returned to establish an agreement with Maga and Ahomadegbe by which the presidency would be rotated between them. Apithy's presidency was scheduled for 1974–6, but the Kerekou coup of 1972 stopped this from happening. He was detained but was finally released in 1981. He went into exile in Paris, where he died in 1989.

43   Joseph Manuel APPIAH

Ghana

Appiah was a leading figure in the CPP who switched to the opposition. Later he cooperated with military governments in the 1960s and 1970s.

Born in 1918 in Kumasi, he later studied law in London, where he became a close friend of Nkrumah and also married the daughter of Sir Stafford Cripps. Back in Ghana he became a leading figure in the CPP, but in 1955 he joined the NLM and was leader of the opposition in the First Republic. He was imprisoned by Nkrumah in the early 1960s. In the first period of military rule he worked for the governing NLC and in the Second Republic he was a major opposition figure once more. In the second military period he was advisor to the head of state, Acheampong, and supported his unpopular proposals for UNIGOV. When Acheampong was overthrown, Appiah was again arrested but was subsequently released. He retired from politics and wrote his memoirs. He died in 1990.

44   Jean-Hilaire AUBAME

Gabon

Aubame was a major Gabonese politician of the early independence period and was briefly head of state, in 1964.

Born into a Fang family in 1912, he began training as a priest but left to join the colonial civil service, where he made rapid progress. In 1946 he was elected to the French National Assembly and was subsequently re-elected in 1951 and 1956. In 1947 he founded a political party, the Gabonese Democratic and Social Union. He was elected to the territorial assembly in 1952 and 1957. In the pre-independence elections he was defeated by his main rival, Leone M'ba, but in 1961 he joined the latter's coalition government as foreign minister.

Relations between the two men deteriorated and in 1962 Aubame was demoted and in 1963 dropped from the government. In 1964 the military staged a coup to depose M'ba and replaced him with Aubame. Soon afterwards French troops intervened to reinstate M'ba and Aubame was arrested. Although there was no evidence that the latter had any foreknowledge of the coup, he was sentenced to ten years' hard labour. In 1972 he was pardoned and went into exile in France.

45   Babikir AWADALLAH

Sudan

Awadallah was the first prime minister in the Numeiri regime and also served in several other key posts.

Born in 1917 in El Citaina, he qualified as a lawyer in London and worked as a district judge before entering politics. He was parliamentary speaker from 1954 to 1957 but then rejoined the judiciary. He was chief justice of Sudan from 1964 to 1967, when he resigned over the issue of banning communists from parliament. Following the Numeiri coup of 1969, he became prime minister, but he retired in 1972 for reasons of health.

46   Obafemi AWOLOWO

Nigeria

Awolowo was one of the major figures of post-independence politics in Nigeria and, arguably, the greatest head of state that Nigeria never had.

Born in 1909 in Ikenne, he was educated locally before becoming a journalist with several Nigerian newspapers. He gained a degree in commerce from London University through correspondence courses before going to Britain to qualify as a barrister. He was the founder of Egbe Omo Oduduwa, a major Yoruba cultural–political grouping. Returning to Nigeria in 1947, he became one of the major leaders of the nationalist movement. In 1949 he launched the *Nigerian Tribune* as a vehicle for nationalist demands. In 1951 he founded his own party, the AG, which was to become the major party of the Western Region and one of Nigeria's most important political groupings. In 1954 he became premier of the Western Region government, a post he held until 1959. As premier he was responsible for the introduction of universal free primary education in the Region. The expansion of basic education to all remained a cause to which he was deeply committed all his political life.

Following independence in 1960, he became leader of the opposition in the federal parliament. A major conflict with Akintola led to splits in the AG and eventually to the arrest and detention of Awolowo. He was released following the 1966 coup and was a major participant in the federal grouping which tried unsuccessfully to persuade the Eastern Region leadership not to secede as the state of Biafra. He was appointed federal commissioner for finance, a position he held throughout the civil war until his retirement in 1971 to work in his legal practice. In 1975 he was appointed to the CDC which was to draw up a draft constitution for the Second Republic, but declined to take up his appointment.

When the ban on political parties was lifted in 1978, his party, the UPN, was the first to declare itself. Although Awolowo worked hard to extend the ethnic base of the party it was viewed by many Nigerians as basically a Yoruba grouping. This was reflected in the 1979 election results, when the UPN won the Yoruba-dominated states in the west of the country but, with the exception of victory in the cosmopolitan Lagos State, achieved relatively minor support in the rest of the country. In the presidential election Awolowo came second to Shehu Shagari. He became leader of the opposition, as he had been in the 1960s, but attempts to form a lasting alliance of all the opposition parties failed to develop significant momentum. In the 1983 elections he was again placed second in the presidential contest and the UPN again failed to make much headway in non-Yoruba areas. The coup at the end of 1983 which brought the Second Republic to an end also effectively ended his political career.

Awolowo died in May 1987. His death brought tributes from all parts of Nigeria and the University of Ife was renamed after him. In terms of leadership skill and intellectual ability he was undoubtedly one of Nigeria's greatest leaders, perhaps *the* greatest, but he never quite bridged the gap between being a leader of the Yoruba and being a truly national leader. He was never a narrow ethnic sectionalist, but neither was he able to gain the trust of the majority of Muslim northerners or indeed the Ibos of the east. The ethnic configurations of Nigerian politics in the end denied him the top leadership position which his talents otherwise probably merited.

47 Joseph Chongwain AWUNTI

Cameroon

Awunti was one of the few senior Cameroonian political leaders successfully to bridge the Ahidjo and Biya periods.

Born in 1932, he completed his education in Nigeria and Britain where he gained a masters degree in forestry. After university his early career was in this field and he became director of the Centre for Tropical Forestry in western Cameroon. In 1972 Ahidjo appointed him vice-minister of agriculture and in 1979 vice-minister of territorial administration. In 1984, Biya promoted him to the post of minister of general inspection and administrative reform. In 1986 he was further promoted to the position of minister delegate at the presidency in charge of relations with

the National Assembly. In this post he was the vital link between the president and the mass of elected MPs. Unofficially he also provided a major point of linkage between the anglophone and francophone political communities and was developing as one of the key figures in the political system. His early death, from natural causes, in 1987 deprived Cameroon of an able politician.

48 Ismael al-AZHARI

Sudan

Al-Azhari was the first post-independence prime minister and a leading figure in both government and opposition until his death in 1969.

Born in Omdurman in 1902 into a wealthy family, he qualified locally as a teacher and later graduated from the American University in Beirut. He worked in education until turning to politics full-time in 1942, when he formed and led the AP. The AP favoured union with Egypt and in 1952 joined with other parties favouring this solution to form the NUP. In 1953 the NUP won the elections and al-Azhari became prime minister. The policy of union with Egypt was abandoned in favour of demands for an independent Sudan, which came into being in January 1956. He continued as prime minister. Following splits within the NUP he was forced to resign and after the 1958 elections he became leader of the opposition. Following military intervention at the end of 1958, he went into private business, but began campaigning for a return to civilian rule. He was arrested and detained in 1961. With the return to civilian rule in 1964 the NUP again did well and he became president of the five-man Supreme Council which acted as a collective head of state. In May 1969 he was ousted in a further coup and died of a heart attack in August the same year.

49 Nnamdi AZIKIWE

Nigeria

Azikiwe was the first president of Nigeria and a major figure in the pre- and post-independence periods.

Born in 1904 in Zungeru into the Ibo ethnic group, he was educated in Nigeria before going to the USA for his higher education. Here he obtained an MA and lectured in political science. He returned to Nigeria in 1934, but lived in Ghana from 1935 to 1938. On returning home again he established a newspaper, the *West African Pilot*. In 1944 he was a founder of Nigeria's first major political party, the NCNC, and in 1946 became its leader. The NCNC developed as the major party in the Ibo-dominated Eastern Region and Azikiwe became regional premier. At independence the NCNC became the minor coalition partner of the NPC and he became governor-general of Nigeria, a largely ceremonial post. When Nigeria became a republic in 1963 he became its first president, but under the constitution of the First Republic this was a relatively powerless position.

During the civil war he supported the Biafran cause and was a member of the rebel government, but he abandoned this in 1969 and supported reunification. After the civil war he temporarily retired from politics but, with the lifting of the ban on political parties in 1978, he joined the NPP and became its leader

and presidential candidate. In the 1979 elections support for the NPP and for Azikiwe was confined largely to Ibo areas of the country and so power at the national level was not gained. The 1983 coup which ended the Second Republic effectively brought his active political career to an end, although he remains an influential figure in Nigerian political affairs. His success in combining Ibo nationalism with wider Nigerian nationalism was always partial and advanced age would appear to preclude significant future participation in Nigerian public life.

50 Martin Dohou AZONHIHO

Benin

Azonhiho has long been regarded as a key figure in the Kerekou regime and as a militant hardliner.

A long-time supporter of Kerekou, he came to prominence in 1974, when he was appointed to the cabinet as minister of information and national orientation. Following the killing of his rival, Aikpe, he was appointed minister of the interior in 1975. In this position he was much feared by his fellow army officers and the mass of the population. He was reassigned to the ministry of information, where he became the main exponent of the Marxist ideology of the regime. In 1982 he was dropped from the cabinet and appointed prefect of Mono Province. In 1987 he returned to the cabinet as minister of rural development and in 1988 was appointed minister of equipment and transport. He is generally regarded as one of the hardest members of what has been a tough and ruthless regime.

B

51 Babacar BA

Senegal

Ba was a senior figure in the government until he fell from power in 1978.

Born in 1930 in Sine-Saloum, he was educated in France before joining the civil service at home. He began his administrative career in the ministry of the interior in 1959 and was subsequently promoted to director of the cabinet under Mamadou Dia. From 1962 to 1966 he worked for the foreign ministry and then became a diplomat in Brussels in charge of relations with the EEC. In 1971 he was appointed to the cabinet as minister of finance and economic affairs, a post he held until 1978. He was elected to parliament in 1973. In March 1978 he became foreign minister but in September the same year he was forced to resign from the government.

52 Ousmane BA

Mali

Ba was a leading figure in the post-independence government of Modibo Keita, serving as foreign minister.

Born in 1919 in Segou, he qualified as a medical doctor in Senegal. After returning home to practise medicine he became involved in politics and trade union activities. He served as minister of labour in the government of the short-lived Mali Federation and when this collapsed two months after independence he was brought into the Keita cabinet. He was a close ally of Keita and one of the regime's most outspoken left-wing ideologues. He held the portfolios of public function (1961–2), the interior (1962–4) and was appointed foreign minister in 1964, a post which he held until the regime was overthrown. Following the 1968 coup he was jailed for several years, before being released and going into exile in France.

53 Kofi BAAKO

Ghana

Baako was one of the dominant figures in the government of the first republic in Ghana.

Born in 1926 in Saltpond into the Ga ethnic group, he began training as a surveyor but abandoned this to go into full-time politics. He was a member of the Ghana League of Patriots and, as a founder-member of the CPP, was very close to Nkrumah. In 1949 he became editor of the party's *Cape Coast Daily Mail* and was first elected to the Legislative Assembly for his home town in 1954, retaining his seat until the 1966 coup.

After independence he held a variety of senior government and party posts. In the cabinet he was successively minister of information and broadcasting, minister of parliamentary affairs and minister of defence. He also served as CPP leader in parliament and general secretary of the party. More than any other individual he was responsible for the creation of the personality cult surrounding Nkrumah. After the 1966 coup he was arrested and detained until 1968, when he was released on grounds of ill health. In spite of his poor health he survived in retirement until 1984, when he died of natural causes. His funeral became a grand reunion for all the surviving veteran leaders of the CPP.

54 Ibrahim Gbadamosi BABANGIDA

Nigeria

Babangida has been military head of state in Nigeria since 1985.

Born in 1941 in Minna in Niger State, he joined the army in 1963 and received military training in India, Britain and the USA. He distinguished himself on active service during the civil war but came to public prominence in 1976, when he played a major part in the defeat of the Dimka coup attempt. He held a number of senior military appointments, including command of the armoured corps, and in 1983 was a participant in the coup which brought Buhari to power. In 1984 he was appointed chief of army staff.

In August 1985 he led an internal coup which ousted Buhari, becoming military head of state and commander-in-chief of the armed forces. He was the first of Nigeria's military leaders to formally adopt the title of president. Since then his attempts to improve the economy with his austerity-based SAP have met with some success, but have been bitterly resented by many urban groups. Initially he announced a return to civilian rule by 1990, but this was later deferred until 1992. Political parties were permitted to form, but in October 1989 he scrapped

those which had done so and said that he would establish two parties to contest the elections. He banned all those who had previously held high political office, including himself, from participating in the coming Third Republic. He reaffirmed his commitment to the return to civilian rule following a major coup attempt in April 1990, when he narrowly escaped assassination.

55 Abdul Rahman Mohammed BABU

Tanzania

Babu was a leading figure in the government until he was detained in 1972 and has since become the leading critic in exile of the government.

Born in 1924 in Zanzibar of mixed Afro-Arab descent, he received university education in Uganda and England and worked as a bank clerk in London before returning home to become a full-time politician. In 1957 he became leader of the ZNP but subsequently quarrelled with its other, more conservative, leaders and in 1963 formed his own new party, the UP. He was arrested and detained after organizing trade union opposition to the government, but later escaped to Dar-es-Salaam on the mainland. Following the Zanzibari revolution in 1964, he returned to become minister of defence and external affairs, but his relationship with the other island political leaders was poor and he moved into the mainland government within a few months. He then served in several very senior government posts, becoming minister of commerce (1965–7), health (1967–8), commerce and industry (1968–70).

In 1970 he was appointed minister of economic affairs and development but, with policies well to the left of the majority of government members, his position was not entirely secure. In 1972 he was implicated in the assassination of the Zanzibari leader, Abeid Karume, and was detained until 1978. On his release he went into exile and has lived mainly in the USA and Britain, earning his living through teaching and writing. He has been the most important of the exiled opponents of the Tanzanian government, calling for a restoration of the multi-party state.

56   Tiecoro BAGAYOKO

Mali

Bagayoko was a leading figure in the military government from 1968 until 1978, when he was involved in a failed coup.

Born in 1937 in Goundam, he trained as a pilot in the Malian army. He was a leading member of the military group which staged the 1968 coup which brought Moussa Traore to power. He became a member of the ruling Military Committee of National Liberation. He was regarded as a military hardliner and, as director of security services, was the most widely feared member of the ruling group because of his brutal treatment of opponents of the regime. In 1978 he became involved in a plot to overthrow the president, but when this failed he was arrested. He was tried and sentenced to death but this was later commuted to life imprisonment. In 1979 he was further tried on charges of large-scale corruption during his period in power. He was found guilty and received

an additional jail sentence. He was detained in the Taoudeni salt mines, where he died in 1983.

57   Jean Baptiste BAGAZA

Burundi

Bagaza was the military head of state in Burundi from 1976 to 1987.

A Tutsi and a kinsman of President Michel Micombero, he was born in 1946. After joining the army he received military training in Belgium and by 1972 had risen to become army chief of staff and, effectively, the second most important man in the country. In 1976 he seized power in a relatively bloodless coup and became president.

He established a Supreme Revolutionary Council and promised a return to civilian rule. Initially he abolished the only political party, UPRONA, but later re-established it with himself as leader. In 1982 elections were held for a new National Assembly but Bagaza remained firmly in control of what was still a resolutely military government. A referendum in 1984 claimed 99.6 per cent of popular support for Bagaza's leadership. Whilst he did appoint some Hutu (the majority ethnic group) to his government, it remained Tutsi-dominated. He launched a campaign against the Catholic church, which had established a record as a defender of human rights in Burundi, and expelled many church leaders. In 1987 he was overthrown in a military coup led by Major Pierre Buyoya while he was attending an international meeting in Canada. In 1988 he made an unsuccessful attempt to return to Burundi but when this failed he returned to exile in Libya.

23

58   Djibo BAKARY

Niger

Bakary was the leader of the government in the period just before independence and has remained an influential figure since.

Born in 1922, he trained as a teacher in Senegal and on his return home became active in trade union affairs. In 1950 he founded the UND, a political party which later changed its name to the Sawaba (Freedom) Party. In the 1957 elections the UND emerged as the majority party in the territorial assembly and he became prime minister. In the 1958 referendum on de Gaulle's proposals for a French Community he campaigned for immediate independence, but was defeated and in the election later in the year he lost his parliamentary majority. His party was banned and he went into exile to launch a guerrilla campaign against the regime of Hamani Diori. The campaign ended in 1965, when foreign backing from Ghana was withdrawn. Following the overthrow of Diori in 1974 he returned to Niger but was arrested a year later in connection with a coup plot. He was released in 1980. When Ali Saibou became president in 1987 he persuaded Bakary to join him in a public call for political reconciliation and the return of exiles. Bakary has remained an important figure in the politics of Niger in spite of the fact that he has never been a member of any post-independence government.

59   Abubakar Tafawa BALEWA

Nigeria

Balewa was the first prime minister of post-independence Nigeria before being assassinated in 1966.

Born in 1912 in Bauchi State into a low-status family (his father was a slave), he initially trained and worked as a teacher. He was a founder-member of the Bauchi General Improvement Union in 1943 and in 1947 became a member of the Northern House of Assembly. In 1951 he became a member of Ahmadu Bello's NPC which became the dominant party in Nigeria. He became deputy leader of the party and minister of transport in the pre-independence government. He was knighted by Britain in 1960 and became prime minister at independence in October the same year.

His elevated position rested largely on Ahmadu Bello's preference for remaining premier of the Northern Region and it was the latter, rather than Balewa, who exerted most power in the First Republic. Balewa was a diligent and honest man but was unable to control the increasingly violent and conflict-ridden nature of Nigerian politics. He was assassinated during the first Nigerian coup of January 1966.

60   Canaan Sodindo BANANA

Zimbabwe

Banana was the first post-independence president, from 1980 until 1987.

Born in 1936 in Esiphezini, he was educated locally before becoming a Methodist clergyman. In 1971 he was a founder-member of Muzorewa's ANC which was formed to oppose the Anglo-Rhodesian agreement of that year and later became its vice-president. From 1973 to 1975 he studied at a theological seminary in the USA, where he gained a masters degree. He was detained for three months in 1976, but then released to attend the abortive Geneva Conference. Whilst there he joined the ZANU and became its publicity secretary. On his return home he was again arrested and was held in detention until November 1979. At independence in April 1980 he became the country's first president, but this was largely a ceremonial role. He played an important part in the politics of reconciliation after independence. When the constitution was changed in 1987 to create an executive presidency he stepped down in favour of Robert Mugabe.

61   Hastings Kamuzu BANDA

Malawi

Banda has been president of Malawi since independence and has been the dominant force in the country's politics for the entire period.

Born in 1902 (the date is frequently disputed and several others have been given) into a poor peasant family of the Chewa ethnic group in Kasunga district, he received his initial education in a local missionary school. He left Nyasaland at the age of 12 to work in Rhodesia and South Africa before going to the USA, where he gained a first degree in political science. He later qualified as a medical doctor in the USA and in Scotland. He practised medicine in several places in England and made contacts with other African nationalist leaders, including Nkrumah and Kenyatta. He acted as a nationalist leader in exile, lobbying against the creation of the CAF which was created in 1953 and included Nyasaland. In 1953 he went to Ghana and worked there as a doctor for five years.

After living abroad for over 40 years he returned home in 1958, following requests that he should lead the African nationalist movement. He immediately became leader of the NAC. The following year, following disturbances, the NAC was banned and Banda was detained. He was released from jail in 1960 and assumed the leadership of the MCP which had been formed while he was in detention. He forced the break-up of the CAF and led the country to independence in 1964, when he became prime minister. With the adoption of a republican constitution in 1966, he became president and in 1971 this was altered to president for life.

In 1964 serious rifts appeared between Banda and most of the more radical members of his government. He reacted by dismissing his opponents, most of whom fled into exile or were arrested. Since then his domination of the Malawian political system has been virtually unchallenged and one-man rule has been developed to a quite remarkable extent. Most of the important government portfolios are held by the president personally. His style of rule has become one of despotic paternalism and policy making lies almost entirely in his hands, with little autonomy for subordinates. Under his leadership the country has been largely stable and has enjoyed a reasonable level of economic development. His external policies have made him a controversial figure in African circles, especially the establishment of full diplomatic relations with South Africa in 1970, a move which brought considerable material gain to Malawi. Despite his great age, Banda has refused to consider the question of political succession.

62   Antoine BANGUI

Chad

Bangui's erratic career has included senior government office, diplomatic postings and imprisonment.

Born in 1932, a member of the Sara ethnic group, he trained as a teacher in France and taught mathematics. He later became a civil servant and then minister of education in Tombalbaye's government in 1962. This lasted for only three months before he became minister of public works. In 1964 relations between Bangui and the president cooled and he was appointed ambassador to Italy and West Germany. By 1966 the relationship had improved and he returned home, serving as Tombalbaye's right-hand man in several senior ministerial positions. His position became so strong that he was regarded as heir-apparent, but this proved dangerous to him as the president came to regard him as a rival. In 1972 he was arrested and charged with a variety of crimes and plots, only narrowly escaping execution. In 1975 he was released and partly rehabilitated. After Habre came to power in 1982 he was made ambassador to Romania.

63   Sylvestre BANGUI

Central African Republic

Bangui has had an erratic and uneven political career, achieving prominence in most post-independence governments but usually losing his position quite rapidly.

As a general in the CAR army he first came to prominence in the early 1960s as an aide to President Dacko when his main task was to look after relationships between the president and the armed forces. At the end of 1965, Dacko was overthrown and Bangui was arrested and detained by Bokassa. He was later released. His political rehabilitation was completed when he was named as ambassador to Paris of the, then, Central African Empire in 1978. The following year he resigned in protest at government atrocities at home and remained in Paris, where he established an opposition movement entitled the Ubanguian Liberation Front. In 1979, with Bokassa overthrown and Dacko back in power, he returned home and was made foreign minister. In November 1980 he was sacked from this post and lost his place in the government. In 1983 he returned to high office when Dacko's successor, General Kolingba, appointed him minister of finance. In 1984 he was again sacked following a dispute with the head of state over economic policy. He was subsequently detained and imprisoned.

64   John Ahmadu BANGURA

Sierra Leone

Bangura was briefly head of state in 1968 but was subsequently executed following a failed coup attempt.

Born in 1930 in Kalangba in the north of the country, he was educated locally before joining the army as a private in 1950. He later received officer training at Sandhurst and became the first Sierra Leonean to graduate from there. In 1963 he served with the UN peace-keeping forces in the Congo. He was detained briefly following the 1967 coup but then released and appointed to a diplomatic post in the USA. Instead he went to Guinea to plot against the military government and, following a further coup in 1968, he returned to head an interim military government. One week later he placed Siaka Stevens at the head of the government and was later promoted to brigadier and appointed army commander. Although he had brought Stevens to power and was thought to be a loyal supporter, he led an attempted coup against Stevens in 1971. When the coup failed he was tried and executed.

65   Teferi BANTI

Ethiopia

Banti was the leader of the military government which followed the overthrow of Haile Selassie in 1974. Following a violent power struggle within the ruling group he was assassinated in 1977.

Born in 1921 into the Galla ethnic group, he joined the army as a private in 1941. During a long military career he gradually rose through the ranks and by the time of the 1974 coup he was a brigadier-general. He gained a reputation as an efficient soldier who was critical of the government. Following the 1974 coup he became chairman of the governing Provisional Military Administrative Council (later known as the *Derg*) and effectively head of state.

Banti supported the goal of creating a socialist state in Ethiopia but consistently argued for greater civilian participation in government than was desired by the other military leaders who were eventually to kill him. He made several unsuccessful attempts to come to an agreement with the Eritrean nationalist movement by offering them greater autonomy within the Ethiopian state. In 1976 structural changes within the government appeared to have strengthened his position but in fact produced an even greater power struggle within the military leadership. In February 1977 the faction led by Mengistu shot Banti; popular demonstrations against this act were violently suppressed.

66   Alexandre BANZA

Central African Republic

Banza was a significant supporter of Bokassa, a senior member of his government and, ultimately, one of his victims.

Born in 1932, he joined the army in 1950 and rose through the ranks to become a captain and commander of an infantry battalion. He formed a close attachment to Bokassa and was one of the main organizers of the coup which brought the latter to power at the beginning of 1966. Promoted to lieutenant-colonel, Banza was appointed minister of finance. In this post he administered a crackdown on corruption which was, in a way, too successful and in 1968 he was downgraded to minister of health. In 1969 Bokassa began to eliminate any possible rival to himself and Banza was arrested in April on spurious charges.

Within two days of his arrest Banza was dead. It is widely believed that Bokassa personally tortured to death his former close colleague.

67   Elijah BARAYI

South Africa

Barayi is the president of the Congress of South African Trade Unions (COSATU), the largest trade union organization in the country.

Born in 1930 in Cradock in the Eastern Cape, he was educated to secondary level. As a teenager he joined the Youth League of the ANC and became one of its organizers. He was arrested and detained on several occasions. In the 1970s he became a mineworker and was involved in union affairs, at first illegally. In 1982 he was instrumental in establishing the NUM and became its vice-president. When COSATU was founded as a multi-racial federation of trade unions in 1985, he was elected president, a post which he still holds. The movement now has up to one million members and in 1988, when it organized a political protest stay-away from work, up to two million participated. Under Barayi's leadership COSATU has played an important political role in the anti-apartheid movement.

68   Omar Hassan Ahmad al-BASHIR

Sudan

Al-Bashir has been head of state since coming to power in a coup in June 1989.

Born in 1944 in the north of the country, he was educated locally before joining the army and training as a para-trooper. By 1989 he had risen to the rank of brigadier and was serving in the remote El Muglad area of south Kordofan, but enjoyed no public prominence. This situation changed dramatically at the end of June 1989, when he seized power from the democratically elected government of Sadiq al-Mahdi in a coup. He established a military Revolutionary Command Council for National Salvation with himself as chairman and effectively head of state. He also appointed a cabinet with himself as prime minister and minister of defence. He dissolved all existing institutions, political parties and trade unions. At the time of taking power he issued a number of conciliatory statements which suggested that he wanted to reduce the severe regional and religious tensions. However, his subsequent actions were in marked contrast to his initial statements. He appointed a majority of Islamic fundamentalists to his cabinet and pursued a policy of ruthless coercion towards all political opponents. At the end of April 1990 he survived a major coup attempt which resulted in the execution of large numbers of senior men within the military hierarchy. There would appear to be no evidence to suggest that he is capable of finding a solution to the country's chronic political conflicts.

69   Louis Lansana BEAVOGUI

Guinea

Beavogui was a leading figure in the regime of Sekou Toure, holding the post of prime minister for 12 years. He was, very briefly, acting president following Toure's death but was ousted in a coup.

Born in 1923 into the Toma ethnic group, he trained as a doctor in Dakar. He worked as chief medical officer in Kissidougou, of which was elected mayor in 1954. In 1956 he was elected to the French National Assembly. Following independence in 1958 he was a senior member of the government, serving as minister of economic affairs from 1958 to 1961 and 1969 to 1972 and as foreign minister from 1961 to 1969. In 1972 he was appointed to the newly created post of prime minister, which he held until 1984. Throughout the period he was Toure's closest and most trusted ally, but remained dependent on the president, lacking an independent power base. Following the death of Toure, in March 1984, he became acting president but was deposed by a coup a few days later and was detained. He died in prison of natural causes a few months later.

70   Ahmadu BELLO

Nigeria

Bello was the dominant political figure of the First Republic in Nigeria until his assassination in the first coup of January 1966.

Born in 1910 in Rabbah, near Sokoto, into the ruling family, he was the grandson of the great Fulani leader Usman Dan Fodio. He initially trained as a teacher and taught for a time in Sokoto. He failed in his bid to become sultan in 1938, but was appointed to the traditional post of Sardauna (leader of war). In 1948 he studied local government in England.

In 1951 he founded the NPC which was to become the leading party in Ni-geria. The NPC was a conservative party with its roots in the northern traditional aristocracy and was able to use the extensive structure of the traditional political system for party purposes. In 1954 Bello became premier of the Northern Region. He held this position beyond independence until the time of his death, preferring to be based in the north and leave the running of the central government in Lagos to his subordinates, such as Balewa. He was effectively the ruler of Nigeria during the period of the First Republic. He was assassinated in January 1966 during the coup. His death provoked great anguish in the north of the country but some celebration elsewhere.

71   Paul BERENGER

Mauritius

Berenger is the most important figure in the neo-Marxist political movement in the country and a leading trade unionist. In 1982 he led the opposition to electoral victory.

Born in 1945 into an affluent Franco-Mauritian family, he graduated from the University of Wales in 1968. Whilst a student he became heavily involved in the 1968 student rebellions, especially in France, which radicalized his political thinking. Back in Mauritius he became a leader of left-wing opposition to the government and, in 1970, founded the MMM, of which he is still secretary-general. The MMM appealed for support along class lines, rejecting more traditional communal bases of support, and rapidly built up a large following, especially amongst trade unionists. Berenger was first elected to parliament in 1976.

In June 1982 a coalition led by the MMM won a general election, the first time that an incumbent government had been ousted from office through the ballot box in post-independence Africa. Berenger became minister of finance in the new government but, the following year, as a result of MMM defections and fractures in the coalition, the MMM lost a further election and he returned to opposition politics. In the 1987 general election he failed to win a seat in parliament but he remains a significant figure in the political system.

72 Frank George BERNASKO

Ghana

Bernasko has been both a senior member of military regimes and a civilian political party leader.

Born in 1931 at Cape Coast into the Fanti ethnic group, he graduated from University College Legon before joining the army. Subsequently he qualified as a barrister through part-time study, making him one of the best educated officers in the army. After the 1966 coup he became director of education in the Ministry of Defence. Following the 1972 coup he was appointed commissioner of the Central Region and later he held the agriculture and cocoa affairs portfolios. He was also director of the 'Operation Feed Yourself' campaign. In 1975 he quarrelled with Acheampong and was sacked and forcibly retired from the army.

In 1979 he formed his own ACP to contest the inaugural elections of the Third Republic. The ACP had strong support in the Central Region but performed poorly elsewhere. Following the 1981 coup the ACP was banned, along with all the other political parties.

73 Stephen BIKO

South Africa

Biko was the founder and leader of the Black Consciousness Movement (BCM). He was murdered in 1977 whilst in police custody.

He was born in 1946 in King William's Town, in the Eastern Cape. His schooling was interrupted by political activities and school closures. In 1966 he went to read medicine at the University of Natal but was expelled in 1972 before completing his studies. Whilst at university he founded and led the BCM, a very loose political grouping which asserted that political liberation had to be based on the assertion of black (which in the South African context included Africans, Asians and Coloureds) identity and struggle and could not be achieved by white liberals and radicals. The BCM produced a very wide range of political movements, most of which Biko led or was closely associated with. The most important amongst these were the black SASO which was founded in 1969 and the BPC which was founded in 1972.

Following his expulsion from university, Biko was involved in organizing Black Community Programmes in several parts of the country but his political work was hampered by frequent arrests and detentions. He also became a 'banned' person, which meant that he could not attend gatherings, political or otherwise, and was constantly watched by the security police. He died in detention in September 1977 from multiple injuries following torture and beatings by the police and prison authorities. He achieved posthumous international fame from the feature film *Cry Freedom* made about his life by Richard Attenborough, which was shot on location in Zimbabwe in 1986 and completed in England in 1987. Although he was only in his early thirties at the time of his death he remained a powerful and charismatic symbol of the struggle against apartheid.

74 Godfrey Lukwongwa BINAISA

Uganda

Binaisa was a leading figure in the First Republic and was, briefly, president following the ousting of Amin.

Born in 1920 in Kampala into the Baganda ethnic group, he was educated at Makerere University before going to London University, where he qualified as a lawyer. He was involved in party politics to a limited extent as a member of the ruling UPC but did not stand for election to parliament. In 1962 he was appointed attorney-general by President Obote and remained in this government post until 1967. He became increasingly opposed to the authoritarian style of rule of Obote and especially to the latter's suspension of the constitution. In 1967 he resigned from the government and the following year became president of the Uganda Law Society. He went into exile in the USA when Amin came to power and did not return to Uganda until the latter was overthrown in 1979. In June of that year Binaisa was chosen as interim president, but held that position for just under one year. He proved relatively ineffectual in resolving the con-

flicts and uncertainties which followed the end of the Amin period and was ousted in May 1980. He was placed under house arrest until 1981, when he again went into exile.

75 Sookdeo BISSOONDOYAL

Mauritius

Bissoondoyal was a leading figure in both government and opposition in the early post-independence period.

Born in 1911, he trained as a teacher and was a follower of Mahatma Gandhi. He was first elected to parliament in 1948 and in 1953 formed his own political party, the IFB. The party gradually increased its support, especially in the rural areas, and in the 1962 elections was the second most important. In 1963 he joined the coalition government and became minister of information and, later, minister of local government. He remained in the latter position after independence in 1968 but in 1969 he resigned from the government and became leader of the opposition. Gradually his party fragmented and he failed to win a seat in the 1976 elections. He died two years later.

76 Paul BIYA

Cameroon

Formerly a close associate and supporter of President Ahidjo, Biya took over the presidency when the latter retired in 1982 and has remained in office since then.

Born in 1933 in Mvomeoka, he received his higher education in France, where he graduated in law. On his return to Cameroon he rapidly rose through the ranks of Ahidjo's UNC and became very close to the president. In the context of political cleavages in Cameroon they complemented each other because Biya was a southern Christian whilst Ahidjo was a northern Muslim. By 1968 Biya was minister of state and secretary-general at the presidency. He was further elevated in 1975, when Ahidjo recreated the post of prime minister and appointed him to it, making him quite clearly second-in-command. From then on Biya was groomed by Ahidjo as his hand-picked successor.

In 1982 Ahidjo retired from the presidency, although he remained leader of the party. Biya became president and it was widely expected that he would pursue a policy of continuity regarding the composition of the government. This expectation proved false and in 1983 Biya began a process of easing out most of the older cabinet members who had been close to his predecessor. Relations between the two men became strained and were further damaged with the discovery later in the year of a coup plot involving Ahidjo supporters. Biya forced Ahidjo to resign his party leadership and installed himself as leader whilst Ahidjo retired to France. Biya then accelerated the replacement of Ahidjo supporters in the government and bureaucracy with his own supporters. In April 1984 a major coup attempt came very close to overthrowing Biya and was only defeated with considerable loss of life. Major purges in the army and civil service followed as Biya re-established his hold on power.

In 1985 a major congress was held by the ruling single party and its name was changed to CPDM. Biya promised a return to democracy in Cameroon but initial hopes that this would include the legalization of opposition parties were soon dashed. Even a decision to allow independent candidates to stand in elections was largely nullified by the creation of a nomination procedure so complex and difficult as to make nominations virtually impossible and none have, so far, succeeded. In 1988, Biya was re-elected to the presidency in an uncontested election and only CPDM candidates contested the parliamentary seats. Although the personnel of the government has changed beyond recognition since Biya took control there have been no significant changes in economic policy or foreign relations. Following widespread popular protest opposition parties were legalized in February 1991 but Biya retained considerable personal power.

77 Allan BOESAK

South Africa

Boesak is the president of the World Alliance of Reformed Churches and one of the main church leaders in the anti-apartheid campaign.

Born in 1945 in Kakamas, in the Cape, into the Coloured community (those of mixed racial ancestry) he was educated at a local seminary and in Holland, where he obtained a doctorate. He is a minister in the Dutch Reformed Mission Church in South Africa, where, with people like Archbishop Tutu, he has been an outspoken critic of the apartheid system. His appointment, in 1982, as the president of the World Alliance of Reformed Churches makes him the spiritual leader of the Reformed

Churches and has given him a useful platform for his political activities. When the UDF was formed in 1983 as a broad-based alliance of anti-apartheid groups Boesak was chosen as its patron. He has been arrested and detained on a number of occasions, although his international prominence has given him some protection against police harassment.

78   Jean-Bedel BOKASSA

Central African Republic (Empire)

A brutal and ludicrous tyrant, the self-styled Emperor Bokassa was a figure of great embarrassment for the whole of Africa. His squalid 13-year rule was wholly negative for his country.

Born in 1921, he received only a rudimentary education and his childhood was marred by the violent death of his father and the suicide of his mother, after which he was raised by a very strict paternal grandfather. In 1939 he joined the French colonial army and was awarded no less than 12 citations for bravery in the second world war and, subsequently, in the war in Indochina. His undoubted personal fearlessness led to promotion and he became a lieutenant in 1958, captain in 1961 and colonel in 1964. He was appointed chief of staff in the ministry of defence by President Dacko but on New Year's Eve, 1965, Bokassa led a coup which overthrew Dacko and installed himself as head of state.

The coup was not unpopular and for a short time it appeared that Bokassa might attempt to govern in the national interest. He donated his first month's salary to the hospital in Bangui and several development projects were started. Within a short time, however, his rule degenerated into an excessively brutal and highly personalized dictatorship. By the late 1960s he was organizing the murder of all possible opponents, including many figures in the army who had previously been his closest collaborators. His personal megalomania reached unprecedented proportions. Not satisfied with declaring himself president for life, he decided that he wished to become an emperor. In 1977 the republic was retitled 'empire' and Bokassa organized a stupendous but bizarre coronation ceremony for himself which cost at least one-third of the national revenue for the year. Having converted to Islam on a trip to Libya the previous year, he announced his reconversion to Christianity.

Following his coronation his rule seemed to become ever more barbarous. In 1979, following a minor demonstration, hundreds of young schoolchildren were rounded up and were brutally tortured and murdered. As on previous occasions, Bokassa himself was a major participant in the brutality. His personal delight in torturing and killing his victims and of indulging in ritual cannibalism are well documented. In addition to his brutality, Bokassa was staggeringly corrupt, amassing a personal fortune of hundreds of millions of dollars from his poverty-stricken country.

Throughout the 1970s a number of coup attempts had failed to dislodge him but in September 1979 French paratroops finally deposed him. Bokassa tried to enter exile in France but on being rejected went to Ivory Coast. In 1986 another bizarre twist in the story occurred when he voluntarily returned to the CAR, saying he was homesick. A lengthy public trial ensued and in 1987 he was sentenced to death for his crimes. In 1988 this was commuted to hard labour for life in a gesture of leniency by the government which was at odds with Bokassa's own period in power. Future historians may find something positive to say about Bokassa, but this does not appear likely.

79   El Hadj Omar BONGO

Gabon

Bongo has been president of Gabon since 1967 and has dominated the politics of the country for the whole period, developing a highly personalized style of rule.

Born in 1935 in Lewai, his first names were Albert Bernard until he converted to Islam in 1973. He entered the civil service in 1958 and rose quickly in public life, owing to the extensive patronage of President M'ba. Between 1962 and 1965 he served as assistant director and then director of the cabinet and also held the information and defence portfolios. By 1966, M'ba was seriously ill and began to engineer the succession of Bongo, whom he favoured to take over. He created a new post of vice-president and appointed Bongo to it. In elections held in March 1967 the president and vice-president were re-elected and when M'ba died in November the same year Bongo became president.

In 1968 he abolished all existing political parties and created his own GDP as the only legal party, with himself as leader. At the same time he released a number of political detainees. This tactic of combining highly authoritarian rule with a policy of reconciliation with defeated political opponents has been a marked feature of his time in power. He has been re-elected president on several occasions: in 1986 the official results gave him 99.97 per cent of the votes in a 99.9 per cent turnout. Personal loyalty to the president has long been a primary prerequisite for senior appointments in the government, bureaucracy and army and Bongo does not hesitate to expel anyone whom he regards as being less than totally loyal. In 1988 he appointed his nephew, major-general Oyini, as commander-in-chief of the armed forces.

With legal opposition to Bongo impossible inside Gabon until recently, the main group hostile to him, known as MORENA, existed underground and in exile. Although the group supported only peaceful change and the restoration of democracy, those of its members who were captured were given harsh sentences. According to Amnesty International, torture has been used on opponents of the regime. Apart from occasional riots and a few ill-planned coup plots, there has been no serious challenge to the regime in recent years.

In spite of its negative aspects, Bongo's regime is not to be listed amongst the most oppressive in Africa. One of the reasons for the level of political stability which exists is the president's skilled balancing of ethnic interests. The country has also been relatively prosperous, mainly owing to its oil revenues, although the latter have declined in recent years. With a population of little more than one million it has one of the highest per capita incomes in Africa. Bongo himself is reliably known to have great personal wealth and his presidential palace is rumoured to have cost more than thirty million dollars. Still a relatively young man, Bongo may well rule Gabon in his highly personal way for some time to come. Some modification of the political system occurred in late 1990 when, following mass demonstrations, opposition parties were legalized. In the October legislative elections Bongo's party emerged with a small overall majority and he appointed some opposition figures to posts in the government.

80 Martin BONGO

Gabon

Bongo has held a number of important bureaucratic and ministerial appointments and has been foreign minister since 1981.

Born in Lekei in 1940, he completed his education in Ivory Coast before entering the Gabonese civil service. He established close links with his namesake, President Bongo, and received rapid promotion. In 1972 he was appointed minister of education. In 1981 he became foreign minister and has since worked to diversify Gabonese foreign links, especially with the USA and the People's Republic of China. Like all senior Gabonese politicians, he is largely controlled by the president.

81 Nazi BONI

Burkina Faso

Boni was a major figure in the pre-independence nationalist movement and subsequently an opposition leader.

A member of the Bwa ethnic group, Boni was born in 1910. After completing his education in Senegal he became a teacher in Ouagadougou. Following the war he entered politics and was a member of several political parties before forming the MPEA which he led. He was three times elected to the French National Assembly, where he served from 1948 to 1960. During this time he was also a member of the Territorial Assembly and was its president from 1957 to 1958.

Boni was most closely associated with the anti-Mossi faction and campaigned against what he saw as Mossi domination. This included the attempt, unsuccessful in the end, to have the territory split into two separate states with Mossi and non-Mossi majorities. At independence he was a bitter opponent of President Yameogo and when the latter started to crush the opposition Boni went into exile in Mali, where he wrote a novel, *The Twilight of Former Times*. Following the 1966 coup he returned home, but was killed in a car crash three years later.

82 Harish BOODHOO

Mauritius

Boodhoo has been a controversial figure in Mauritian politics in both government and opposition.

Trained as a schoolteacher, he joined the then dominant MLP, for whom he was elected to parliament in 1976. He became a dissident figure within the MLP and after leading a backbench revolt in 1978 he was expelled from the party in 1979. In 1982 he formed his own party, the PSM, which combined with the major opposition MMM to win the general election of that year. In 1983 he and his party defected to support the newly formed MSM. This alliance won the 1983 general election and shortly afterwards the MSM and PSM merged to form a single party. Boodhoo became government chief whip but resigned from this post in 1985. In 1986 he resigned from parliament following a drugs scandal. In 1988 he revived the PSM as a separate party and became its leader.

83   Bertin BORNA

Benin

Borna was one of the most important of the politicians of the independence period, a member of several governments, including a spell as Minister of Finance, but has spent most of his later life in exile.

Born in 1930, Borna gained a degree in law before entering politics in the 1950s. He was vice-president of the National Assembly from 1959 to 1960 and minister of public works in the pre-independence government. In 1960 he was appointed minister of finance in the independence government and survived in that post until the 1963 coup. In spite of being charged with gross corruption, he was brought back as minister of finance in 1966 in the military regime of Soglo until that government was overthrown by a coup in 1967. He then worked abroad, mainly in Senegal. In 1975 he was sentenced to death *in absentia* for involvement in an attempted coup, but remained in exile in Togo and the Ivory Coast. In 1982 the

United Nations appointed him director of its Regional Bureau for the Sahel Region, even though he was unable to return to Benin.

84   Pieter Willem BOTHA

South Africa

Botha was the dominant figure in the government from 1978 until 1989, serving as prime minister and as president. Although he introduced some reforms to the apartheid system he was basically a conservative who was unwilling to countenance any ending of minority rule.

Born in 1916 on a farm in the Paul Roux District of the Orange Free State, he was the son of a nationalistic Afrikaner father who had fought as a commando against the British in the Boer War. In 1934 he became a law student at Grey University College in Bloemfontein but dropped out the following year to organize the NP in Cape Province. He was the NP campaign manager in the 1948 election which brought the party to power and also won a seat in parliament himself. Over the next decade and a half he served in a number of relatively junior ministerial posts, including minister of Coloured affairs and minister of public works. In 1966 he was appointed minister of defence and also became NP leader in the Cape. As defence minister he presided over the strengthening of the armed forces, which gave them the capacity to intervene widely in other states in the region during the 1970s and 1980s. He also worked to make South Africa self-sufficient in basic arms production and a net exporter of arms, in the face of sanctions over weapons. He also established very close personal links with the military establishment which was to prove important in his future political career.

Botha succeeded Vorster as prime minister in 1978, but retained the defence portfolio as well until 1981. In 1984 a new executive presidency was created (following a whites-only referendum the previous year) and Botha became the first occupant of the role. During his time in office he was an ambivalent figure, earning the nickname of the 'old crocodile'. He was keen to present himself as a reformer following an 'adapt or die' philosophy and announcing that old-time apartheid would be brought to an end. Some genuine reforms did take place, such as the legalizing of black trade unions, an end to the ban on inter-racial marriages, the granting of some land rights to urban blacks and the dismantling of much of the structure of petty apartheid. In 1984 limited participation in government was granted to the Asian and Coloured racial groups, although the black African majority remained excluded.

His reform programme was important enough to alienate the right wing of his party, which in 1982 broke away to form the CP, but was never enough to satisfy the genuine reformers in the white political elite and, even less, the black nationalist opposition. He continued to use coercion as the main tactic against his internal opponents and enemies, real or perceived, in neighbouring states. In spite of increasing pressure to release Nelson Mandela and unban organizations like the ANC, actions which many saw as a vital precondition

for future progress, he continued to resist such moves. In January 1989 he suffered a stroke and the following month he resigned from the leadership of the NP, to be replaced by F.W. de Klerk. In August the same year he announced his retirement from the presidency and from active politics. Following his retirement he became increasingly critical of the reformist moves of his successor and in May 1990 he announced that he was resigning his party membership in protest.

85   Roelof Frederik ('Pik') BOTHA

South Africa

Botha is one of the more liberal members of the white government and has been foreign minister since 1977.

Born in 1932 in Rustenburg in the Transvaal, he qualified as a lawyer at Pretoria University before joining the diplomatic service, for whom he worked in Sweden and West Germany. He was elected to parliament for the ruling NP in 1970 and in 1975 he was appointed ambassador to the USA. In 1977 he became foreign minister, a post he has held ever since. One of his greatest successes came with the signing of the Nkomati Accord with Mozambique in 1984. In 1986 he told reporters that he could accept the possibility of a black president in South Africa, a statement which was much attacked by the hardliners within his party. In 1989 he was a candidate to succeed P.W. Botha (no relative) as leader of the NP but did not have enough support within the party to win. He was retained as foreign minister by F.W. de Klerk and played a major role in the discussions that took place after the legalization of the ANC in 1990. He is generally seen as one of the most able and personally charming figures within the government as well as one of the most favourably disposed towards reform.

86   Kojo BOTSIO

Ghana

Botsio was a loyal supporter of Nkrumah and a leading figure in the government of the First Republic. He also played a significant role in party politics in the Third Republic.

Born in 1916, he studied at Oxford and became one of the founder-members of the CPP and was first elected to parliament in 1951. He was the first minister of education and later became minister of foreign affairs. In 1965 he was appointed chairman of the State Planning Commission.

Following the 1966 coup which ousted Nkrumah, Botsio went into exile with his leader and after Nkrumah's death in 1972 he made the arrangements for the return of the body to Ghana. In 1973, Botsio was sentenced to life imprisonment for plotting a coup, but was released in 1977. In the 1979 elections he was banned from running for office but was in charge of the campaign of the victorious PNP. Following the 1981 coup he again went into exile and became one of the most vociferous critics of the Rawlings regime.

87   Ahmed Ould BOUCEIF

Mauritania

Bouceif was prime minister of Mauritania for a short period in 1979 before being killed in a plane crash.

Born in 1934 in Kiffa into the Moorish ethnic group, he joined the army in 1962 and received military training in France. On his return home he served in several top level administrative posts, including governorship at F'Derik. In 1976 he was appointed army chief of staff. Following the coup of July 1978 he became minister of fisheries. In April 1979, conflict within the ruling military group brought a change of leadership and he became prime minister and vice-president of the Military Committee for National Salvation. Although he was in power for only a very short period, he was instrumental in ending Mauritania's participation in the war in Western Sahara through an agreement with the POLISARIO guerrilla movement. Less than two months after coming to power he was tragically killed when his plane crashed into the sea in a sandstorm at Dakar airport in Senegal.

88   Muhammadu BUHARI

Nigeria

Buhari was military head of state from 1983 until 1985, when he was ousted in a further coup.

Born in 1942 in Daura into the Hausa ethnic group, he joined the army in 1962 and received officer training in Britain. He served briefly in the UN peace-keeping force in the Congo. He was director of supply and transport for the Nigerian army from 1974 to 1975. He was a participant in the 1975 coup and became military governor of North East State. Following the reorganization of the federal structure he was appointed governor of Borno State in 1976. Later that year he was appointed federal commissioner for petroleum and energy. In 1979 the military returned to the barracks.

In December 1983, Buhari led the coup which overthrew the Second Republic and became the new military head of state. His performance in office was not impressive and his regime became increasingly unpopular and repressive. In August 1985 he was ousted in a further coup led by Babangida and placed under house arrest. He was forcibly retired from the army but was finally freed from all restrictions on his liberty in September 1989.

89   Kofi Abrefa BUSIA

Ghana

Busia was a leading politician and a leading academic who was prime minister of Ghana's Second Republic from 1969 to 1972, when he was overthrown by a coup.

Born in 1913 into the royal family of Wenchi in the Brong-Ahafo Region, he was educated locally and at Oxford, where he gained a doctorate in social anthropology. After a brief spell in the colonial administration he became a lecturer at University College Legon in 1949 and remained there until 1956. During this period he wrote several books and was also an elected member of the legislative assembly. He then turned to politics full-time and was a major figure in the opposition to Nkrumah. In 1959 he was forced into exile and for the next few years held academic posts in the USA and Britain.

In 1966, following the overthrow of Nkrumah, Busia returned to Ghana and became chairman of the Political Advisory Committee of the NLC military government. He held several important posts for the NLC and was one of the most important figures in drawing up the Second Republic constitution. In 1969 he formed the PP to participate in the elections which were a prelude to the withdrawal of the military. When the elections were held in August the same year the PP emerged as the majority party and he became prime minister in the new civilian government (under the constitution the prime minister was the most important figure, whereas the president had a largely ceremonial role).

The period of the Second Republic was dominated by a struggle with the problems of the economy and Busia's policies of austerity and currency devaluation proved unpopular with many urban dwellers and with military leaders. In January 1972 he was in Britain receiving medical treatment when a further coup took place and his government was toppled. He stayed in exile in Britain, where he returned to an academic career. He died in Oxford of a heart attack in August 1978 and his body was returned to Ghana for a state funeral. Busia represented a curious combination of the mild-mannered academic and the tough grass-roots politician.

90   Mangosuthu Gatsha BUTHELEZI

South Africa

Buthelezi is the chief minister of KwaZulu and the president of the Inkatha movement and is one of the most important black leaders in South Africa.

39

Born in 1928 in Mahlabathini, the son of a Zulu chief, he is the great-grandson of the famous King Cetshwayo. After local education he enrolled at Fort Hare University, but was expelled two years later for political activities. He subsequently completed his degree at Natal University. At this time he was an active member of the ANC and participated in its militant Youth League. In 1953 he returned to Zululand to take up his hereditary chieftaincy. With the founding of the KwaZulu Territorial Authority in 1970, he became its chief executive officer and in 1976 its chief minister. He repeatedly refused to give in to government pressure to accept 'independence' for his homeland under the now totally discredited Bantustan scheme.

In 1975 he established Inkatha as a political party. Despite its anti-apartheid stance, Inkatha remained a legal organization during the period when most black groups opposed to apartheid were banned. Although the party is open to all South Africans, it has remained predominantly Zulu in its membership and in its character. It is known to have a vast membership, although the actual figures are a matter of dispute. Buthelezi's support for the capitalist system and his opposition to the imposition of economic sanctions on South Africa have made him a popular figure amongst sections of the white population. In recent years there have been an increasing number of violent clashes between supporters of Inkatha and of the ANC which have led to a large number of deaths. Although Buthelezi remains a controversial figure it is difficult to see how a solution to the South African crisis can be obtained without his participation.

91 Pierre BUYOYA

Burundi

The current head of state in Burundi, Buyoya came to power in a military coup in 1987.

Born in 1949, he was educated in Belgium and received military training in France and West Germany. By the mid-1980s he was in charge of logistics in the Burundian army. He was on the central committee of the ruling Uprona party and was considered to be a close colleague of President Bagaza. In 1987 he overthrew the latter and became president, establishing himself as chairman of the Military Committee of National Salvation and minister of defence. He abolished Uprona and promised an eventual restoration of democracy. Buyoya, a Catholic, abandoned the campaigns against the Catholic church which his predecessor had launched. Himself a Tutsi, he promised a fairer deal for the Hutu majority, but in August 1988 his army was heavily involved in widespread massacres of Hutu civilians. Buyoya recreated the post of prime minister and appointed a Hutu, Adrien Sibomana, to it, but it remained clear that Tutsi domination remained in place in Burundi.

40

C

92 Amilcar Lopes CABRAL

Guinea–Bissau

Cabral was the leading theoretician of the liberation movements of Lusophone Africa. He founded the PAIGC and was its leader until his murder in 1973.

Born in 1924 in Bafata to a Cape Verdean father and Guinean mother, he was educated locally before going to Lisbon University, from which he graduated in 1950. Whilst in Lisbon he met and married his Portuguese wife, Anna Maria. Returning home he joined the colonial service and from 1952 to 1954 carried out the first agricultural census in the territory, which gave him a detailed knowledge of conditions in the rural areas. He became involved in the covert nationalist movement and in 1956 founded the PAIGC. Given the unwillingness of the Portuguese to consider decolonization, he determined that the path to independence had to be through guerrilla war fought from the rural areas. He wrote prolifically on this and related matters and his publications became extremely influential in many parts of Africa.

In 1963 the PAIGC launched a campaign of guerrilla insurgency and within a few years the movement was in control of most of the countryside, with the Portuguese controlling little outside of the capital, Bissau. By 1973 the PAIGC was able to declare itself the government of an independent state, although formal independence did not come until after the coup in Lisbon in 1974. Cabral was not only the main organizer of the struggle but spent a great deal of time in diplomatic work around the world building support for the liberation movements in all the Portuguese territories. Tragically he never lived to see his country independent because he was assassinated in January 1973 in an attempt by the Portuguese secret police to undermine the liberation movement. His death deprived Guinea–Bissau of a leader of great stature and integrity and it is widely argued that the post-independence history of the country would have been markedly happier if he had lived to govern it.

93 Luis de Almeida CABRAL

Guinea–Bissau

Luis Cabral was the younger brother of Amilcar and became the first president of independent Guinea–Bissau in 1974. He was ousted by a coup in 1980.

Born in Bissau in 1931, he trained as an accountant before entering politics. He was one of the founder-members of the PAIGC and in 1961 became the founding secretary general of the pro-PAIGC trade union movement. In 1965 he became a member of the PAIGC war council and alternated between guerrilla activity in the territory and exile abroad. Following the murder of his brother he became president in 1974, when the departing Portuguese colonialists recognized the independence of the territory under his leadership. He favoured friendly ties with Portugal and in 1978 became the first leader of a Lusophone African state to pay a state visit to Lisbon.

At home his period of rule was marked by increasing economic crisis, bureaucratic inefficiency and corruption and political authoritarianism. In 1980 he was overthrown in a coup and evidence was produced of the mass graves of 500 political opponents. He was tried and sentenced to death but was later allowed to go into exile, eventually settling in Lisbon. His leadership was in some ways an unfortunate accident of history and he certainly lacked the stature of his brother.

94   Vasco CABRAL

Guinea–Bissau

Cabral (who is not a relative of Amilcar or Luis Cabral) was a senior figure in the war of liberation and in the post-independence period has served in governments both before and after the 1980 coup.

Born in Bissau in 1924, he went to the University of Lisbon in 1950, finally graduating in economics in 1959 after spending nearly six years in prison for political offences. He joined the PAIGC in 1962 and soon became a member of its central committee. He was a leading figure in the guerrilla campaign and a member of the war council. At independence he was appointed minister of economic coordination and planning, a position he held until 1982, surviving the 1980 coup. Since 1984 he has been secretary of the council of state, the third most powerful position in government, and permanent secretary of the central committee

of the PAIGC, the second most powerful position in the party.

95   Assan Musa CAMARA

The Gambia

Camara was vice-president of The Gambia from 1973 to 1982 and now leads an opposition party.

Born in Basse in 1923, he was called Andrew David Camara before his conversion to Islam. He was educated locally and worked as a teacher before entering politics. He was elected to the House of Assembly in 1960 as an independent candidate and briefly switched to the United Party. In 1962 he moved again, this time to the PPP which became the ruling party at independence. He was a member of the government from 1963, holding the education portfolio and, subsequently, foreign affairs. In 1973 he became vice-president, a move which pleased his supporters amongst the Fula and Serahuli of Upper River Division. In 1981, with President Jawara out of the country, it was Camara who led the early resistance against the attempted coup.

Following the 1982 election he was dropped from the cabinet after rumours that he had covertly supported successful independent candidates against his own party in the up-river areas. He remained an increasingly critical backbench member of the PPP until 1986, when he broke away to form the GPP and become its leader. Although the new party attracted reasonable support in the 1987 elections it failed to win any seats. The main asset of the GPP is undoubtedly Camara's deserved reputation for competence and honesty.

96   Mama CHABI

Benin

A major northern politician, Chabi has been a senior figure in several post-independence governments.

Born into one of the most important chiefly families in the Parakou area in 1921, Chabi worked in the civil service before entering politics. His powerful traditional support base made him an important ally for other major leaders. Initially he was closely linked with Maga, serving as vice-president of the National Assembly when the latter was in power. After Maga's overthrow he was appointed foreign minister in the Soglo military regime. Following a disagreement with Soglo he was sentenced to 20 years' imprisonment after leading anti-government demonstrations, but his power in the north meant that it was impossible to enforce the sentence. In 1969, President Zinsou appointed him minister of education and when Zinsou was overthrown he was appointed minister of rural development. Although he lost his government position following the 1972 coup by Kerekou, and was briefly imprisoned on corruption charges, he has remained a major political figure amongst northern conservatives.

97   Koenyama CHAKELA

Lesotho

Chakela was a major opposition leader at home and in exile who attempted to reconcile the conflicting political groups in Lesotho before he was assassinated in 1982.

Born in 1935 in Leribe District, he became a migrant labourer in South Af-

rica in 1951. During the 1950s and early 1960s he became the main BCP organizer amongst the migrants in South Africa. In 1965 he returned to Lesotho and was elected as a BCP MP. In 1967 he became secretary-general of the party. He was arrested following the 1970 coup and on his release in 1974 went into exile in Zambia.

In 1977 he led a faction of the exiled BCP which tried, unsuccessfully, to oust Mokhehle as leader. In 1980 he returned to Lesotho under a government amnesty to rally the internal section of the BCP behind him. He tried to act as a unifying force in national politics but rejected the offer of a cabinet post in Jonathan's government. He campaigned for a restoration of democracy in which legal opposition would be permitted. In 1982 he was assassinated, most probably by South African forces or the LLA, or a combination of the two.

98   Gwanda Chikanzi CHAKUAMBA PHIRI

Malawi

Chakuamba Phiri was a leading figure in the Banda government and was viewed as the president's right-hand man until he was imprisoned for treason.

Born in Nsanje District in 1935, he was educated locally before being awarded a scholarship to study in the USA. He abandoned his studies to work for the nationalist movement and became a branch secretary for the Nyasaland African Congress. Along with other nationalist leaders he was detained from 1959 to 1960. On his release he was elected to the legislative council and subsequently to the national assembly. He was a member of successive cabinets and held a large number of different portfolios, including minister for the Southern Region. He was widely regarded as one of Banda's closest allies, but in 1981 he was sentenced to 22 years' imprisonment with hard labour following charges of treason.

99 Momodou Cadija CHAM

The Gambia

Cham has been an important, and often controversial, politician and government minister since independence.

Born in Basse in 1938, he worked in the civil service before entering parliament in 1962 as the elected member for the Tumana constituency, which he has represented ever since. Initially a member of the opposition United Party he switched to the ruling People's Progressive Party in 1970 and became minister of education and then minister of economic and industrial development. In 1977 he was appointed minister of finance but lost this post following a corruption scandal in 1981. He remained an MP and after the 1987 election he returned to the government as minister of works and communications. A powerful orator, with strong grass roots support, he has been one of the more colourful personalities of Gambian politics.

100 Chea CHEAPOO

Liberia

Cheapoo has had an erratic political career, alternating senior government office with periods of imprisonment and exile.

Born in 1942 in Tawohkehn, he received his higher education in the USA, where he graduated in law. On returning to Liberia he worked as a civil servant and was appointed assistant minister of justice by Tolbert. He was also elected as a senator for Grand Gedeh County. Following disagreements with the TWP leadership he lost all his official positions. After a short period in his private law practice he joined the PAL as its legal advisor and was instrumental in turning the PAL into the opposition PPP. When the latter was banned in 1979 he was imprisoned and charged with treason.

Following the 1980 coup he was released and appointed minister of justice in the new government. In September the following year he was sacked from the cabinet and went into exile in Côte d'Ivoire. In 1987 he was politically rehabilitated and was appointed chief justice. In this post he began a lively campaign against corruption within the judiciary which led to the arrest of several judges but which made him many enemies. Ten months later he was dismissed from his position.

101 Richard CHIDZANJA NKHOMA

Malawi

Chidzanja Nkhoma was a senior figure in the government and ruling party until his death in 1978.

Born in 1921 in Mtimuni in Lilongwe district, he received little formal education and worked as a bus inspector before entering politics. He was an active member of the nationalist movement and, along with many of his colleagues, was detained from 1959 to 1960. On his release he became Central Region chairman of the MCP, the dominant party. In 1964 he became minister for home affairs and for the Central Region. Subsequently he held a variety of portfolios, including agriculture, labour and transport. He also held diplomatic posts in Bonn and Nairobi. He was a close ally of President Banda. He died of natural causes in 1978.

102 Bernard Thomas CHIDZERO

Zimbabwe

Chidzero has been the government minister in charge of economic development since shortly after independence.

Born in 1927 in Mashonaland, he received higher education in universities in South Africa, Canada and Britain and earned a doctorate in political science. During the 1960s and 1970s he lived in exile and took no direct part in the guerrilla war. During this time he worked for the United Nations in several important posts and was still working for this organization at the time of independence in 1980. In 1981 he was appointed minister of economic planning and development and the following year the finance portfolio was added to his responsibilities. He has retained these posts ever since. He has had primary responsibility for the, generally successful, development of the Zimbabwean economy since independence and is generally regarded as a pragmatist rather than an ideologist.

103 Gaositwe Keagakwa CHIEPE

Botswana

Having reached the post of foreign minister, Chiepe is one of the few women to have attained high government office in post-independence Africa.

Born in Serowe in 1922, Chiepe established a successful career as an educationalist before entering politics. By 1968 she had risen to the position of director of education for the whole country. In 1970 she switched to a diplomatic career when she was appointed High Commissioner to the United Kingdom in London, where she was also responsible for Botswana's relations with several other west European states.

In 1974 she was brought into the government at home as minister of commerce and industry, a post she held for three years. Her success in this post led, in 1977, to her appointment as minister of mineral resources and water affairs. In the context of Botswana's rapidly growing, and later hugely successful, mineral extraction industry, combined with the perennial problem of aridity, this was a key post in the search for economic growth and development. Chiepe retained this portfolio until 1984 and is rightly credited with making a substantial contribution to the outstanding record of economic success in Botswana. When President Seretse Khama died in 1980 she was even tipped by some as a possible successor.

In 1984, Chiepe became minister for external affairs, a position which demands high levels of political skill given Botswana's geographical location in the heart of the southern African region. She has had considerable success in the difficult task of balancing Botswana's detestation of apartheid with its vulnerability to the might of neighbouring South Africa.

104   James Robert Dambaza CHIKEREMA

Zimbabwe

Chikerema was a leading figure in the nationalist movement, but faded from importance after independence.

Born in 1925 in Kutama, he was educated locally and in South Africa, where he became active within the African National Congress (ANC) of South Africa. He returned home in 1950 and in the late 1950s became vice-president of the African National Youth League (ANYL). In 1961 he joined Nkomo's Zimbabwe African People's Union (ZAPU), where he became an influential figure, acting as president when Nkomo was absent. In 1971 he was a founder of FROLIZI, an ephemeral organization which attempted to unify the nationalist movement. He then joined Muzorewa's ANC, soon renamed UANC and was a member of the government which followed the ill-fated internal settlement of 1978, serving as minister of transport. He then clashed with the UANC leadership and left to form his own ZDP. The ZDP gained little support and failed to win any seats in the 1980 independence elections. The party collapsed soon afterwards and Chikerema retired from politics to become a private businessman. His rapid

movement from one grouping to another had eventually left him politically isolated.

105   Josiah Mushore CHINAMANO

Zimbabwe

Chinamano was a leading figure in ZAPU and for a short time was a member of the post-independence government.

Born in 1923 in Epworth, he qualified as a teacher and later became a school manager. In the early 1960s he became involved in nationalist politics and was vice-president of ZAPU. He was arrested in 1964 and spent most of the next decade in detention. Following his release, he acted as the main negotiator between ZAPU and the other nationalist movements. In the post-independence government he served as minister of transport but was dropped in 1982, along with the other ZAPU members. He died from natural causes in 1984.

106   Henry Masauko CHIPEMBERE

Malawi

Chipembere was a leading figure in the nationalist movement and a member of the first post-independence government. He later led an abortive rebellion against the Banda regime.

Born in 1930 in Mangochi into the Yao ethnic group, he received higher education in South Africa and worked as a teacher before entering politics. He was a militant member of the Nyasaland African Congress and, later, of the Malawi Congress Party, serving as treasurer of both. In 1956 he was elected to the Legislative Council, where he campaigned against the Central African Federation. He was responsible for inviting Banda to return home and lead the nationalist movement in 1958. Like most of the nationalist leaders he was jailed from 1959 to 1960, but unlike the rest he received a further three year sentence from the colonial courts three months later. On his release he was appointed minister of local government in the pre-independence government.

In the post-independence government he was minister of education but resigned from the cabinet following the clash between the president and the younger radicals in 1964. In 1965 he led an armed uprising which was crushed by government forces. He went into exile in Tanzania and then to the USA, where he died in 1975.

107   Daniel Julio CHIPENDA

Angola

Chipenda was a top-ranking guerrilla leader in the MPLA during the war of liberation who later defected to the FNLA.

Born in 1931, he was the son of Jesse Chipenda, the first General Secretary of the Church Council of Central Angola. The latter was arrested by the Portuguese for dissident activity and died in prison. Daniel was an important early leader of the MPLA and in 1964 became head of its youth wing, as well as serving on most of its top committees. He was the leading Ovimbundu within the movement. He commanded the guerrilla army on the eastern front,

where most of his men owed personal loyalty to him rather than to the national leadership.

In 1973 he split with Agostinho Neto, taking most of his guerrilla fighters with him, and was expelled from the MPLA. In 1975 he joined the FNLA of Holden Roberto who made him secretary-general of the movement. Unlike most of the FNLA, Chipenda's forces fought against the South African invasion in 1975, but his grouping subsequently disintegrated and he went into exile in Zaire and Portugal. In 1986 the Angolan government decreed that he could return to the country as a free man following his declaration of support for the MPLA.

108   Jeremiah CHIRAU

Zimbabwe

Chirau was a major traditional chief who was closely involved in attempts at an internal settlement in the 1970s.

Born in 1924 in Makonde, he was very much a conservative traditional chief with little liking for the more modern nationalist movements. He emerged as an ally of Ian Smith and in 1973 he became president of the Council of Chiefs, the body which the white minority government regarded as representative of the black majority within the population. In 1978 he was a signatory to the ill-fated internal settlement. In the same year he founded a political party, ZUPO, in an attempt to mobilize conservative black support, but it had little impact and folded the following year. By the time of independence in 1980 he was isolated from the political mainstream and looked a somewhat anarchronistic figure. He died from natural causes in 1985.

109   Orton Edgar Ching'oli CHIRWA

Malawi

Chirwa was a leading figure in the nationalist movement and founder of the MCP who later clashed with President Banda.

Born in 1919, he qualified as a teacher and taught at Domasi Teachers' College. He later qualified as a barrister in London, the first Malawian to do so. He returned home to support the nationalist movement and in 1959 he founded the MCP, which was to become the ruling party. The following year he handed the leadership of the party to Banda when the latter was released from detention. He became the legal adviser to the MCP and played a prominent role in the independence negotiations. During this period he also established the local court system. At independence in 1964 he became minister of justice and attorney-general. Along with most of the younger radical members of the cabinet he clashed with Banda shortly after independence and was sacked in September 1964.

He went into exile in Zambia, where he established an exiled opposition group, MAFREMO. In 1981 he was back in Malawi: it is alleged that he was kidnapped from Zambia by Malawian secret police. In 1983 he was sentenced to death for treason. Following an international outcry the sentence was commuted to one of life imprisonment. In the late 1980s he was accused of planning continued MAFREMO ac-tivity from prison and warned that he would be held responsible for future actions of the movement. In effect this made him a hostage of the state.

110   Yatuta Kaluli CHISIZA

Malawi

Chisiza was a leading figure in the nationalist movement and the first post-independence minister of home affairs before clashing with Banda.

Born in 1926 in Karonga District, he was educated locally before moving to Tanzania in 1948 to join the colonial police force. He rose to the rank of inspector of police but in 1957 rejected the offer of remaining in Tanzania to head the country's post-independence police to return home to join the nationalist movement. He became a full-time politician with the Nyasaland African Congress and was jailed for his nationalist activities from March 1959 to September 1960. On his release he was appointed administrative secretary of the newly-formed MCP which became the dominant party. At independence in 1964 he was appointed minister of home affairs but, like most of the radical members of the cabinet, he clashed with Banda shortly after independence and was dismissed. He went into exile in Tanzania, from where he led an armed invasion in 1967. The attempt to overthrow the government failed and Chisiza was killed.

111   Joaquim Alberto CHISSANO

Mozambique

Chissano has been president of Mozambique since the death of Samora Machel in 1986.

Born in 1939 in Chibuto, he was an early recruit to the nationalist movement, FRELIMO, when it was established in 1962. He rose rapidly within its ranks: from 1963 to 1966 he was in charge of education and then became secretary to the leader of the movement, Eduardo Mondlane, until 1969. From then until 1974 he was the chief representative of the movement in Tanzania, which was FRELIMO's most important base. Following the Portuguese coup of 1974, which effectively ended Portuguese colonial rule in Africa, he became prime minister of the provisional government of Mozambique until 1975, when formal independence was introduced. He was very close to the FRELIMO leader Samora Machel and when the latter became president in 1975 he appointed Chissano foreign minister. Because of the difficulties posed to Mozambique in the southern African region, especially its hugely problematic relationship with South Africa, the post of foreign minister was arguably the most important within the government. In an attempt to solve the grave security problems Chissano was instrumental in the signing in 1984 of the Nkomati Accord with South Africa whereby in return for the closing of ANC bases in Mozambique, the South Africans agreed to stop supporting the RENAMO guerrillas who were fighting the FRELIMO government. Evidence suggests that Mozambique was the more punctilious in honouring its side of the bargain.

Following the death in a plane crash of Samora Machel in 1986, Chissano became president of both the country and FRELIMO. Since then he has shown himself to be both skilful and pragmatic in attempting to solve the huge economic, political, diplomatic and security-related problems which have afflicted the country. He has attempted with some success to change Mozambique's pro-Soviet foreign policy to one of genuine non-alignment. In 1987 he visited leaders of most of the important western states to cement this new policy. Mozambique was granted observer status at the Commonwealth Conference, in spite of the fact that it had never been subjected to British imperialism. The problems posed by the RENAMO rebels proved more difficult. An amnesty granted to rebels in 1987 failed to produce the desired results. In 1989 and 1990 he agreed to talks with RENAMO and accepted that South Africa was no longer supporting them. In July 1989, Chissano formally renounced Marxism as the guiding ideology of Mozambique and in November 1990 he introduced a new multi-party constitution.

112   Herbert Wiltshire Hamandini CHITEPO

Zimbabwe

Chitepo was a leading figure in the nationalist struggle and chairman of ZANU until his assassination in 1975.

Born in 1923 in Bonda, he gained a degree in South Africa and later qualified as a lawyer in London, becoming Rhodesia's first black barrister. He joined ZANU on its formation in 1963 and later became its chairman. He was largely responsible for the formation of ZANU's military wing, ZANLA, and for the early conduct of the guerrilla campaign against the Smith regime. In 1975 he was assassinated by a car bomb in the Zambian capital, Lusaka. There is still considerable controversy surrounding the identity of his assassins. A Zambian government commission blamed his death on a factional dispute within ZANU, but others have claimed that he was murdered by Rhodesian secret agents.

113 Victoria CHITEPO

Zimbabwe

Chitepo (who is the widow of Herbert Chitepo) is the most senior woman in the government.

Born in 1927 in Natal, South Africa, she received higher education in South Africa and Britain before working as a teacher in the country of her birth. After marrying she moved to Rhodesia, where she was a social worker and became involved in nationalist politics. In 1962 she went into exile in Tanzania, where she did welfare work with Zimbabwean exiles and refugees. She returned to Zimbabwe after independence and in 1982 joined the government as minister of natural resources and tourism, a position she has held ever since.

114 Kanyama CHIUME

Malawi

Chiume was a leading figure in the nationalist movement and Malawi's first minister for external affairs before he clashed with Banda.

Born in 1929 in Usisya, he was educated in Tanzania and Uganda, where he dropped out of medical school. During the 1950s he was an active member of the NAC for whom he was publicity secretary in spite of periods spent teaching in Tanzania. In 1956 he was elected to the legislative council. He was a keen supporter of pan-Africanism and before independence a close ally of Banda. At independence in 1964 he was appointed minister of external affairs but, like most of the radical members of the cabinet, he was sacked a few months later.

He fled to Zambia and later moved to Tanzania. He established the Congress for a Second Republic, an exiled opposition movement which is based in Tanzania.

115 Jean COLIN

Senegal

Colin, who is a white Senegalese of French origin, was a senior member of the government from independence until his retirement in 1990.

Born in Paris in 1924, he was educated there before joining the colonial administration in 1946. He first worked in Cameroon, before moving to Senegal in 1947. Between 1949 and 1957 he worked in Paris and again in Cameroon before returning to Senegal. After independence in 1960 he remained in Senegal, taking Senegalese citizenship and marrying a niece of Leopold Senghor. He retained high political office for the whole post-independence period under both Senghor and, later, Diouf. In 1964 he became minister of finance and retained this post until 1970, when he became minister of the interior. He has also been an elected member of parliament and the elected mayor of Thies. In 1981 he became minister of state and secretary-general to the presidency, a position he held until his retirement in

1990. He was generally regarded as the second most influential person in the government after the president.

116   Blaise COMPAORE

Burkina Faso

Currently head of state in Burkina Faso, Compaore was a close friend and associate of his predecessor, Thomas Sankara, until he overthrew him in a coup in 1987.

The son of a Mossi chief, Compaore was born in 1952. He first met Sankara in 1978, when they were in Morocco for parachute training, and from then on their military and political careers were closely entwined. Although only a captain he became the commander of the National Training Centre for Commandos in Po. When Sankara was arrested in May 1983, Compaore organized resistance to the government from his base in Po and in August led a military force to Ouagadougou to release Sankara and install him as head of state. From then until 1987 he was Sankara's second-in-command, serving as minister of state and justice and as a member of the National Council of the Revolution.

Because the two men seemed so close it surprised and shocked many observers when, in October 1987, Compaore led the coup in which Sankara was overthrown and killed and proceeded to install himself as president. Compaore subsequently claimed that Sankara had been plotting to kill him, although no evidence was ever produced. In power Compaore has followed a less radical approach to domestic and international affairs with his Popular Front government. The local Committees for the Defence of the Revolution were scrapped and their functions returned to the traditional chiefs. Government spending has been reduced and state controls on the economy relaxed.

Compaore is married to a niece of President Houphouet-Boigny of Côte d'Ivoire.

117   Lansana CONTE

Guinea

Conte has ruled Guinea since seizing power in a coup in April 1984.

Born in Dubreka into the Susu ethnic group, he was an unknown figure before 1984. He had risen to the rank of captain and was military commander of Boke Region. In April 1984 he led the coup which occurred a few days after the death of Sekou Toure, establishing himself as president with a military government entitled the CMRN. Initially the new government embarked on a series of liberal measures, including the ending of censorship and the release of large numbers of political prisoners. Following a failed coup attempt in 1985, however, the regime adopted a more authoritarian style of rule, although promising an eventual return to democratic government. Some improvement in the country's economic performance has taken place.

118   Paulo Alexandre Nunes CORREIA

Guinea–Bissau

Correia was the second most important leader in the Vieira regime until he was executed for attempting a coup.

He was a close associate of Vieira and played a leading role in the coup which brought the latter to power in 1980. Immediately following the coup he was a member of the ruling Council of the Revolution and minister of the armed forces. In 1984 he became first vice-president and effectively the second most powerful man in the regime. At the same time he held the post of minister of justice. In November 1985 he led an attempted coup against Vieira which, although having significant support, was defeated. He was tried and in July 1986 he was executed.

119　Manuel Pinto da COSTA

Sao Tome and Principe

Costa has been president of this tiny island state since independence from the Portuguese in 1975.

Born in 1937 in Agua Grande, he spent much of his early life in exile. In 1972 he founded the MLSTP to campaign against continued Portuguese rule. The movement was based in Gabon until 1975. Costa has continued to lead the movement since its foundation. In 1975 independence from colonial rule was secured (owing almost entirely to events elsewhere) and he became the first, and so far only, president of the tiny republic. The MLSTP was until late 1990 the only legal party, although it was possible for independent candidates to contest elections with those of the ruling party. There have been several unsuccessful coup attempts, the most serious being in 1988. Costa has followed a non-aligned, non-ideological path since independence. He is also commander-in-chief of the armed forces.

In late 1990 a new multi-party system was introduced. In legislative elections in January 1991 the MLSTP was defeated by the opposition PCD. Costa announced that he would not stand in the presidential elections due later in the year.

120　Mamadou COULIBALY

Côte d'Ivoire (Ivory Coast)

Coulibaly was a major figure in the colonial period and in the post-independence period until his death in 1985. He was the most important Muslim in the government.

Born in 1910 into the Malinke ethnic group in the north of the country, he was educated in Dakar and at the University of Paris. He returned home to work as a headmaster before entering politics. He was a senior member of the PDCI and acted as party treasurer from 1959 to 1980. He was elected to the territorial assembly in 1959 and became vice-president at independence. From 1961 to 1963 he was Ivoirian ambassador to Tunisia. He was appointed president of the Economic and Social Council (the main advisory body to the president) in 1963 and held that post until his death in 1985.

121　Maurice CURE

Mauritius

Cure was the founder and president of the MLP, which dominated Mauritian politics until the 1980s, when it was ousted through the ballot box.

Born in 1886 into the Creole group, he qualified as a medical doctor in England in 1913. On his return home he

52

campaigned for Mauritius to be transferred from British colonial control to French but the idea never gained much support. In 1936 he founded the MLP and became its leader. The party, which was to a large extent modelled on the Labour Party in Britain, was the main vehicle for nationalist demands. Cure resigned from the party as early as 1941 but remained a significant figure in Mauritian politics until independence. He was nominated to the legislative council in 1964. After independence in 1968 he took little active part in politics but remained a very influential figure in the background. The party which he had founded ruled until 1982. Cure died in 1978.

D

122 David DACKO

Central African Republic

Dacko was president of the CAR for two separate periods, the first in the 1960s and the second in the late 1970s and early 1980s. Both periods of rule were ended by military overthrow and neither could be considered a success.

Born in 1930, he originally worked as a schoolteacher. In the 1950s he entered politics in association with Barthelemy Boganda, the most able of the nationalist leaders. In the latter's pre-independence government he served as minister of agriculture and minister of the interior. Following Boganda's death just before independence, Dacko became government leader and, at independence in 1960, president. His first period in office was marked by economic stagnation and increasing authoritarianism as he suppressed the opposition. On New Year's Eve, 1965, having lost all support within the country, he was overthrown in a coup by his kinsman, Jean-Bedel Bokassa.

Dacko spent a long period in detention following his overthrow, but was rehabilitated in 1976, when Bokassa appointed him as one of his advisors. When Bokassa was ousted by French paratroops in September 1979, Dacko resumed his presidency with the support of the French. In 1981 Dacko was accredited with 50 per cent of the votes in a presidential election contested by several candidates, but his opponents claimed that electoral malpractice had occurred. Scheduled competitive legislative elections which would have included opposition parties were postponed by Dacko. By now whatever credibility he might have had had evaporated and Dacko faced increasing opposition from labour unions, students and other urban groups. Attempts to respond to this with oppression and censorship were to no avail and in September 1981 he was easily overthrown in a coup by Kolingba. On the occasion of his second military overthrow Dacko retired to his farm.

123 Moktar Ould DADDAH

Mauritania

Daddah was the first president of independent Mauritania and remained in office until overthrown in a coup in 1978.

Born in 1924 in Boutilimit into a Berber family of Islamic teachers, he was educated locally and then worked for the colonial administration before studying in France, where he obtained a law degree. In 1957 he was appointed president of the Government Council of Mauritania. In 1959 he was elected to the first national assembly and became prime minister. At independence in 1960 he became head of state and in 1961 was elected as the country's first president. He was subsequently re-elected to this post in 1966, 1971 and 1976.

Following his election in 1961 he formed a new political party, the PPM and banned all opposition parties. From 1971 to 1972 he served as chairman of the OAU. In 1974 he asserted Mauritania's claim to part of Western Sahara as the Spanish colonial administration was withdrawing from the territory, which brought his country into conflict with the POLISARIO guerrilla movement. Involvement in this war brought economic disaster for the country and was very unpopular with the army. In 1978, Daddah was overthrown in a coup and placed under house arrest. He was released shortly afterwards and went into exile in Paris. In 1980 he was sentenced, *in absentia*, to hard labour for life but in 1985 he was given an official pardon by President Taya.

124   Joseph Kwame Kyeretwi Boakye DANQUAH

Ghana

Danquah was one of the major nationalist leaders in Ghana and leader of the opposition after independence.

Born in 1895 into the royal family of Akyem Abuakwa, he was the outstanding Ghanaian scholar of his generation. In England he gained first degrees in both philosophy and law and a doctorate in philosophy, winning several important academic prizes and scholarships. He published several scholarly books on law, sociology, philosophy and religion. In 1931 he returned home, where he founded and ran the *West African Times* and became involved in nationalist politics. In 1947 he founded the UGCC, which was the major party until Nkrumah broke from it to form the CPP. In 1951, Danquah was elected to parliament and from then on was the most important of the opposition leaders before and after independence in 1957.

After independence the opposition parties joined together to form the UP and Danquah was the UP presidential candidate in the 1960 elections, when he lost to Nkrumah. Although he was never tried for any crime he was arrested in 1961, released in 1962 and re-arrested in 1964. In 1965 he died in prison, one of the many victims of Nkrumah's authoritarian style of rule.

125   Sadou DAOUDOU

Cameroon

Daoudou was a close associate of President Ahidjo and considered by many to be the strong man of the regime.

Born in 1926, he was educated in Chad and initially worked in the colonial administration before becoming principal secretary in the prime minister's office in 1958. In 1960 he became minister of information and in 1961 minister in charge of the armed forces. He retained this key position for two decades and played a vital role in keeping the armed forces loyal to President Ahidjo and thus keeping the latter in power. By 1981 his relationship with the president had become a little more distant and he was demoted to the politically less important post of minister of public services. When Biya replaced Ahidjo as president, Daoudou was initially given the important post of permanent secretary to the presidency but a year later, in 1983, he was sacked as part of the purge of old Ahidjo supporters. Officially he retired from public life, but in 1988 he was partly rehabilitated when Biya gave him a prominent role in the organization of the ruling party's election campaign.

126 Bakary Bunja DARBO

The Gambia

Following a brilliant bureaucratic and diplomatic career, Darbo became vice-president of The Gambia in 1982, a post he still holds.

Born in 1946, he was educated at the University of Ibadan (Nigeria) and did postgraduate work in Ivory Coast. On returning home he joined the civil service and in 1971 was appointed director of economic and technical affairs. In 1974 he became manager of the Gambia Commercial and Development Bank. From 1979 to 1981 he was ambassador to Senegal, a key diplomatic posting considering The Gambia's geographical position. In 1981 he was nominated to parliament by President Jawara and appointed minister of information and tourism.

In 1982 he was elected to parliament as PPP member for the Western Kiang constituency. In the same year he was appointed vice-president and was confirmed in this post following the 1987 election. His rapid promotions were part of the president's strategy to rejuvenate the cabinet by bringing in younger men with exceptional ability. The vice-president acts as leader of government business in parliament and Darbo is also minister of education. He is seen as a possible successor to President Jawara.

127 Tamunoemi Sokari DAVID-WEST

Nigeria

David-West has been a prominent figure in several areas of public life and was a senior member of the government in the Buhari period.

Born in 1936 in Buguma, Rivers State, he received higher education at universities in Nigeria, the USA and Canada. He joined the academic staff of Ibadan University and became professor of virology. He served as commissioner for education in the Obasanjo period and was also a member of the Constitution Drafting Committee which produced the draft of the constitution for the Second Republic. In early 1984 he was appointed minister for petroleum and energy in the Buhari regime, a key post because of Nigeria's economic dependence on oil. He was dropped in 1986 by Buhari's successor, Babangida.

128 Zacharias Johannes DE BEER

South Africa

De Beer is the co-leader of the liberal opposition DP.

Born in 1928 in Cape Town, he was educated at Cape Town University, where he qualified as a medical doctor. In 1953 he became the youngest MP when he won the Maitland seat for the UP. In 1959 he was one of the group of more liberal UP members who broke away to form the PP. He lost his seat in the 1961 election, as did all the PP members apart from Helen Suzman. In 1977 the PP merged with one section of the disintegrating UP to become the PFP and de Beer was one of 17 PFP members elected to parliament in the same year. He also became an executive director of the Anglo American Corporation, which dominates the private sector of the South African economy. In 1988 he became the leader of the PFP and in 1989 led the party into a new merger of liberal opposition parties to form the DP, of which he became co-leader. In the 1989 election the DP won 33 seats and one-fifth of the votes.

129   Aquino DE BRAGANCA

Mozambique

De Braganca was a leading academic, diplomat and advisor to FRELIMO until his death in the plane crash which also killed Samora Machel in 1986.

Born in 1925 in the Portuguese colony of Goa in the Indian sub-continent, he trained as a physicist before becoming involved with the struggle against Portuguese colonialism. As well as working for FRELIMO he was instrumental in bringing together the liberation movements in all the Portuguese African colonies to form the umbrella organization, CONCP. Following independence he rejected a career in government to set up and act as director of the Centre of African Studies at Eduardo Mondlane University in Maputo which had an important role in government policy formation. He also acted as a diplomat for the government and was the closest advisor of Samora Machel. In October 1986 he was killed in the same unexplained plane crash which took the life of Machel.

130   Joseph William Swain DE GRAFT-JOHNSON

Ghana

De Graft-Johnson was an important academic and political leader who was vice-president in Ghana's Third Republic.

Born in 1933 into an important Cape Coast family, he received his university education in Britain and the USA where he gained his doctorate in engineering. While holding an academic post at the University of Kumasi he served on several important commissions, including the one which drew up the constitution of the Third Republic. He was a senior member of the PNP and its successful vice-presidential candidate in the 1979 elections. After the coup at the very end of 1981 he was arrested and detained for two years. He then went into exile in Britain to campaign for the restoration of democracy in Ghana.

131   Frederik Willem DE KLERK

South Africa

De Klerk has been leader of the NP since February 1989 and president of South Africa since September 1989. Although he had previously been regarded as a cautious and conservative figure, he rapidly embarked on a series of reforms which completely changed the face of South African politics.

Born in 1936 in Johannesburg into a family with a long history of political involvement, he trained as a lawyer at Potchefstroom University, where he was actively involved in the youth section of the NP. He was first elected to parliament in 1972 as the member for Vereeniging and joined the cabinet as minister of posts and telecommunications in 1978. After holding other portfolios he was appointed minister of home affairs and national education in 1984. Following the breakaway of the Conservative Party in 1982, he became the leader of the NP in the Transvaal, which gave him a powerful political base. Following the resignation of P.W. Botha from the NP leadership in February 1989, de Klerk was elected as the new leader of the party at the national level. In August 1989 he became acting president on the retirement of Botha and the following month he led the NP to victory in the general election and was elected to the presidency.

Although he had claimed to be a reformer during the election campaign, few observers were prepared for the developments which followed his coming to power. In October 1989 a number of important political prisoners, including the veteran ANC leader Walter Sisulu, were released from jail. In February 1990 most remaining political prisoners, including Nelson Mandela, were released and most previously illegal opposition groups, including the ANC, the PAC and the SACP, were unbanned. In May de Klerk's government began discussions with the ANC, with the declared aim of restructuring the South African political system. In June he announced the lifting of the state of emergency (except in Natal) and in September he declared his wish to see the NP open to members of all racial groups. Many other more minor reforms were also introduced during this period. In early 1991 he announced that most remaining apartheid legislation, including the Group Areas Act, would be scrapped. Although he was bitterly attacked by the far right of South African politics, he succeeded in carrying his party with him on the path to reform of the system.

By the end of de Klerk's first year in office the South African political system had been very considerably reformed. Although many problems remained, a predominantly peaceful solution to the long-standing crisis in South Africa appeared a real possibility.

132   Afonso DHLAKAMA

Mozambique

Dhlakama is the leader of RENAMO.

Born in 1953 into the Ndau ethnic group (a Shona subgroup), he originally fought with FRELIMO in the guerrilla war against Portuguese colonialism. He joined the RENAMO movement when it was launched by the Rhodesian army in 1976 to pressurize the FRELIMO government in Mozambique, which was supporting the Zimbabwean nationalist guerrilla movement by allowing them bases in that country. After the independence of Zimbabwe in 1980, the South Africans took over the financing of RENAMO in an attempt to destabilize the FRELIMO government. South African support was supposed to terminate with the Nkomati Accord between Mozambique and South Africa in 1984, although evidence suggests that support continued for at least a time afterwards. In 1982 Dhlakama became president and supreme commander of RENAMO, a position he retains.

RENAMO is a very shadowy organization about which remarkably little is known in spite of its continued ability to wage guerrilla war against the government in Mozambique. Its opponents portray it as little more than a series of extremely brutal armed gangs with no serious political aims. Dhlakama claims it as a genuine nationalist movement with widespread support in the rural areas of Mozambique which is fighting an anti-communist struggle for democracy. Whichever view is taken, the evidence of widespread brutality is overwhelming. Negotiations between RENAMO and the government of Mozambique aimed at resolving the crisis began in 1989 and continued in 1990, without making much progress.

133   Mamadou DIA

Senegal

Dia was the first prime minister of Senegal and was subsequently an opposition leader.

Born in 1910 in Khombole, he was educated in France and later worked as a teacher. After the second world war he co-founded, with Senghor, the Democratic Bloc of Senegal (BDS), and was elected to the French Council of the Republic from 1948 to 1956. Before independence he formed a pattern of joint leadership with Senghor and at independence in 1960 he became prime minister. In 1962 his partnership with Senghor disintegrated and he was accused of plotting a coup. He was imprisoned from 1962 to 1974. With the liberalization of the Senegalese political system in the early 1980s, he formed the MDP in 1981 and has been party leader ever since. He contested the 1983 presidential election but came a very poor third. Neither Dia nor his party contested the 1988 election and, given his advanced age, it would appear unlikely that he will play a prominent role in the future.

134   Yoro DIAKITE

Mali

Diakite was a leading figure in the government following the 1968 coup, serving as vice-president and prime minister. Four years later he was jailed following a coup attempt.

Born in 1932 at Bangassi-Arbala, he joined the French army in 1951 and received officer training in 1958. He later saw active service with the UN peacekeeping forces in the Congo. He was involved in the 1968 coup and although he was Moussa Traore's senior in army ranking, he became second to the latter in the military government. He became vice-president of the ruling Military Committee of National Liberation and leader of the provisional government. In 1969 he was demoted to minister of transport but in 1970 he was promoted to minister of defence. At the end of 1971 he was accused of plotting a coup and the following year he was sentenced to hard labour for life. He died in detention in 1973.

135   Boubacar Telli DIALLO

Guinea

Diallo was a senior government figure in Guinea and was also the first secretary-general of the OAU.

Born in 1926 at Poredake into the Fulbe ethnic group, he went on to earn a doctorate in law in Paris before returning to work as a colonial magistrate at home. After independence he was appointed as Guinea's permanent representative at the United Nations. In 1964 he became the first elected secretary-general of the OAU and held the post until 1972, when he returned home to become minister of justice. In 1976 he was implicated in a coup plot and imprisoned. He was never tried and died of starvation in prison the following year.

136 Ange DIAWARA

Congo

Diawara was one of the major political figures in the Congolese government and ruling party in the late 1960s and early 1970s, before he led a failed coup and was killed.

Born in 1941, the son of a Congolese mother and Malian father, he received higher education in Cuba and the USSR but claimed to be a Maoist. On returning to the Congo he was appointed commander of the civil defence corps. In 1967 he became a leader of the youth movement of the ruling MNR. In 1968 he joined the army and was named vice-president of the CNR and minister of defence. In 1969 he added the crucial post of political commissar of the army to his other responsibilities and became a senior member of the politburo of the newly-formed PCT. He was a key member of the Ngouabi regime and one of its major ideologues. Motivated by a mixture of ideology and personal ambition, he led an attempted coup against Ngouabi in 1972. When this failed he managed to escape and for a time organised a successful guerrilla movement against the government, but the following year he was caught and executed. His body was put on public display in Brazzaville as a warning to other opponents of the regime.

137 Sheriff Mustapha DIBBA

The Gambia

Dibba was vice-president of The Gambia from 1970 to 1973 and since 1975 has been the leader of the main opposition party.

Born in 1937, the son of a chief, at Salikini, he worked briefly as a clerk before becoming a full-time politician in 1959. In that year he was one of the founder-members of the PPP and leader of its youth wing. He was first elected to parliament in 1960 and became minister of labour in 1964. He was also, successively, minister of local government, works and communications, and finance. In 1970 he was appointed vice-president while retaining the finance portfolio. He was clearly the second most important political leader in the country after President Jawara, but his position as a potential rival to the latter caused a split between the two. In 1973, Dibba was dismissed from his government post and expelled from the PPP.

In 1975 he founded the NCP which rapidly became the major opposition party. Dibba rallied support amongst fellow Mandinka in the rural areas, especially in the Baddibus, who felt that Jawara (himself a Mandinka) had neglected their interests, and in the urban coastal areas. In the 1977 elections the NCP won five seats (out of 34) and Dibba became the official leader of the opposition in parliament. In 1981 he was arrested and charged with being implicated in the attempted coup which had taken place. In 1982 he was brought to trial, found not guilty and released. He was in prison during the 1982 elections and, although he and his party were candidates and gained nearly one-third of the votes, he lost his own seat. In the 1987 elections the NCP won five seats but Dibba again failed to secure election in his own Central Baddibu constituency. Although he remained leader of the party, one of his colleagues took over the role of leader of the opposition in parliament. During 1989 there were strong rumours that Jawara and Dibba were discussing the possibility of the latter rejoining the PPP, but nothing materialized.

138 Umaru DIKKO

Nigeria

Dikko was a major figure in the government of the Second Republic and came to international fame when an attempt was made to abduct him from Britain in a wooden crate.

Born in 1936 in Kaduna State, he was educated locally and later graduated from London University. From 1967 to 1972 he was commissioner for finance in North Central state and later commissioner for information. He was a senior figure in the ruling NPN and after the return to civilian rule in 1979 became minister of transport. He was subsequently appointed chairman of the Presidential Task Force to oversee the importation of essential commodities. He gained a reputation for large-scale corruption and after the 1983 coup he fled to exile in Britain. In 1984 an attempt was made to abduct him from Britain in a crate whilst in a drugged condition, to stand trial in Nigeria, but the attempt was discovered at the airport and failed. Lengthy legal proceedings concerning his extradition followed and in May 1989 his request for refugee status was finally rejected by the British, leaving him in an extremely vulnerable position.

139 Buka Suka DIMKA

Nigeria

Dimka was a figure of total obscurity until he fronted the 1976 coup attempt.

Born around 1940 into the Angas ethnic group, he was an unknown junior officer in the physical education corps of the army until February 1976, when an attempt to overthrow the government of Murtala Muhammed took place. Dimka was the man who announced the coup on the radio. The attempt, which was very unpopular, failed but Muhammed was assassinated. The affair was complicated by Dimka's kinship ties to Yakubu Gowon, who had been ousted the previous year. Dimka was caught and executed the following month. Although other, more senior, figures are known to have been involved, the event is usually referred to as the 'Dimka coup'.

140 Cheikh Anta DIOP

Senegal

Diop was one of Africa's leading scholars and a major opposition leader in Senegal.

Born in 1922 in Diourbel, he was educated locally before going to France to study in 1946. He remained there until 1960, engaged in research and student politics. He published a large number of books and articles and was best known for his controversial thesis that ancient Egypt was basically a black civilization. Back in Senegal in 1961 he founded a radical opposition party, the BMS but the party folded in 1963 when most of his party colleagues defected to the ruling party. He founded a further party, the FNS, but this was banned in 1965. In 1973 he founded another party, the RND, but because of the restrictions on numbers of parties it was not legalized until 1981. In 1983 the RND came a poor third in the general election. Diop led the party until his death from natural causes in 1986, but it never succeeded in building a support base outside of the urban areas and remained somewhat intellectually remote from the mass of the Senegalese population.

141 Hamani DIORI

Niger

Diori was president of Niger from independence in 1960 until he was overthrown in a coup in 1974.

Born in 1916 near Niamey into the Djerma ethnic group, he was educated locally before qualifying as a teacher in Senegal. He subsequently worked as a schoolteacher and as an instructor in African languages for colonial administrators. In 1946 he founded the PPN and later the same year was elected as deputy for Niger in the French National Assembly. During the 1950s Diori and his party were engaged in political competition with his main opponent, Djibo Bakary, with the balance of power fluctuating between the two groups. Diori succeeded in gaining the support of most of the traditional leaders and also of the most numerous ethnic group, the Hausa. In 1958 he achieved two important victories, first in the referendum on de Gaulle's plans for autonomy in the French Community (which Bakary opposed) and second in the December general election which gave his party a substantial majority in the legislature. He became prime minister and with full independence in 1960 he was elected to the presidency of the new republic.

Diori's period in power was marked by an increasingly authoritarian style of rule punctuated by several attempts to overthrow or assassinate him. Opposition was banned and evidence grew of significant levels of government corruption. Relations with France were generally harmonious, although they were strained at the time of the Nigerian civil war, when he backed the federal forces whilst the French favoured the Biafran side. His hold on power was seriously weakened in 1973 when serious drought led to economic collapse and he was finally overthrown in a coup in 1974. His wife was killed in the coup and he was imprisoned. He remained in jail until 1980, when he was transferred to house arrest. In 1987 he was finally released and went into exile in Morocco, where he died in April 1989.

142 Abdou DIOUF

Senegal

Diouf has been president of Senegal since 1981, when he succeeded Senghor.

Born in 1935 in Louga, he was educated locally and at the University of Paris, where he graduated in law in 1960. On his return home he joined the civil service and earned a reputation as an extremely able administrator. In 1970 the post of prime minister was re-established and Diouf was appointed by Senghor. This was correctly seen as the beginning of Senghor's attempt to choose his own successor, although at the time Diouf was seen as an able technocrat but lacking in political skill and without an independent power base. These doubts still remained when, at the end of 1980, Senghor announced his retirement. Diouf became president in January 1981 and, shortly afterwards, leader of the ruling PS, but many believed that he would only be a temporary replacement. Since then Diouf has proved these doubts to be unfounded.

Less than three months later he extended the democratization process started by Senghor by allowing for the free formation of political parties without ideological restrictions. In the elections of 1983 and 1988 he was elected to the presidency and the PS won a healthy parliamentary majority on each occasion. In 1982 he formed the Senegambian Confederation between Senegal and the small neighbouring state of The Gambia and became president of its council of ministers, but confederal arrangement proceeded very slowly and the project was abandoned in 1989. In 1987 he faced a major crisis when the police force went on strike, but he was able to defuse the situation without undermining his own position. Within the ruling PS he has strengthened his position through a gradual and peaceful purging of potential opponents and through strengthening his ties with the Muslim leaders in the rural areas who supply much of the support base for the party. Although there are still strains within the Senegalese political system, Diouf has proved since coming to power that he is a highly skilled political operator who prefers conciliation to conflict. He was chairman of the OAU from 1985 to 1986.

143   Emmanuel DIOULO

Côte d'Ivoire (Ivory Coast)

Dioulo has been a major figure in politics and banking, although his career received a major setback after a scandal in the mid-1980s.

Until 1985 he was one of the most influential people in the country. He was a senior figure in the PDCI and a member of the steering committee of the party. He had been president of the Southwest Region Authority and in 1985 was mayor of the capital, Abidjan. He was also president of a major bank and several other companies. Following a major financial scandal in 1985 he fled to Paris, from where he threatened to expose malpractice in the higher levels of the government. In 1986 he was given a presidential pardon and flown back to Côte d'Ivoire in the president's personal plane to begin a process of rehabilitation. He had previously been tipped as a possible successor to the president, but it remains to be seen whether or not he can overcome the incident.

144   Dono-Ngardoum DJIDINGAR

Chad

Djidingar is a master of the art of political survival. In the violent and unstable world of Chadian politics he has managed to emerge as a senior figure in successive governments.

Born in 1928 in Dono-Manga in the far south of the country, he received little formal education, an omission which has never been a handicap in his political career. He was first elected to the Territorial Assembly in 1957 and to the new Legislative Assembly in 1959. After independence he was appointed to a series of important ministerial positions in President Tombalbaye's government. In 1961 he became minister of finance, being switched to posts and telecommunications in 1965, to public works in 1966 and to agriculture and rural development in 1971. He was one of the very few people to survive the frequent purges which took place over this period.

He then survived the 1975 coup which overthrew the government of which he was a member and temporarily withdrew from national politics to become mayor of his home town. In 1982 he became prime minister in Goukouni's government and when the latter was violently overthrown by Habre he was appointed to the new government as minister of agriculture and rural development. In 1989 he was appointed minister of state, a position which in formal terms is second in importance to the presidency.

Unlike most Chadian political leaders Djidingar has never attempted to create his own armed grouping and his continued survival has rested on his abundant skills as a politician, with genuine popular support.

145   Mamari Ngakinar DJIME

Chad

Djime has been a senior figure in the Chadian army and has held important positions in several governments.

A member of the Sara-Kaba ethnic group, he was born in 1934 and received his secondary education in Brazzaville. He joined the French colonial army in 1952 and fought in Algeria. He received senior military training in France from 1958 to 1960 and again in 1962 and from 1969 to 1970. In the late 1960s and early 1970s he was frequently promoted and held several important military posts, including command of the gendarmerie. In 1975, along with sev-

eral senior officers, he was arrested by the Tombalbaye government. His detention, combined with his popularity amongst the troops, was one of the factors which led to the coup which toppled the government shortly afterwards.

In the post-coup government Djime was minister of the interior and security and regarded as one of the strong men of the regime. When Habre took control in 1978 he was appointed minister of defence and managed to retain this post when the former was ousted by Goukouni. He finally lost his position when Habre resumed power in 1982.

146   Negue DJOGO

Chad

Generally regarded as one of the most able military leaders in the country, Djogo has remained an important figure in most of the post-independence governments owing to his willingness to negotiate new alliances.

Born into the Sara-Kaba ethnic group in 1932, he joined the French colonial army at an early age and received military training in France before seeing action in Algeria. In 1964 he was appointed deputy chief of staff in the Chad army and commander of the First Infantry Battalion. In 1965 he fell from favour and was made commander in the remote Faya-Largeau area, but his competent handling of this difficult assignment earned him political rehabilitation. In 1972 he was appointed head of Tombalbaye's cabinet, a position he held until he was arrested in 1975. Within weeks he was released, following a coup which ousted Tombalbaye, and became minister of finance and later minister of health, labour and social affairs. When Goukouni came to power Djogo became vice-president in the GUNT government. In 1982, following Habre's ousting of Goukouni, he became the leader of one of the main armed factions opposed to the new government and commander in chief of the anti-government forces. However in 1985 he switched sides and declared his support for Habre and, in 1986, was appointed minister of justice by the latter. In 1988 a cabinet reshuffle resulted in him becoming minister of transport and civil aviation.

147 Bhekimpi DLAMINI

Swaziland

Dlamini was prime minister from 1983 until he was dismissed by the king in 1986.

Born in 1924 in Hhohho into the traditional Swazi ruling clan, he received his schooling locally and in South Africa. He fought for the British army in North Africa and Italy in the second world war, rising to the rank of sergeant. After the war he worked as a storekeeper. On the death of his father he became a senior chief and was elected to parliament in 1967, the year before independence. Before the death of King Sobhuza in 1982 he served in only minor government positions, but during the regency of the queen mother, Dzeliwe, he was rapidly promoted, becoming prime minister in 1983. Even by the standards of the Swazi aristocracy he was considered to be an arch traditionalist. Following King Mswati's succession to the throne in 1986 he was dismissed. He was known to have opposed Mswati's succession and in 1987 he was arrested and charged with treason. He was sentenced to 15 years in jail but was pardoned and released in 1989.

148 Makhosini DLAMINI

Swaziland

Dlamini was the first post-independence prime minister, serving from 1968 to 1976.

Born in 1914 in Enhletsheni into the traditional Swazi ruling clan, he trained as a teacher in Swaziland and South Africa. He enjoyed a career in teaching and became a headmaster before resigning in 1947 to devote his time to business and politics. On the death of his father in 1950 he became a senior chief and began working for the colonial authority as a rural development officer. He was involved in the constitutional talks with the British in the late 1950s and early 1960s and in 1964 he became the founder and chairman of the INM. The INM was the political wing of the traditional Swazi aristocracy which was formed to respond to the advent of electoral politics in the late colonial period. It was from the start the dominant political party, winning all the seats in the pre-independence elections. At independence in 1968, Makhosini Dlamini became prime minister and retained this position when King Sobhuza scrapped the constitution in 1973. He was replaced as prime minister in 1976 and died of a heart attack two years later.

149 Maphevu DLAMINI

Swaziland

Dlamini was prime minister from 1976 until his death in 1979 and was also the commander of the armed forces.

Born in 1922 in Egocweni into the traditional Swazi ruling clan, he received his education locally before working for a short time as private tutor in the royal residence. He then worked in South Africa in a number of minor clerical posts. In the 1950s he returned to Swaziland to train as a veterinary assistant. By the time of independence in 1968 he had risen to become Chief Stock Inspector. In 1973 he joined the newly formed army, the Umbutfo Defence Force, and became its commander in January 1976. In March of the same year he was appointed prime minister. He remained in this post until 1979, although for part of the time he was unable to work because of serious injuries sustained in a car crash in 1977. He died in October 1979.

150   Mfanasibili DLAMINI

Swaziland

Dlamini was one of the most powerful figures in government until he was ousted in 1985.

Born in 1939 in Embekelweni into the traditional Swazi ruling clan; his early education was interrupted by periods of work as a herdboy. He later worked in the South African mines. In 1963 he was nominated to the powerful traditional Swazi National Council. He was elected to parliament in 1967 and joined the cabinet in 1972 as minister of commerce. He remained in the cabinet for many years but his more important power base was as the recognized leader of the lineage which expected to provide the successor to King Sobhuza. In the power struggle following the death of the latter he lost out and was sacked by the Queen Regent in 1985.

The following year he was sentenced to seven years in jail following strong rumours of a coup plot.

151   Jackson Fiah DOE

Liberia

Doe (who is no relation of S.K. Doe) was a senior figure in the pre-coup hierarchy and a major opposition leader in the post-1985 period.

Born in 1934 in Glolay, he received higher education in Liberia and the USA before becoming a teacher and headmaster. He was elected to parliament in 1967 and served until 1972, when he joined the government as deputy minister of education. From 1975 he also served as a senator. He was a leading figure within the ruling TWP and became first national vice-chairman of the party in 1979.

Following the 1980 coup he was imprisoned for four months. In 1982 he was appointed special advisor to the head of state on national and international affairs. When the ban on political parties was lifted in 1984 he founded and led the LAP. In the 1985 elections he was placed second in the presidential election with a little over one-quarter of the votes. In the legislative elections the LAP emerged as the largest opposition party. Despite harassment from the government, including periods in detention, he has continued to lead his party.

152   Samuel Kanyon DOE

Liberia

Doe was the leader of the 1980 coup and the winner of the presidential election of 1985. His regime was constantly threatened by coup attempts.

Born in 1950 in Tuzon into the Krahn ethnic group, he completed his primary education but dropped out of secondary school in 1967. Two years later he joined the army and by 1979 had risen to the rank of master-sergeant. In 1980 he led a group of low ranking enlisted men in a coup which overthrew the government of President Tolbert and resulted in the assassination or execution of many leaders of the ousted regime. Doe became chairman of the People's Redemption Council (or PRC) and head of state. The coup broke the long-term dominance of the Americo-Liberian elite and Doe became the first Liberian ruler to come from an indigenous Liberian ethnic group. His first cabinet included a number of academics and professionals who had previously been identified with parties and groups in opposition to the ousted TWP regime. The inclusion of such people gave the government a degree of administrative competence which was lacking in the ill-educated soldiers who had seized power in the coup. Many were also identified with radical left-wing ideologies, which led observers to believe that this would bring a significant change of direction in government policies.

The uneven composition of the government led to considerable tensions and within a couple of years almost all the educated radicals had been expelled by Doe and many had gone into exile. Government policy came to closely resemble that of the ousted TWP government, although a doubling of army pay secured support from most soldiers.

Doe promised a return to civilian rule but it became obvious that the change

was not meant to diminish his own position. When the ban on political parties was lifted in 1984 he formed his own NDPL as a vehicle for his political ambitions. In the 1985 elections he won just over half of the votes in the presidential election, while the NDPL won a majority of seats in the legislature. The fairness of the elections and the accuracy of the results were strongly contested by the opposition parties and many neutral observers, but in January 1986 he was sworn in as president.

After 1986 he presided over a regime noted for its incompetence, authoritarianism and venality. There were numerous violent attempts to overthrow him every year he was in power. In 1990 armed rebellion broke out and the country degenerated into civil war. Doe was killed by the rebels in September 1990, leaving no agreed successor.

153   Jose Eduardo DOS SANTOS

Angola

A senior figure within the MPLA, dos Santos was a prominent member of the post-independence government and in 1979 became president of Angola following the death of Agostinho Neto.

Born in 1942, the son of a bricklayer, dos Santos joined the MPLA as a teenager and became vice-president of its youth wing. He joined the guerrilla army in 1962 and in 1963 was awarded an MPLA scholarship to study in the Soviet Union, graduating with a degree in petroleum engineering in 1970. He returned to Angola and was elected to the Central Committee of the MPLA in 1974.

In 1975 he became foreign minister in the first post-independence government and then first vice-prime minister. In 1978 the latter post was abolished in a restructuring of the government system and dos Santos was appointed to the key position of minister of national planning. In 1979, following the death of President Neto, he was elected as leader of the ruling MPLA Workers' Party and president of Angola. Having previously been designated leader of government business when Neto was abroad, dos Santos was viewed as the chosen successor of the deceased president. Given the prior history of factionalism within the MPLA, the unanimity of support for dos Santos was most striking. He has a reputation for combining Marxism with a high level of pragmatism and is regarded as a party moderate.

For most of the 1980s Angola was plagued with a civil war which involved a high level of foreign intervention. In 1988, dos Santos achieved a major breakthrough when, following talks between Angola, South Africa and Cuba, an agreement was reached which provided for independence for neighbouring Namibia, the ending of South African support for UNITA and the withdrawal of Cuban troops from Angola. In 1989, dos Santos signed a peace agreement with Jonas Savimbi at a meeting held in Zaire. There is no doubt that Angola needs internal peace if economic development and social reconstruction are to take place. In an attempt to achieve peace he instituted a multiparty system at the end of 1990.

154   Marcelino DOS SANTOS

Mozambique

Dos Santos was a top leader in FRELIMO during the struggle against Portuguese colonialism and has been a senior figure in government and party since independence.

Born in 1931 in Lourenco Marques (now Maputo) he received higher education in Lisbon and Paris before devoting himself to the FRELIMO cause. At the inaugural conference in 1962 he was chosen as secretary for external affairs. He held this post until independence in 1975 and was responsible for much of the diplomatic work in promoting the cause of anti-colonialism. In 1970 he also became vice-president of FRELIMO. After independence he became minister of economic planning but his sometimes erratic policies of state control produced little success in the economic field, even allowing for the extra problems caused by Mozambique's troubled position in the Southern African region, and have subsequently been modified or abandoned.

Following the death of Samora Machel in 1986 he was viewed by some as a possible contender for the presidency, but he did not press his claims and supported Joaquim Chissano. In 1987 he was appointed to the newly created post of chairman of the People's Assembly, the equivalent of leader of parliament. He retains his position on the political bureau of FRELIMO.

155 Kissima DOUKARA

Mali

Doukara was a senior figure in the military government from 1968 to 1978, when he was jailed following a coup plot.

He was a leading actor in the 1968 coup and became a member of the ruling Military Committee of National Liberation. In 1970 he became minister of defence and security. In this post he earned the reputation of a military hardliner owing to his brutal treatment of opponents of the regime. In 1972 he was placed in charge of Mali's drought-relief campaign, a position which placed him in control of large amounts of funds from foreign donors. Evidence shows that he embezzled large amounts of this money. In 1978 he clashed with President Traore over the issue of a return to partial civilian rule, which he opposed. The president tried but failed to expel him from the government. Later in the year Doukara organized a coup attempt against Traore and was sentenced to death. In 1979 he was also tried on corruption charges and found guilty of embezzling nine million dollars of drought-relief money, for which he received another death sentence. The sentences were commuted to life imprisonment and he died in 1983 in the Taoudeni salt mines.

156 Charles Gaetan DUVAL

Mauritius

Duval has been a central figure in Mauritian politics and has occupied most of the senior government positions.

Born in 1930 into the Creole community, he qualified as a lawyer in Britain, returning home in 1956. He joined the rather conservative PM. He rose within the party ranks to become its leader and in 1965 changed the name of the party to PMSD. The party was opposed to independence from Britain but when decolonization became inevitable Duval accepted it. In the 1967 elections the PMSD was the second best supported party and he became leader of the opposition. In 1969, a year after independence, he took his party into the newly formed coalition government and became foreign minister. In 1976 the coalition split and for a time Duval returned to legal work after rejecting the post of attorney-general. He remained in politics and after the 1983 election returned to government as deputy prime minister. In 1987 he was implicated in a drug scandal and offered to resign, but his offer was rejected by the prime minister. In 1988 he did resign and in 1989 he was accused of murder but after a short period in detention he was released.

E

157 Krobo EDUSEI

Ghana

Edusei was a senior figure in the government of the First Republic in Ghana and an influential figure in the Third Republic.

Born in Kumasi in 1915, he was educated locally before becoming a journalist on the *Ashanti Pioneer*. In 1947 he founded the Ashanti Youth Association and in 1949 joined Nkrumah's CPP, becoming one of its leading figures and its propaganda secretary. He held many important ministerial portfolios both before and after independence, including justice, the interior, industry and agriculture. He was a strong supporter of Nkrumah's authoritarian style of leadership and also was involved in several corruption scandals, which included the purchase of a golden bed.

After the 1966 coup he was arrested for corruption and was not released until 1970. Because of his record he was banned from standing for office in the 1979 elections but became a leading figure in the ruling PNP, serving on the central committee of the party and as chairman of the Ashanti Region branch. After the 1981 coup he was again jailed for corruption. In 1983 he was released on grounds of ill health and he died the following year.

158 Mohamed Haji Ibrahim EGAL

Somalia

Egal was a senior figure in the post-independence government and was prime minister from 1967 until the 1969 coup.

Born in 1928 in Berbera, he was the son of a wealthy merchant and was privately educated in England. He was elected to parliament in 1960 for the SNL which he had led since 1958. At independence in the same year he became minister of defence and was subsequently minister of education. In 1967 he became prime minister but was ousted and detained in the 1969 coup. His major achievement whilst in office was in improving Somalia's relations with its neighbours.

He was released in 1975 and appointed as ambassador to India. The following year he was again arrested and this time remained in jail until 1982. After his release he became chairman of the local Chamber of Commerce.

159 Imoru EGALA

Ghana

Egala was a major government figure in Ghana's First Republic and one of the most influential politicians of the Third Republic.

Born in 1914 into a wealthy family in Tumu in the northern part of the country, he became one of the most important Muslim politicians. He was first elected to parliament as an independent in 1954, but then joined the dominant CPP. He served in several cabinet posts in the First Republic and was chairman of the notably inefficient and corrupt Cocoa Marketing Board. He was minis-

70

ter of industry at the time of the 1966 coup. In 1969 he was banned from participation in the elections which ushered in the Second Republic.

In 1979 he founded the PNP, which was to become the ruling party in the Third Republic, but, because of his past record, was once again banned from standing for public office. To get around this he succeeded in getting his nephew, Hilla Limann, elected as president. Egala was appointed as adviser to the president and was widely recognized as the 'power behind the throne'. He died suddenly of a heart attack in April 1981.

160 Colin Wells EGLIN

South Africa

Eglin was the leader of the liberal opposition (PP, later PFP) from 1971 to 1979 and from 1986 to 1988.

Born in 1925 in Sea Point, he was a student at the University of Cape Town. Although his studies were interrupted by war service, he graduated in 1946. In 1958 he was first elected to parliament as a UP MP. In 1959 he was one of the liberal group within the UP which broke away to form the PP. In the 1961 election Eglin, like all the PP members except Helen Suzman, lost his seat in parliament. He continued to work for the PP as party leader in the Cape and by assisting the party's sole MP. In 1971 he became national leader of the party. In the 1974 election he led the party to a moderate success when it increased its number of MPs from one to six and he was elected for the Sea Point constituency. In 1977 he led the PP into an alliance with other liberal groups from which the PFP was constructed, with

him as leader of the new party. In November the same year the party won 17 seats in a snap general election and he became leader of the official opposition in parliament. In 1979 he stepped down from the party leadership in favour of F. van Zyl Slabbert, but continued as national chairman. In 1986, when van Zyl Slabbert resigned as party leader, Eglin again took over, but himself resigned in 1988 although he remained in parliament.

161 Vangah Mathieu EKRA

Côte d'Ivoire (Ivory Coast)

Ekra has been a senior member of the Ivoirian government and of the ruling PDCI since independence.

Born in 1917 into the Dan ethnic group, he had wide experience in the colonial civil service before entering politics. In 1947 he became a member of the executive committee of the PDCI but in 1949 he was detained by the colonial authorities for three years. In the late 1950s he worked for the French overseas ministry in Paris. In 1959 he was elected to parliament and the following year he briefly headed the Ivory Coast delegation at the United Nations.

When he returned from New York in 1961 he joined the government and has since held a wide range of important portfolios, including public service and the interior, whilst retaining an important position within the party. Since the late 1970s he has been minister of state in charge of state enterprises. In this role he has played an active part in getting rid of less efficient heads of parastatals and imposing more resolute government budgetary control over this sector. In doing this he has earned a certain amount of respect but has also made a number of political enemies. He is viewed by many as one of the more likely candidates to succeed Houphouet-Boigny.

162 Cyprian EKWENSI

Nigeria

Ekwensi is a major Nigerian novelist who was a participant on the Biafran side in the civil war.

Born in Minna in 1921 into the Ibo ethnic group, he was educated locally before training as a pharmacist in England. Best known as a novelist of acute political and social observation, he has published many books, from *People of the City* (1954) to *Beneath the Convent Wall* (1987). During the civil war he was a strong supporter of the Biafran cause and worked for the rebel government as director of information services in Enugu. Since the war he has also been a major publisher and has held a number of important academic posts.

163 Alex Ifeanyichukwu EKWUEME

Nigeria

Ekwueme was vice-president of Nigeria during the period of the Second Republic.

Born in 1932 in Oko into the Ibo ethnic group, he was educated locally before going to the USA and Britain for higher education. He earned a doctorate from the University of Strathclyde in Scotland. He built up a large architecture practice in Nigeria and became very wealthy. With the lifting of the ban on

political parties in 1978 he joined the NPN and was chosen as its vice-presidential candidate. In 1979 he was elected to the vice-presidency and was re-elected in 1983. Following the coup at the end of 1983 he was detained. He was released in 1986, when it was decided that there was no evidence of corruption to bring against him. In 1989 he commenced a postgraduate course in law.

164 Anthony Eronsele ENAHORO

Nigeria

Enahoro was one of the major politicians of the First Republic and has continued to play a prominent role in public affairs ever since.

Born in 1923 in Uromi, Bendel State, he was educated in Lagos before becoming a journalist. He was editor of several newspapers, including the *Southern Nigerian Defender* (1944) and the *Nigerian Star* (1951). In 1951 he was a founder-member, with Awolowo, of the Action Group (AG) and was subsequently elected to the House of Representatives. He was the mover of the 'self-government in 1956' motion in parliament. In the pre-independence government he was minister of home affairs.

After independence he was chief opposition spokesman on foreign affairs. In 1962 he was arrested but escaped and fled to Britain, from where he was extradited following a controversial court case. He was sentenced to jail but was released in 1966 after Gowon came to power. In 1967 he was appointed federal commissioner of information, labour and cultural affairs. During the civil war he was engaged in top-level diplomatic activities on behalf of the federal government. In 1975 he was put in charge of the arrangements for FESTAC, the major continental gathering, but was sacked from his post after Gowon was ousted. In 1978 he joined the NPN, which was to become the ruling party of the Second Republic, and was elected chairman of the party in his home state. This marked a major break with his old partner Awolowo, who was leader of the opposition. Following the demise of the Second Republic in 1983, he remained an influential figure but his active political career came to an end.

165 Gnassingbe (Etienne) EYADEMA

Togo

Eyadema has ruled Togo since he came to power in a coup in 1967.

Born in 1937 in Pya into the Kabre ethnic group, he did not complete his education before joining the French army at the age of 16. He fought for the French in Algeria and Indochina. He was a participant in the 1963 coup, when he personally assassinated President Olympio. He then led the 1967 coup which brought him to power as president. In 1969 he established a new political party, the RPT, which he has led ever since and which is the only legally permitted party. In practice the party has been little more than a front for Eyadema's domination, although some limited pluralism has been allowed within the party since the mid-1980s. A new constitution did not appear until 1979. Under it Eyadema was elected president, as the sole candidate, in 1979 and again in 1986. In 1974 he launched a campaign of 'African authenticity' which largely consisted of changes in names, including his own from Etienne to Gnassingbe.

In his long period in office his regime has a mixed record. In spite of several poorly organized coup attempts, the political system has been largely stable. He has developed a highly personalized authoritarianism and there have been large numbers of political prisoners with seemingly reliable accusations of the use of torture against opponents. Although Eyadema himself is poorly educated, he has appointed sufficient well-educated technocrats to ensure that Togo is one of the more efficiently administered states of the region. The economy has also been relatively stable, with some signs of development and growth. Beyond an ill-defined nationalism the regime has indicated no ideological preferences. In spite of more than two decades in power, Eyadema looks more than averagely secure in office.

F

166   Henry Boima FAHNBULLEH

Liberia

Fahnbulleh was a leading opposition figure before the 1980 coup and a senior member of the government afterwards, before losing his position in 1983.

Born in 1949 in Monrovia, he received his higher education in Liberia and the USA, where he earned a doctorate in political science. In 1978 he returned home to an academic post at the University of Liberia. He became involved in left-wing opposition to the government and was a founder member of the MOJA. In 1979 he was arrested and detained for a few weeks.

Following the 1980 coup he was appointed minister of education, in which post he was active in trying to reform the school system. In 1981 he was appointed foreign minister, but in 1983 he lost this position in confusing circumstances. He claimed to have resigned over government policy of establishing diplomatic links with Israel, but the head of state claimed to have sacked him for supporting an unacceptable ideology.

167   Adekunle FAJUYI

Nigeria

Fajuyi was a senior figure in the Ironsi government in 1966, until his assassination.

Born in 1926 in Ado Ekiti, Ondo State, he was educated locally before entering the army. After officer training in England he was commissioned in 1954. He served with the UN peace-keeping forces in the Congo, where he was military assistant to the UN supreme commander. At the time of the January 1966 coup he was commander of the Abeokuta garrison. He was appointed military governor of the Western Region by Ironsi. During the July 1966 coup he was assassinated alongside Ironsi, whom he had tried to defend.

168   Remi Ade FANI-KAYODE

Nigeria

Fani-Kayode was a senior political leader in the First Republic and was prominent in the Second Republic.

Born in 1921 in London, he was educated in Lagos and at Cambridge University, where he graduated in law. He was called to the bar in 1945. He went into politics as a member of the NCNC and was first elected to parliament in 1954. At independence in 1960 he became leader of the opposition in the Western Regional House of Assembly. In 1963, following an alliance with Akintola, he became deputy premier of the Region. Following the 1966 coup he returned to his legal practice and business activities. After the lifting of the ban on political parties in 1978 he joined the NPN, which was to become the ruling party of the Second Republic, and became a national vice-president of the party until the further coup of 1983.

169   John Colley FAYE

The Gambia

Faye was a major political leader in the pre-independence period and a major religious leader who remained influential in public life until his death in 1985.

Born in Bathurst (now Banjul) in 1908, he qualified as a teacher and became a minister in the Anglican church. He was the leading figure in the attempt to bring education to the previously neglected up-river rural areas. He represented the latter on the Legislative Council throughout the 1950s and also acted as minister of works and communications. In 1951 he created the DP, which was the country's first political party. In 1960 he united the DP with the Muslim Congress Party to form the DCA. The latter marked the coming together of Christian and Muslim political leaders and although it never became a major force it set the tone for the religious political tolerance which has existed in the country ever since. During 1963–4 Faye was the Gambian Commissioner to the United Kingdom. In 1964 he retired from active politics but remained provost of St Mary's Cathedral in Banjul. Combining his roles of Christian leader and religious conciliator, he was an extremely important public figure until he died in 1985.

170   Winston FIELD

Zimbabwe

Field was prime minister of Southern Rhodesia from 1962 until 1964.

Born in 1904 in Bromsgrove, England, he emigrated in 1921 to Southern Rhodesia where he worked his way up from being a farm assistant to becoming a major independent tobacco farmer and the president of the powerful Rhodesian Tobacco Association. He enlisted in the British army during the second world war and participated in the Normandy landings. He became leader of the Dominion Party in 1955 and stayed leader when it changed its name to the RF in 1962. When the RF won the election later the same year he became prime minister and began by releasing most of the black nationalists then in detention. Although he was by no means a progressive on matters of race, he was ousted by the right wing of the RF in 1964 and replaced by Ian Smith. He retired from politics and died from natural causes in 1969.

171   John Ngu FONCHA

Cameroon

Foncha was prime minister of West Cameroon and a strong supporter of the unification of Anglophone and Francophone Cameroon.

Born in 1916 in the former British Cameroons, he was educated in Nigeria and later became a schoolteacher. From 1951 to 1954 he was a member of the Eastern Nigerian Assembly. In 1955 he founded the KNDP, which he led until its dissolution in 1966. He enjoyed a reputation as a good grass roots politician, often using a bicycle to reach the more remote villages. When the KNDP won the 1959 election he became prime minister of West Cameroon with a mandate to seek unification with Eastern Cameroon. Following the 1961 plebiscite of 1961, which supported the merger, he became vice-president of the new

Cameroon Federal Republic, as well as remaining prime minister of the west. In 1965 he was re-elected to the federal vice-presidency, but was unenthusiastic about President Ahidjo's plans to move from a federal to a unitary form of government. In 1970 he formally retired from politics but continued to exercise considerable background influence amongst the Anglophone politicians.

172   Lawrence Shang FONKA

Cameroon

Following a steady, but not especially distinguished, political career, Fonka was the surprise choice of President Biya for the key post of president of the National Assembly, which in constitutional terms is second only to the presidency.

Born in 1920, he trained as a teacher and taught for several years before entering politics. From 1956 to 1959 he was minister of information in the Eastern Region of Nigeria. Following the merger of Anglophone and Francophone Cameroon he joined the ruling UNC party in the new federal republic. He was active in party organization and built a career as a backbench member of the National Assembly, representing especially Anglophone interests. His rapid elevation to the presidency of the Assembly came in 1988, following the retirement of the leading Anglophone politician Solomon Tandeng Muna.

G

173 Aaron GADAMA

Malawi

Gadama was a senior figure in the Banda government before his mysterious death in 1983.

Born near Kasungu in 1934, he qualified as a teacher and received further training in Scotland and Kenya. In 1971 he was elected to parliament as MP for Kasungu and was rapidly promoted to the cabinet as minister of community development. He subsequently became a powerful figure in government and was appointed minister for the Central Region. He appears to have been perceived as a threat to President Banda and in May 1983 he died (along with Dick Matenje) in circumstances which have never been properly explained. Government sources claimed that the men died in a car crash, but it was widely believed that they were shot while trying to flee the country.

174 John GARANG

Sudan

Garang is the leader of the southern rebels in the civil war in Sudan.

Born in 1943 in Jonglei into the Dinka ethnic group, he was educated in the USA. From 1969 to 1970 he was a member of the Sudanese army but then defected to join the Anya Nya rebels who were fighting against the northern-dominated government. Although this particular period of armed conflict came to a temporary end with the Addis Ababa agreement of 1972, southern resentment continued and in 1983 Garang formed the SPLM, with its military wing, the SPLA. He continues to lead both with support from Ethiopia. Although there have been several ephemeral cease-fires the war between Garang's southern rebels and the Sudanese army continues to have devastating effects on the country. Assessments of Garang vary considerably, from those which see him as a radical nationalist to those which see him as a self-serving Dinka tribalist.

175 Joseph Nauven GARBA

Nigeria

Garba was a major figure in the 1975–79 military regime and has since had a notable career as a UN diplomat.

Born in 1943 in Langtan, Plateau State, he was educated locally before joining the army in 1957. He later received officer training in Britain and served in the UN observer forces in Kashmir. From 1968 to 1975 he was commander of the Brigade of Guards at the Dodan Barracks in Lagos, a crucial military position. He was a leading participant in the 1975 coup which overthrew Gowon, for which he made the official announcement on the radio. In the Muhammed–Obasanjo regime he was commissioner for external affairs. He retired from the army in 1980 and was appointed Nigerian ambassador to the United Nations in 1983. In 1989 he was elected president of the UN General Assembly.

176 Ibrahim Momodou GARBA-JAHUMPA

The Gambia

Garba-Jahumpa was a major educationalist, trade union leader and politician who held several senior government appointments in the colonial and post-colonial periods.

Born in Bathurst (now Banjul) in 1912, he trained as a teacher and held a number of senior appointments in the education field. He was also a trade unionist and was secretary of the Gambia Labour Union from 1939 to 1945 and a member of the International Confederation of Free Trade Unions. In 1951 he brought several Muslim groups together to form the MCP. In 1960 he merged the MCP with the Christian-led Democratic Party to form the Democratic Congress Alliance. He later joined the United Party and, in 1968, the ruling PPP. He was appointed minister of health and, in 1973, minister of finance. In the 1977 elections he was defeated in his Banjul South constituency by an opposition candidate and retired from active politics, although he continued to be an influential figure in the community.

177 Bathoen GASEITSIWE

Botswana

After decades as chief of one of Botswana's major tribes, the Bangwaketse, Gaseitsiwe turned to party politics following independence and became the most important opposition leader for a time.

Born in 1908 in the Ngwaketse tribal capital, Kanye, he became chief Bathoen the Second of the Bangwaketse tribe in 1928, holding this position for over 40 years until he abdicated in favour of his son, Seepapitso. In colonial Bechuanaland the major tribal chiefs had considerable power and influence. From 1937 to 1958 he was also chairman of the African Advisory Council, which represented the indigenous people in dealings with the colonial authorities.

At independence power was transferred from the traditional chiefs to the more modern elected political leaders. This change was bitterly resented by the more conservative chiefs like Bathoen, but as the traditional leaders were legally barred from participating in party politics it was difficult for them to challenge the government openly. In 1969 Bathoen resigned his chieftainship and joined the opposition BNF. Established in 1966 by Daniel Kwele and Kenneth Koma, the BNF was at the time an avowedly radical party, making it appear an odd base for the arch conservative ex-chief. In the elections of 1969 all the BNF electoral successes were in the Ngwaketse tribal area and directly attributable to the prestige of Bathoen. In the Kanye South constituency he himself defeated vice-president Quett Masire. He proceeded to reorganize the party, expelling many of the early radicals, but not Koma. From 1970 to 1978 he was president of the party. In 1978 he handed the presidency of the party to Koma but retained the leadership of the parliamentary party. Apart from being a good constituency MP, he used his position in parliament to campaign for the restoration of the traditional powers of the chiefs, without much success. In 1986 he retired from party politics and became president of the Customary Court of Appeal. He died in late 1990.

178   Komla Agbeli GBEDEMAH

Ghana

Gbedemah was a leading member of the Ghanaian nationalist movement and a senior figure in the post-independence government.

Born in 1912 in Nigeria to Ghanaian parents of the Ewe ethnic group, he was educated in Ghana and worked as a teacher and businessman before entering politics full-time in the late 1940s. He was a member of the UGCC, but left the party, along with Nkrumah, to found the CPP in 1949. When Nkrumah was imprisoned it was Gbedemah who ran the party. He was the main organizer of the CPP election victory in 1951 and was a major figure in the pre- and post-independence governments for the next decade.

From 1954 to 1961 he was minister of finance, but in the latter year major disagreements with Nkrumah led, first, to his demotion to minister of health and then to dismissal from the cabinet. He went into exile but returned following the 1966 coup. For the 1969 elections he organized the NAL, which was one of the major opposition parties in the Busia period. He later worked for the military regime of Acheampong but clashed with the latter and was jailed for a short period. His earlier association with the CPP continued to be a major political handicap and he was debarred from standing in the 1979 elections.

179   Hage GEINGOB

Namibia

Geingob has been a senior figure in SWAPO and in March 1990 became the first prime minister of independent Namibia.

Born in 1941 in Otjiwarongo, he qualified as a teacher and worked as a schoolteacher before going to the USA for higher education, graduating with a masters degree in political science. He joined SWAPO in 1962 and his work for the movement was mainly diplomatic and organizational rather than involving participation in the guerrilla warfare. From 1963 to 1964 he was SWAPO representative in Botswana and from 1964 to 1971 served the same role at the United Nations. From 1972 to 1975 he worked for the United Nations. In 1975 he was appointed director of the UN Institute for Namibia in Zambia, an institution which was responsible for training and educating future administrators of an independent Namibia.

In June 1989 he returned to Namibia and was chosen as the leader of SWAPO's election campaign. After the election he became chairman of the Constituent Assembly which had the task of drawing up the post-independence constitution. At independence in March 1990 he became the country's first prime minister.

180   Jeanne GERVAIS

Côte d'Ivoire (Ivory Coast)

Gervais was the first woman minister to be appointed to the Côte d'Ivoire government.

Born in 1922, she became vice-president and later president of the Ivoirian Women's Association. Just after independence she was elected to the national assembly and remained a member until 1976. In that year she joined the government as minister of women's affairs, the first woman to attain government office, albeit of a rather token kind. She remained in this post until 1984.

181   Joseph Deshi GOMWALK

Nigeria

Gomwalk was a senior figure in the Gowon regime from 1967 to 1975 and was later executed for his participation in a counter-coup .

Born in 1935 in Amper, Plateau State, he graduated in zoology from Ibadan University in 1961. He worked as a research officer at the Kaduna Veterinary School before joining the Nigerian police in 1966, rapidly rising to the rank of chief superintendent. In 1967 he was appointed governor of Benue-Plateau State in the Gowon regime. He remained in this post until 1975, but he became one of the most unpopular of Gowon's governors and earned a reputation for serious corruption and maladministration. He was sacked in 1975 after the overthrow of the Gowon regime. In 1976 he was one of the major figures behind the failed Dimka coup. He was arrested, tried and executed in May 1976.

182   Enrique GORI MOLUBUELA

Equatorial Guinea

Gori Molubuela was a leading figure in pre-independence politics and later became foreign minister.

A member of the Bubi ethnic group, he was born in Fernando Po (the offshore island part of the state) in 1924. He entered a seminary but never completed his training for the priesthood. In 1964 he became president of the Fernando Po branch of the main nationalist party, MUNGE. From then until independence in 1968 he was president of the island's assembly and a member of the Spanish Cortes. At independence he became foreign minister. In 1969 he was arrested in connection with a claimed coup attempt and imprisoned. In 1972 he perished horribly in prison when he was left to die of gangrene after having his eyes torn out.

183   GOUKOUNI Oueddie

Chad

Goukouni was president of Chad between 1979 and 1982 and both before and since has been a major leader of armed opposition to several regimes. In recent years his support has dwindled and he has become a rather isolated figure in exile in Libya.

Born in 1947, the son of a major Toubou traditional leader in the remote northern Tibesti region, he worked briefly in the civil service before returning to his home area to form an armed anti-government group entitled the Second Liberation Army, which became loosely allied to the FROLINAT forces. Despite a change of regime in 1975 as the result of a coup, Goukouni continued armed opposition to the central government. He received massive aid from Libya which enabled him, in 1979, to take control of the capital Ndjamena and declare himself president.

The civil war continued and, although formally he was the head of state, Goukouni was never able to control more than a portion of the national territory. In 1982 he lost the military struggle with his arch enemy Habre and was forced to flee to the north with those forces still loyal to him.

Goukouni set up a self-styled Government of National Salvation in Bardai, a town close to the Libyan border. From here he fought the Habre government, but the fighting became dominated by foreign intervention, with the French backing Habre and the Libyans backing Goukouni. The latter was weakened by the defection of most of his more important Chadian supporters and when, after several failed attempts, the Libyans and French negotiated a withdrawal, Goukouni was left fairly isolated. In this weakened position he was unable to prevent further defections and went into exile in Libya. From here he proclaimed himself president of the government in exile in 1988, but more recent reports suggest that he is now virtually under house arrest and has a negligible following.

184   Hassan GOULED Aptidon

Djibouti

Gouled became the first president at independence in 1977 and has remained in power since that time.

Born in 1916 in what was then French Somaliland, he belongs to the Issa ethnic group. He was an elected member of the French Senate from 1952 to 1958 and of the French National Assembly from 1959 to 1967. He was a major leader of the independence movement

and in 1972 became president of the main nationalist party, the LPAI. In 1977 the miniscule territory became independent, with Gouled as president. Tensions have existed between the Somali-oriented Issa ethnic group of Gouled and the minority Ethiopian-oriented Afar group. In 1981 he banned the opposition PPD, which was mainly supported by Afars. In 1982 Gouled's party, now renamed the RPP, was declared the only legal party. Since then he has attempted to placate the Afar community by appointing members of the group to his government, but there are a number of exiled opposition groups and the politically sensitive geographical location of Djibouti makes the situation somewhat fragile. He was last re-elected to a six-year presidential term in November 1987.

185   Abel GOUMBA

Central African Republic

A leading politician, who was also the country's first African qualified doctor, Goumba has spent most of his political career in opposition, often in exile.

Born in 1926, Goumba worked for the French colonial administration before receiving his medical education. He entered politics in the 1950s and became minister of finance in the pre-independence government of Barthelemy Boganda. On the latter's death in 1959 he became interim president but quickly lost this position to his rival, David Dacko, who excluded him from the government. Goumba formed an opposition party, the Movement for the Evolution of Democracy in Central Africa, but this was banned and he was arrested.

81

In 1962 he went to France and began an international medical career which included a period with the World Health Organisation. Continuing his opposition in exile to successive governments at home he formed a body called the Ubanguian Patriotic Front.

Goumba spent a total of 17 years in exile but returned home following the overthrow of the Bokassa regime. He contested the 1981 presidential election but lost to Dacko. After the overthrow of the latter by Kolingba, Goumba was appointed rector of the University of Bangui. In 1982 he was arrested for political activities and sentenced to five years in jail, but was released in 1983. In early 1984 he was again arrested but released at the end of the year.

Given the generally abysmal quality of government leaders in the CAR since independence, it is extremely unfortunate that Goumba has continually found himself so marginalized in the country's political system. A progressive man who is intellectually head and shoulders above his opponents, Goumba is certainly the best president the CAR has never had.

186   Yakubu GOWON

Nigeria

Gowon was military head of state in Nigeria from 1966 until 1975.

Born in 1934 in Lur, Plateau State, into the small Angas ethnic group, he is both a northerner and a Christian, a combination which was important in his political career. He joined the army in 1954 and received officer training at Sandhurst in England. In 1961 and 1962 he served in the UN peace-keeping force in the Congo. He was absent from Nigeria at the time of the January 1966 coup, but was appointed army chief of staff in the new government. He did not participate in the coup which took place in July the same year, but as the senior surviving military figure he was chosen, at the age of 32, to become the new military head of state.

He came to power at a particularly difficult time and, despite his best efforts, was unable to prevent the secession of Biafra and the subsequent civil war. His successful prosecution of the war maintained Nigerian unity. Following the war he embarked on a quite remarkable process of reconciliation under the slogan 'no victors–no vanquished' which was largely successful in reintegrating the Biafran secessionists into the federal republic. In the later part of his period in office his regime became bogged down in corruption and inefficiency, although responsibility for this has to be attributed to some of his subordinates rather than to Gowon himself, who retained a well-deserved reputation for integrity. His indefinite postponement of a return to civilian rule in 1974 greatly weakened his position.

In July 1975 he was overthrown in a bloodless coup while he was attending an OAU meeting in Uganda and went into exile in England, where he enrolled as a student of political science at the University of Warwick. The following year attempts were most unfairly made to associate him with the failed counter-coup which led to the death of his successor, Murtala Muhammed, although no evidence was ever produced. Nevertheless he was dismissed from the army and was declared a wanted person in Nigeria. In 1981 all charges against him were dropped and he finally returned to Nigeria in 1983. The following year he gained his doctorate in political science from Warwick.

Although he came to power virtually by accident, Gowon was, arguably, the most important of Nigeria's post-independence leaders to date and certainly survived in office longer than any other. A man of great intelligence, honesty and dedication, his main fault was an inability to deal with subordinates who did not reach his own high standards.

187   Nicolas GRUNITZKY

Togo

Grunitzky was the president of Togo for four years, from 1963 to 1967.

Born in 1913 in Akatpame to a Polish officer in the German army and a Togolese mother, he received his primary education in Togo and his secondary and higher education in France, where he obtained a degree in engineering. On returning to Togo he worked as a railway engineer before becoming a businessman. In 1946 he founded and led the PTP and from 1951 to 1958 he represented Togo in the French legislature. Following the 1955 elections he became prime minister in the pre-independence government, but in the 1958 elections his party performed poorly and he lost office to his main rival, Olympio. Grunitzky went into exile in Côte d'Ivoire but returned after the 1963 coup had ousted Olympio and was installed as president by the army. His regime lacked a popular support base and in 1966 he responded to pressure by sacking his cabinet and taking personal re-

sponsibility for most ministries. The following year he was overthrown in a further coup and returned to exile in Côte d'Ivoire. In 1969 he was involved in a car crash and shortly afterwards died in a hospital in Paris from the injuries he sustained.

188   Lamine GUEYE

Senegal

Gueye was an early leader of the nationalist movement and remained significant after independence.

Born in 1891 in Mali of Senegalese parents, he studied law in France during the first world war and became Francophone Africa's first black lawyer. He was elected mayor of Saint-Louis in 1925. In 1935 he was a founder member and leader of the PSS, which was the first modern political party in the country. In 1946 he was elected mayor of Dakar. He was the guiding figure in the early political career of Leopold Senghor, but the two men split in 1948 and Gueye was eclipsed by his former protégé. They reunited in 1958 and, at independence in 1960, Gueye became the president of the National Assembly. He retained this post and was an influential figure in government circles until his death in 1968.

189   Archibald Jacob GUMEDE

South Africa

Gumede has been a senior figure within the African National Congress for many years and is a president of the UDF.

Born in 1914 in Pietermaritzburg, he was educated to secondary level and worked mainly as a clerk. He joined the

ANC in 1944 and subsequently became secretary of the Natal branch. In 1966 he qualified as a lawyer. In 1979 he founded the Release Mandela Committee and became its chairman until the committee lost its reason for existence with the release of Mandela in February 1990. When the UDF was founded in 1983 as a broad-based anti-apartheid grouping he was elected one of its presidents. He was arrested and detained on several occasions. His father was a founder member of the ANC back in 1912.

H

190 Hissein HABRE

Chad

Habre served in, and led armed opposition to, several Chadian governments before he seized power and became president in 1982. Subsequently, using a combination of tactical political manipulation and the ruthless application of brute force, he brought to Chad a degree of unity and central government control which had not existed before.

Born in 1936 in Faya-Largeau, in the north of the country, he is the son of a shepherd. He served in the French colonial administration and later in the post-independence bureaucracy, where he made rapid progress, and received further training in Paris. In 1971 he was sent by President Tombalbaye to negotiate secretly with armed opposition groups based in Libya. Instead he deserted the government and joined the fragmented opposition forces. From 1972 to 1976 he operated an alliance with Goukouni, but split from him after policy and personality clashes and then led his own armed group in isolation. In 1978 he made peace with President Malloum and became prime minister in the latter's coalition government. This alliance was weak and ephemeral and soon degenerated into armed conflict which enabled Goukouni to take control in the capital and establish his GUNT government in 1979. At first Habre served in this government as minister of defence, but by 1980 it had broken into warring factions and he was ousted by Goukouni's Libyan support troops. Habre returned to armed opposition, receiving support from the French and the CIA and in 1982 succeeded in ousting Goukouni and installing himself as president.

The first few years of Habre's rule were marked by an escalation of political violence as the Chad civil war drew in substantial foreign intervention, with large numbers of French troops backing Habre and Libyan troops backing Goukouni. Gradually, however, Habre gained supremacy as larger areas of the country fell under his control. His increasing hegemony was based on coercive force rather than popular support. In 1988 he succeeded in negotiating the end of Libyan backing for his opponents, which confirmed his military supremacy. In 1988 and 1989 he consolidated his victory through a series of political manoeuvres in which some of his most influential opponents were brought into his government in important, but subordinate, positions.

By the end of the 1980s internal opposition appeared drastically reduced, although a failed coup attempt in 1989 clearly indicated that it had not been entirely eliminated. For the first time in many years the state of Chad had a central government which exercised a degree of control over virtually the whole country. To achieve this Habre had frequently demonstrated great ruthlessness in the violent situation in which he found himself. The key question which remained was whether or not he had the necessary qualities of leadership to rebuild his war-shattered country. This question was not to be answered because he was overthrown in a further coup in December 1990 and the country was pitched back into violent anarchy.

191   Juvenal HABYARIMANA

Rwanda

Habyarimana has been president of Rwanda since coming to power in a coup in 1973.

Born in 1937 in Gasiza into the northern section of the majority Hutu ethnic group, he received higher education in Zaire before entering the army in 1960 and receiving officer training in Belgium. He enjoyed a spectacular rise within the army, becoming chief of staff in 1963. In 1965 he was appointed minister of defence in Kayibanda's government. Following a deterioration in social and economic affairs he led a bloodless coup against Kayibanda, a fellow Hutu, in 1973 and became head of state. He appointed a cabinet with a civilia̟ majority but with soldiers occupying key posts.

In 1975 he announced the formation of a new political party, the MRND, with himself as leader. All Rwandan citizens automatically become members of the MRND at birth. In 1978 a new constitution was introduced which allowed for the direct election of the president, but with only one candidate. Habyarimana was elected in this way in 1978, 1983 and 1988. Under his rule relations between the Hutu majority and Tutsi minority have been improved, which, in turn, has led to improved relations with neighbouring Burundi, although the relationship was strained in 1988 with the influx of Hutu refugees fleeing Tutsi persecution in Burundi. Internal rule has been authoritarian but generally stable. Rwanda is the most densely populated state in Africa and economic development has remained extremely moderate.

192   Mohammed Khouna Ould HAIDALLA

Mauritania

Haidalla was prime minister from 1979 to 1980 and president from 1980 to 1984.

Born in 1940 in Beir Enzaran into the Aroussi ethnic group, he was educated locally before joining the army. He received officer training at St Cyr in France from 1962 to 1964. During the 1970s he saw a great deal of active service in the struggle with the POLISARIO guerrillas in Western Sahara. He was a member of the military government following the 1978 coup and, when Bouceif was killed in a plane crash in 1979, Haidalla became prime minister. In the same year he became army chief of staff. In January 1980 he led a coup against the leadership of Louly and became president and leader of the Military Committee for National Salvation.

In 1980 he abolished the institution of slavery in Mauritania. He brought an increasing number of civilians into the government but plans for further liberalization of the political system were abandoned after abortive coup attempts. His greatest success was in finally extricating Mauritania from the war in Western Sahara and signing a peace treaty with the POLISARIO movement. In December 1984 Haidalla was overthrown by Taya in a bloodless coup while he was out of the country, following a period of civil unrest. He returned home and was placed in detention until his release in 1988.

193   Emperor HAILE SELASSIE

Ethiopia

Haile Selassie was emperor of Ethiopia from 1930 until he was deposed by the 1974 coup.

Born Tafari Makonnen in 1892 into the royal family, he was appointed governor of Harar province when he was 18 years old. He rapidly established himself as the most able and intelligent member of the royal family and in 1916 became head of the government. He held this position for 14 years and established himself as a progressive reformer by the standards of the very conservative Ethiopian society, working hard to increase contacts with the outside world. Following a period of factional conflict within the court he became emperor in 1930, adopting the name Haile Selassie, which means Lion of Judah. In 1931 he established the first parliament in the kingdom but over the next few years domestic reform was stalled by increasing Italian pressure and eventual invasion following a feeble response from the League of Nations when he appealed to that body for help. He personally led the armed resistance to the Italian invaders, until he was forced to flee into exile in Britain in 1936.

In 1941, with the help of British troops, he was restored to the throne in Ethiopia. He pursued a programme of modernization and cautious reform and in 1955 produced a new constitution which, for the first time, allowed for elected members of parliament. However most real power remained with the emperor, as it did until the time of his overthrow. In 1960 he survived an attempted coup. In 1962 Eritrea was incorporated into Ethiopia, a development which was to cause serious problems for successive Ethiopian governments. Throughout the 1960s he played a major role in inter-African relations, including the founding of the OAU in Addis Ababa in 1963 and acting as a mediator in the Nigerian civil war. At home the old political system came under increasing pressure from more radical sections of Ethiopian society, including the trade unions, students and, most crucially, the army. By now an octogenarian, Haile Selassie was unable to respond effectively to these pressures and in September 1974 he was ousted by the army. He was placed under arrest and was not released before his death in 1975. He was buried without ceremony. He still remains a major figure for the world-wide Rastafarian movement.

194   Abdirazak HAJI HUSSEIN

Somalia

Haji Hussein was prime minister from 1964 to 1967 and subsequently an opposition leader.

Born in 1924 in Galcaio, he was educated at Koranic schools but was forced to leave owing to a lack of finance. In 1953 he went to Cairo to pursue Arabic studies and joined the SYL, serving as its president from 1955 to

1956. He was first elected to parliament in Somalia in 1959 and at independence in 1960 was appointed minister of the interior. In 1964 he became prime minister and pursued a policy of pan-Somali nationalism. In 1967 he was replaced as prime minister by Egal but remained in parliament as an opposition figure. After the 1969 coup he was arrested and remained in detention until 1973. The following year he was appointed ambassador to the United Nations. He remained in this post until 1980, when he retired to live at home in Somalia.

195   Chris Martin Thembisile HANI

South Africa

Hani is a leading figure in the younger generation of leaders of the ANC.

Born in 1942 in Cofimvba in the Transkei, he graduated from Rhodes University and worked as an articled clerk in Cape Town. He joined the ANC Youth Wing in 1957 and when the movement was banned in 1960 he joined its military wing, Umkhonto wi Sizwe (Spear of the Nation). After several arrests and detentions he went into exile with the ANC and also fought with the liberation movement in Zimbabwe. In 1982 he was appointed deputy commander of Umkhonto and in 1987 ANC chief of staff. Following the unbanning of the ANC in February 1990, he returned to South Africa to take part in the negotiations with the government, adopting a much more moderate tone than he had done previously. He is regarded as a possible future leader of the ANC.

196   Emmanuel HANSON

Ghana

Hanson was a leading figure of the radical intellectual left in Ghana who figured prominently, but briefly, in the early Rawlings regime in the 1980s.

Born in 1937, he gained his doctorate in political science in the USA and held academic posts in Ghana, the USA and the United Kingdom while maintaining a critical stance to governments at home. In 1982 he was appointed secretary of the PNDC government of Rawlings, one of the most senior political posts in the regime. By 1983 he had become disenchanted with what he regarded as the government's failure to live up to its radical promise and was sacked. He returned to opposition in exile while working as a consultant for the UN university in Tokyo. In 1987 he was killed in a car crash while visiting Tanzania.

197   James George HASKINS

Botswana

Having held a number of senior government positions, Jimmy Haskins has been the most important white politician in post-independence Botswana.

Born in Bulawayo in 1914, he entered the family business established by his father in Bechuanaland and built up a successful career. In the colonial period he served on the European, and later Joint, Advisory Councils and on the Legislative Council. With the coming of independence Haskins, like most of Botswana's white population, was keen to integrate with the non-racial society which was being created and joined the BDP.

In 1966 he became a specially elected member of the National Assembly. He was appointed minister of commerce from 1966 to 1969, minister of finance from 1969 to 1970, minister of agriculture from 1970 to 1972 and minister of works and communications from 1972 to 1979. In all these posts his efficiency was recognized.

Because of his open and friendly nature he gained political popularity which knew no racial boundaries. He was an active worker for the ruling BDP and was party treasurer from 1970 to 1979. In 1979 he was unanimously elected to the delicate post of speaker of Botswana's highly democratic National Assembly, where his performance has earned the praise and respect of the members of all the political parties represented there.

198   Helenard Joe (Allan) HENDRICKSE

South Africa

Hendrickse is the leader of the (Coloured) LPSA, which participates in the tri-cameral parliament established in 1984.

Born in 1927 in Uitenhage, he trained as a minister in the Congregational Church and also worked as a teacher. In 1969 he founded and led the LPSA which initially was linked with other radical non-white groups in the Black Consciousness Movement. In 1979 the policy of the party changed to that of cooperation with the government, although it still declared itself opposed to apartheid. Following the establishment of the tri-cameral parliament in 1984, which allowed limited government participation by Coloureds and Asians, but excluded black Africans, Hendrickse and his party have been the main Coloured group to take part. In the 1984 and 1989 elections to the House of Representatives (the Coloured parliament) the LPSA has emerged as the dominant party, but the vast majority of those eligible to vote have chosen not to do so. Because of this it is difficult to know how much support Hendrickse has within his community, but it would appear likely that cooperation with the apartheid system has damaged his credibility.

199   Jan Christiaan HEUNIS

South Africa

Heunis was a leading figure in the government of P.W. Botha and was a candidate in the contest to succeed him.

Born in 1927 in Uniondale, in Cape Province, he graduated in law from the University of Stellenbosch in 1948. He became involved in NP politics at local and then provincial level and was first elected to parliament in 1970. He was a member of several cabinets, where his ministerial roles included Indian affairs, economic affairs and transport. In 1982 he became minister of constitutional planning, being responsible for drawing up the 1984 constitution which gave Asians and Coloureds a limited role in government but continued to exclude the black African majority. In 1986 he became party leader in the Cape but his political credibility was dented the following year when he only just retained what had previously been a safe NP seat. He was very close to Botha and when the latter was absent through illness or foreign travel he became acting president. When Botha resigned the party leadership in February 1989, Heunis was a candidate in the election to replace him but lost to F.W. de Klerk. It was well known that Heunis enjoyed an antagonistic relationship with the new party leader, which could not bode well for his political future and he retired from politics in May 1989.

200   Felix HOUPHOUET-BOIGNY

Côte d'Ivoire (Ivory Coast)

Houphouet-Boigny has been the most important and long-lasting of all the politicians of Francophone Africa. He was a major figure in the colonial period and has been president of his country since independence, operating a highly personalized, but not unsuccessful, form of rule.

Born in 1905 in Yamoussoukro into the Baule ethnic group and the son of a chief, he received medical training in Senegal and practised medicine for 20 years before becoming a full-time politician. He also became a prosperous planter and, in 1940, a canton chief. His first involvement in politics came in 1944, when he organized African planters in defence of their interests against the European planters who were favoured under the colonial administration. In 1946 he launched the PDCI, which became the dominant force in Ivoirian politics and which he still leads. Later the same year he was elected to the French Constituent Assembly and once in Paris campaigned strongly for African interests. At this stage he was regarded as a left-wing radical and developed strong links between the PDCI

and the French Communist Party. By 1950 he had decided that the communists were not likely to be a major force in French politics and broke his alliance with them. He continued to organize the PDCI into an effective political grouping, drawing support from a wide range of ethnic, regional and religious groups.

He remained a member of the French National Assembly for 14 years and, in 1956, was also appointed to the French cabinet. In the same year he was elected mayor of Abidjan and in 1957 he became president of the Grand Council of French West Africa. In 1958 he resigned from the French cabinet in order to become prime minister of the Ivory Coast in the pre-independence government. Throughout the 1950s he argued against those African nationalists in other Francophone states who wished for colonial rule to be replaced with a federal structure in West Africa. His support for the idea of a totally separate independence for the Ivory Coast was based on the fact that it was the best endowed territory in terms of natural resources and could only suffer through linking itself with the poorer territories. Although his nationalism was narrower than that of the pan-Africanists it was deeply felt and ultimately more realistic and successful.

In 1960 the Ivory Coast became independent, keeping its very colonial-sounding name, and Houphouet-Boigny was elected president virtually without opposition. Until recently the most outstanding feature of Ivoirian politics was its quite remarkable continuity, with little serious challenge to the status quo. Houphouet-Boigny has developed a style of leadership which is autocratic but not especially repressive and almost entirely dependent on himself. The Ivoirian state has become what one writer describes as 'an administrative–technical agency devoid of structures of representation or participation'. Personal loyalty to the president is vital for advancement but so is competence. 'Le vieux' (the 'old man'), as he is ubiquitously known, has amassed a huge personal fortune (part of which was spent on constructing the basilica at Yamoussoukro), but not at the cost of debilitating the state economy, which has been one of the most prosperous in black Africa in spite of being almost entirely dependent on agriculture. Ties with France have remained strong and, with occasional exceptions, extremely harmonious.

The main problem facing the political system is clearly that of the eventual political succession to 'le vieux'. Houphouet-Boigny repeatedly refused even to contemplate the question until 1990, when he announced that he would not seek a further re-election when his term expired. However, he soon changed his mind. Although opposition candidates were allowed to contest the October 1990 presidential election he was re-elected to the presidency.

I

201 Kashim IBRAHIM

Nigeria

Ibrahim was a major political leader of the First Republic and the first indigenous governor of Northern Nigeria.

Born in 1910 in Maiduguri, he trained as a teacher and had a successful career in education before entering politics. In 1951 he was a founder-member of the NPC and served in both regional and central governments before independence. From 1956 to 1962 he was Waziri (a major traditional office) of the Borno Native Administration. In 1962 he was appointed the first Nigerian governor of Northern Nigeria. He held this post until the coup of 1966, but afterwards served as adviser to the military governor. Later he served as the chancellor of both Ibadan and Lagos universities. He died in 1990.

202 Waziri IBRAHIM

Nigeria

Ibrahim was a senior government figure in the First Republic and a major opposition leader in the Second Republic.

Born in 1920 in Yerwa, Borno State, into the Kanuri ethnic group, he was educated locally and was a successful businessman before entering politics shortly before independence. In the First Republic he served as minister of health and minister of economic development. Following the coup of 1966 he went back to being a businessman.

When the ban on political parties was lifted in 1978 he was instrumental in the formation of the NPP but, following conflicts with other party leaders, he broke away to found the GNPP, of which he became leader and presidential candidate. He lost in the 1979 presidential election, but the GNPP gained control of Borno and Gongola States. He was defeated in the presidential contest again in 1983 and following the coup of the same year went into exile in London, returning to Nigeria in 1986. In April 1989 he took the military government to court to exclude them from his residence, which had been declared an illegal party office. In June the same year he was arrested for illegal political activities but was released the following month. He remains a fairly conservative politician with a strong following in the north-east of the country.

203 Tunde IDIAGBON

Nigeria

Idiagbon was the second most important individual in the Buhari regime from 1983 to 1985.

Born in Kwara State, he did not come to national prominence until he was a major participant in the Buhari coup which brought to an end the Second Republic at the end of 1983. He became chief of staff Supreme Headquarters, the second most important post in the regime, with responsibility for army and government administration. He was widely regarded as the hard man of the regime, especially through his use of the NSO, the secret police, against anyone suspected of potential opposition. He was extremely unpopular and contributed greatly to the downfall of the regime. He was detained when the regime was overthrown in 1985 and forcibly retired from the army. In December 1988 he was released; restrictions on his movements were lifted in September 1989.

204 Bola IGE

Nigeria

Ige was a senior political figure in the Second Republic and an influential individual in previous administrations.

Born in 1930 in Esa Oke, he graduated from Ibadan University in 1955 and after teaching for a year went to London University, where he graduated in law. On his return home he joined the AG and became its publicity secretary. He was detained for a period in 1962. Under military rule he was commissioner for agriculture and for lands and housing. He was appointed a member of the CDC in the build-up to the Second Republic. In 1978 he joined the newly-formed UPN and became its chairman in Oyo State. In the 1979 elections he was elected governor of Oyo State, but was defeated in the 1983 gubernatorial elections. Following the 1983 coup he was arrested and charged with corruption. He was sentenced to 21 years' imprisonment, but was released in 1986.

205 Samuel Gomsu IKOKU

Nigeria

Ikoku was a senior figure in both civilian periods of government in Nigeria.

Born in 1924 into the Ibo ethnic group, he was educated locally and at London University where he gained a higher degree in economics. On his return home he joined the AG and became its secretary-general and party leader in the Eastern Region. He was charged, with Awolowo, with subversion and went into exile in Ghana. He was detained when he returned home but was released in 1966. In 1970 he was appointed commissioner for economic development in East Central State. With the removal of the ban on party politics in 1978, he joined the PRP and became its national secretary. In the 1979 election he was the PRP candidate for the vice-presidency, but lost. Following factional disputes within the party he defected to the ruling NPN in 1982. Following the 1983 coup he was detained but was subsequently released.

206 Michael Ominus IMOUDU

Nigeria

Imoudu has been a major trade unionist and was a significant party leader in the Second Republic.

Born in 1902 in Ora, Bendel State, he joined the Nigerian Railways in 1928 as a labourer and went on to found the Railway Workers' Union in 1932. He was extremely active in trade union affairs during the colonial period and was detained on several occasions. In 1959 he became the first president of the Trade Union Congress of Nigeria. In 1962 he formed and led the Independent United Labour Congress and he was a major leader of the 1964 general strike. He was forcibly retired by the military government in 1976. Two years later, with the lifting of the ban on political parties, he was a founder member of the PRP. In the split in the PRP in 1980 he was the leader of the more radical faction and when the factions were reunited in 1983 he became national vice-president of the party. The coup at the end of 1983 effectively ended his political career.

207   Abdel Hadj ISSAKA

Chad

Issaka was at one time leader of the FROLINAT guerrilla forces, before being ousted and murdered by political opponents.

Born in Batha in 1921, he was a minor Arab chief who worked as a trader and later as a civil servant. On being purged from the civil service by the Tombalbaye regime, he went into exile in the Central African Republic, where he formed an armed group to oppose the government at home. He received guerrilla training in North Korea before returning to Chad. For a time he was one of the most important guerrilla leaders and became commander of the FROLINAT rebel forces after the death of Abatcha. His favouritism towards the Arabs and his corrupt use of funds reduced his stature and in 1970 he lost control of FROLINAT. He continued as a rebel leader, but with a much diminished group of supporters. In 1972 he was assassinated by an unknown political opponent.

J

208 Lateef Kayode JAKANDE

Nigeria

Jakande was a senior politician in the Second Republic and was governor of Lagos State.

Born in 1929 in Lagos, he was educated locally before starting a very successful career in journalism. He became editor of the *Nigerian Tribune* in 1954 and went on to acquire extensive interests in publishing. During the First Republic he was a member of the AG and was one of those jailed with Awolowo from 1963 to 1966. When the ban on political parties was lifted in 1978 he again united with Awolowo to form the UPN, which was to become the major opposition party of the Second Republic. In 1979 he was elected governor of Lagos State and was re-elected in 1983. Although few of those in power in the Second Republic emerged with much credit, Jakande was a notable exception and it was generally agreed that he made an outstanding success of the notoriously difficult job of running Lagos. He was also tipped as the most likely successor to Awolowo as UPN leader whenever the latter decided to stand down. The 1983 coup and the banning of all political parties brought such speculations to an end. Jakande was detained but was released in 1985.

209 Dawda Kairaba JAWARA

The Gambia

Jawara has been the dominant figure in Gambian politics since before independence, preserving a democratic and largely stable political system.

Born in Barajally in 1924, he was known as David before converting to Islam. The son of a Mandinka farmer, he was educated locally and in Ghana before going to the University of Glasgow, where he graduated in veterinary medicine in 1953. He was the first person from the up-river rural areas of The Gambia to hold a university degree. Returning home he worked as a veterinary officer in the colonial administration. In 1959 he was one of the founders of the PPP (Protectorate People's Party – later the People's Progressive Party) which was formed to defend the interests of the rural people who had hitherto been largely neglected. With the extension of the franchise to the whole of the population, the PPP won the 1962 election and Jawara became prime minister in the pre-independence government. He retained this position after independence in 1965. He was knighted by the British in 1966. Shortly after independence he held a referendum on a proposal to change the country to a republic, but it was narrowly defeated. A second referendum on the subject was held in 1970 and this time it received majority support, which meant that Jawara became president of the new republic.

The Gambia has retained a multiparty liberal-democratic political system throughout the post-independence period but, in spite of the existence of lively opposition parties, the PPP under

Jawara's leadership has won a majority of seats in each election. The president has exhibited a strong personal commitment to democracy and has strongly resisted any suggestion that The Gambia should become a single-party state. Although his initial success was based on the support of the up-river rural people, once in power he worked to develop a truly national base for the PPP. This led to accusations that he was neglecting the interests of his own Mandinka ethnic group, who are the largest in the population, but he refused to be drawn into policies of ethnic favouritism. Since independence he has shown enormous skill in balancing the interests of the various ethnic, regional and religious groups within the country.

In July 1981 the political tranquillity of The Gambia was temporarily shattered by an attempted coup led by members of the paramilitary section of the police and discontented urban youths. Jawara was in Britain attending a royal wedding when the coup took place, but several members of his family were taken hostage by the rebels. The president arranged for assistance from the army of neighbouring Senegal, under a mutual defence pact, to help put down the revolt. In the event the rebels were defeated and the hostages released, but many people died in the fighting. In the trials which followed the due processes of law were strictly adhered to and judges were brought in from other Commonwealth countries to help in hearing the cases. The attempted coup appears to have been an isolated, and totally atypical, incident and by the following year general elections were held in the usual manner. During the

elections Jawara narrowly escaped death in a helicopter crash which killed some of his travelling companions.

One of the outcomes of the events of 1981 was the creation of a new confederal structure linking The Gambia and Senegal. This proved difficult to implement because of Gambian fears of becoming dominated by the larger and more powerful Senegalese. After several years of very slow progress and significant disagreement and tension, the confederation finally broke down in 1989.

Although The Gambia is one of Africa's smallest and poorest states, Jawara's record over the long period he has been in power remains impressive. An intelligent, skilful and modest man, he will be a hard act to follow for his eventual successor.

210   Ellen JOHNSON-SIRLEAF

Liberia

Johnson-Sirleaf was one of the most able figures in the opposition to the Doe regime.

Born in 1938 in Monrovia of mixed Americo-Liberian and Gola parentage, she trained as an economist at Harvard University. In 1967 she returned to Liberia to work first as special assistant to the secretary of the treasury and, from 1972 to 1973, as assistant finance minister. In 1973 she became critical of the government and resigned to work abroad for the World Bank. In 1977 she was persuaded to return as deputy finance minister and in 1979 became the first ever female finance minister in Liberia. She was widely regarded as the most honest and able member of the government, which led to her surviving the 1980 coup, when so many of her colleagues were executed.

In 1980 she was appointed president of the Liberia Bank for Development and Investment. She resigned this position at the end of the same year and began to divide her time between international banking appointments and opposition to the government at home, becoming a leading member of the LAP. In 1985 she was sentenced to ten years in jail for sedition but was later released. In 1986 she led a demonstration of 500 women to protest against the jailing of opposition figures. Shortly afterwards she was again arrested on treason charges, but escaped from jail and went into exile in the USA, where she has been a prominent member of the exiled opposition ACDL.

211   Leabua JONATHAN

Lesotho

Jonathan ruled Lesotho from independence in 1966 until his overthrow by the military in 1986.

Born in 1914 in Leribe, he was a member of a junior segment of the ruling family and second cousin to the present king. After working on the South African mines and in local government in the Basutoland Protectorate he entered politics in the 1950s as a member of the BCP. In 1959 he founded his own BNP and in 1962–3 was part of the Basotho delegation to London which made the arrangements for the granting of independence. In the pre-independence elections of 1965 the BNP emerged with a small majority of seats in the legislature, much to the surprise of most ob-

servers. Campaigning on a conservative manifesto, Jonathan gained the support of the influential Roman Catholic church and many women voters, persuading the latter that if the more radical BCP were elected their vital remittances from migrant male Basotho in South Africa would be in jeopardy. Although the BNP won the election, Jonathan lost in his own constituency, but entered parliament shortly afterwards following a specially arranged by-election.

At independence in 1966 he became prime minister of Lesotho. After independence he received considerable South African support, especially in the period leading up to the 1970 election, when he obtained money, vehicles and the services of a South African chief electoral officer to run the election. In spite of this the BNP lost the election, but Jonathan, backed by the paramilitary police, staged a coup to stay in power. In 1974 and 1975 he survived armed attempts by the outlawed opposition to force him from office.

In the late 1970s he made some attempt at domestic political reconciliation and brought former opposition members into his cabinet. Free elections were promised on several occasions, but never took place. At the same time he embarked on a more radical foreign policy, establishing full diplomatic relations with the Soviet Union and Cuba. He became increasingly critical of his former ally, South Africa, and allowed ANC refugees to reside in Maseru. In 1982, South African military forces attacked ANC bases in Lesotho, killing ANC refugees and Basotho civilians. In 1986, Jonathan was overthrown by a military coup and placed under house arrest. Although South African involvement was suspected, no evidence was produced to suggest that this was anything but an internal political development. In 1987, Jonathan died of cancer in a South African hospital.

212 Aneerood JUGNAUTH

Mauritius

Jugnauth has been prime minister of Mauritius since 1982 and remains the dominant figure in Mauritian politics.

Born in 1930 in Quatre Bornes, he qualified as a lawyer in Britain and was called to the bar in 1954. On his return home he joined Bissoondoyal's IFB, for whom he was elected to parliament in 1963. In 1965 he was appointed minister of labour but in 1967 resigned, working as a magistrate until 1969, when he became a crown counsel in the attorney-general's office. In 1971 he joined the more radical MMM, becoming its chairman. Following the 1976 election he became leader of the opposition in parliament.

Following the victory of the MMM in the 1982 election he became prime minister. In 1983, following factional splits within the MMM, he broke away to form his own MSM which, in alliance with other parties, won the 1983 general election and he was once again prime minister. He retained this position when, in alliance with other parties, the MSM won the 1987 election. While in office he has survived a number of political scandals, involving drug dealing and, in November 1988 and March 1989, two assassination attempts. He has also presided over a quite remarkable growth and diversification of the economy. As well as being prime minister he is also minister of defence. Jugnauth is a highly skilled politician and has maintained the pluralistic democratic system of Mauritius in a situation of continued party factionalism.

213 Aboud JUMBE

Tanzania

Jumbe was the president of Zanzibar and thus vice-president of Tanzania from 1972 until 1984.

Born in 1920 in Zanzibar, he was educated locally and in Uganda before embarking on a career as a teacher. In 1953 he became the leader of the ZNU, but when the party folded he switched to the ASP, becoming a member of its central committee in 1961. Following the 1964 revolution he became minister of health. After the unification with mainland Tanganyika to form the state of Tanzania he remained in the government of the island rather than moving to the mainland. Following the assassination of the Zanzibari leader Abeid Karume in 1972, Jumbe became president of Zanzibar and, automatically, vice-president of Tanzania. Unlike his predecessor he favoured a strengthening of the links between the island and the mainland and in 1977 he merged the ASP with the mainland TANU to form a new single party, Chama cha Mapinduzi (CCM – Party of the Revolution) becoming its vice-chairman. He retained his positions in both party and government until 1984, when growing unrest in Zanzibar resulted in his resignation and retirement from politics.

98

214   Salia JUSU-SHERIFF

Sierra Leone

Jusu-Sheriff has been a senior government figure for most of the time since independence, apart from a period in the late 1960s and 1970s when he was leader of the opposition.

Born in 1929, he was educated locally before going on to higher education in England, where he graduated in 1954 and then trained as a chartered accountant. He was elected to parliament for the SLPP in 1962 and immediately joined the government as minister of agriculture. Until the ousting of the SLPP regime in 1968 he remained in government, holding consecutively the trade and industry, education and health portfolios. He was detained briefly following the 1968 coup.

From 1968 until the introduction of the single-party state in 1978 he was leader of the opposition to the APC government of Siaka Stevens and led the SLPP. When the SLPP was banned he joined the APC and in 1982 was appointed finance minister. In 1985 he became minister of development and economic planning. When Momoh came to power in November 1985, Jusu-Sheriff turned down the health portfolio, but in 1987 he became minister of lands and, shortly afterwards, second vice-president. He still holds the latter position, which makes him the third most important figure in the government hierarchy.

215   Andrew JUXON-SMITH

Sierra Leone

Juxon-Smith was military head of state from 1967 to 1968 and later became a leader of the opposition in exile.

Born in 1931 in Freetown, he was educated locally before joining the army and receiving officer training at Sandhurst. Following the ousting of Lansana in 1967 he became chairman of the NRC and head of state. In 1968 he was overthrown in a further coup and was sentenced to death. He was reprieved and was released in 1972. He went into exile in the USA, where he formed an exile opposition group, the NAP, which he still leads.

K

216 Cecilia KADZAMIRA

Malawi

Kadzamira has no official government position but is widely believed to be one of the most influential people in the country.

Born in Dedza District into the Chewa ethnic group, she is the niece of John Tembo. She trained as a nurse but her special position is the result of her unique relationship with President Banda. She acts as his personal secretary, official hostess and close companion. She is regarded as the nation's 'first lady'. It is widely held that she is one of the very few people who can influence Banda in any significant fashion.

217 Abubakar KAMARA

Sierra Leone

Kamara is the first vice-president and was previously attorney-general.

Born in 1929 in Mabanta, he was educated locally before studying law in London, where he qualified as a barrister. He was appointed minister of finance in 1978 and the following year became attorney-general and minister of justice. In 1982 he was demoted to minister of trade, but in 1984 he was reappointed attorney-general and minister of justice, only to be demoted to minister of health in 1985. In 1986, after President Momoh came to power, he was appointed second vice-president and minister of lands. The following year he was promoted to first vice-president, the second most important post in the government hierarchy. He is viewed as a man of ability but one lacking a strong autonomous political power base. In February 1991 he announced his intention of retiring in the near future because of ill health.

218 Christian Alusine KAMARA-TAYLOR

Sierra Leone

Kamara-Taylor was a senior figure in government from 1968 until his retirement in 1984.

Born in 1917 in Kai-Hanta in the north of the country, he was educated locally and later gained an external diploma in accountancy from the London School of Accountancy through a correspondence course. He joined the civil service as a messenger in 1937 and later became a clerk. He met Siaka Stevens in the same year and became a lifelong political ally. He fought with the allied forces in the second world war in Burma but returned to a civilian job in the civil service when the war was over. He later joined the United Africa Company and by 1958 had worked his way up to become its public relations officer. In 1960 he joined Stevens to establish the APC and became secretary-general of the party. He was first elected to parliament in 1962 and was a leading figure in the APC opposition.

When the APC came to power in 1968 he was appointed minister of mines. He remained a senior figure in the government until his retirement. He was finance minister from 1971 to 1975, when he became prime minister and minister of the interior. Following the constitutional changes of 1978, he became second vice-president and for a time was also minister of housing. He retained his vice-presidential position until his retirement due to ill health in 1984. He died in 1985 and was given a large state funeral.

219 Wadal Abdelkader KAMOUGOUE

Chad

Kamougoue is a senior military figure who has held significant positions, including the vice-presidency, in several Chadian regimes.

Born in Gabon in 1938 of southern Chadian parents, he was educated in Chad and Brazzaville before joining the army. He was trained in France from 1963 to 1964 and in the early 1970s was a senior leader of government forces fighting rebels in northern Chad. In 1975 he was one of the main participants in the coup which overthrew President Tombalbaye, leading the assault on the troops who resisted the coup. Following the coup he became foreign minister in Malloum's government, a position he held until the overthrow of the latter in 1978. He kept control of a large fighting force which was personally loyal to him and in 1979 joined the GUNT coalition government of Goukouni, becoming vice-president. When this government was ousted by Habre in 1982, Kamougoue initially remained loyal to Goukouni, fought on his side in the civil war and was made vice-president in the latter's government in exile.

By 1986, Kamougoue realized that he was supporting the losing side and resigned from the government in exile. In 1987 he declared his support for Habre and in 1988 he returned to Ndjamena to be publicly welcomed by the president. Later the same year he was appointed minister of agriculture in Habre's government.

220 Shehu Mohammed KANGIWA

Nigeria

Kangiwa was a major politician of the Second Republic and was governor of Sokoto State.

Born in 1939 in Kangiwa, Sokoto State, he trained and worked as a teacher. He later joined the civil service and was private secretary to the prime minister, Balewa. In 1966 he qualified as a lawyer in Lagos and subsequently held a number of senior bureaucratic posts, including permanent secretary in the Sokoto State military government. In 1978 he was appointed federal commissioner for mines and power. In 1978 he joined the NPN, which was to become the ruling party of the Second Republic. In the 1979 election he was elected governor of Sokoto State, the heartland of the NPN. In his time in office he presided over a significant expansion of secondary education within the state. He died in 1981 after falling from his horse in a polo match.

221 Muhammed Aminu KANO

Nigeria

Kano was one of the major political figures of post-independence politics, although he spent more time as an opposition leader and critic than he did in government.

Born in 1920 in Kano into the Fulani ethnic group, he trained as a teacher. He combined western and Islamic learning and was popularly referred to as 'Mallam' (teacher). He became involved in union affairs and was the founder and first leader of the Northern Teachers' Association in 1948. In 1949 he joined the NPC, but the following year decided that the party was too conservative and left to form the NEPU, of which he remained leader until it was banned in 1966 following the first coup. The party was opposed to the dominant NPC in the First Republic and represented the interests of the poorer sections of society. Under military rule Kano was a senior government figure and was appointed federal commissioner for communications and, later, health. He was a member of the Constituent Assembly from 1977 to 1978, the body which finalized the constitution of the Second Republic.

When the ban on party politics was lifted in 1978 he formed the PRP, which was the most radical of the parties to contest the 1979 election. Kano was the PRP presidential candidate, but lost. Although the party had a multi-ethnic leadership and tried to put forward an ideological image rather than a sectionalist one, most of its support was confined to the north, especially Kano and Kaduna States. Following the elections the PRP split into two factions which Kano tried hard to reunite. He died, before achieving his aim, in April 1983. He remains one of the most respected figures in Nigerian political history.

222   Clemens KAPUUO

Namibia

Kapuuo was traditional chief of the Herero people and figured prominently in the internal settlement engineered by the South Africans before his assassination.

Born in 1923 in Ozondjona in Okahandja district, he trained as a teacher and, in 1950, became president of the South West Africa Teachers Association. He later worked as a businessman. In 1970 he became chief of the Herero with the full support of his people. He subsequently became leader of the conservative NUDO. In 1975 he supported the Turnhalle Conference which the South Africans organized in an attempt at an internal settlement which excluded SWAPO. The following year he became president of the DTA which dominated the government. The government lacked broad-based internal legitimacy. In March 1978 Kapuuo was assassinated. Although SWAPO was suspected of being behind the assassination no conclusive evidence was ever presented.

223   Simon Mwansa KAPWEPWE

Zambia

Kapwepwe was the second most important figure in the government and ruling party at independence but later became a major opposition figure.

Born in 1922 in Chinsali into the Bemba ethnic group, he was a childhood friend and long-term political ally of Kenneth Kaunda. He trained as a teacher and taught on the Copperbelt, where he helped to found the Northern

Rhodesian ANC in 1951. With Kaunda he broke away from the ANC in 1958 and, when the former became president of the UNIP in 1960, Kapwepwe became treasurer. At independence in 1964 he became foreign minister and in 1967 he was promoted to vice-president. He was also deputy leader of UNIP. Until the end of the 1960s Kapwepwe's role was very much that of the junior partner in the very successful alliance with Kaunda, but he then started to challenge Kaunda. In 1970 he left UNIP and the government to found his own party, the UPP, which gained strong support, especially amongst the Bemba on the Copperbelt. In 1972 the UPP was banned and Zambia became a single-party state. Kapwepwe was arrested and imprisoned and although he was later released he was the victim of government harassment and arrest on several subsequent occasions. In 1978 he rejoined UNIP and tried to challenge Kaunda for the presidency. Although his action was perfectly constitutional he was prevented from mounting a challenge. He died of a stroke in 1980 and was given a state funeral.

224 Josephat Njuguna KARANJA

Kenya

Karanja is a leading businessman, diplomat and politician who served for a short time as vice-president before being dropped by President Moi.

Born in 1931 into the Kikuyu ethnic group, he was educated locally, in Uganda and in the USA, where he gained a doctorate. He was a university lecturer in the USA and in Kenya until he switched to a diplomatic career on his appointment, in 1963, as high commissioner in the United Kingdom. He remained in this post until 1970, when he became vice-chancellor of Nairobi University.

His political career was very slow to get going and although he was a Kikuyu he never developed a strong personal support base. He failed to get into parliament in his first two attempts but finally secured a place in a by-election in 1986. He was brought into the cabinet as minister of research, science and technology and then promoted to minister of home affairs. In 1988 he was surprisingly promoted to vice-president, a move which some interpreted as an attempt by the president to downgrade the post. He proved very unpopular with the party and many saw him as arrogant and insensitive to national problems. In May 1989, after less than a year in office, he was forced to resign after losing a parliamentary vote of confidence and the support of the president.

225 Josiah Mwangi KARIUKI

Kenya

Kariuki was a senior politician and government member who became critical of the regime and was later murdered in suspicious circumstances.

Born in 1929 in Rift Valley province, he became an active member of Mau Mau after leaving school. He was detained by the colonial authorities from 1953 to 1960. On his release he published an autobiographical work, *Mau Mau Detainee*. From 1961 to 1963 he was Jomo Kenyatta's private secretary. He was first elected to parliament in 1963 and was subsequently re-elected three times. He was a member of the government from 1966 to 1974. He became increasingly critical in public of the widening gap between rich and poor and was dropped from the government in 1974. He remained on the backbenches and became an increasingly dissident member of the ruling KANU party. In March 1975 his bullet-riddled body was found in the Ngong hills close to Nairobi. The precise circumstances of his murder were never established but it caused considerable popular resentment.

226 Abeid Amani KARUME

Tanzania

Karume was the president of Zanzibar and vice-president of Tanzania until his assassination in 1972.

Born in 1905 in Zanzibar, he was unable to complete his schooling when his father died, and became a merchant seaman for 17 years. In 1938 he founded and led a trade union called the Syndicate for Dockers and Sailors. In 1954 he became the leader of the African Association, which in 1957 merged with the Shirazi Association to form the ASP under his leadership. In 1961 he was minister of health in the pre-independence coalition government and in 1963 broke the coalition to become leader of the opposition in parliament. Following the 1964 revolution he was chairman of the Revolutionary Council and, following the declaration of a republic, the first president. Later the same year he negotiated the union of Zanzibar with mainland Tanganyika to form the Republic of Tanzania, of which he became vice-president. Under his leadership Zanzibar functioned as a semi-autonomous part of the state and was run in a much more authoritarian manner than the mainland. His dictatorial and increasingly arbitrary style of rule became very unpopular and he was assassinated in 1972.

227 Joseph KASAVUBU

Zaire

Kasavubu was the first president of Zaire (then Congo Republic) from independence in 1960 until he was overthrown in a coup in 1965.

Born in 1913 in Tshela, he originally trained for the priesthood but later left the seminary and became a schoolteacher. In 1942 he joined the colonial administration, for which he worked in the treasury department. Throughout the 1940s he was active in various cultural associations of the Kongo ethnic group which in 1950 led to the formation of a political party, the Alliance of Bakongos (known as Abako). Kasavubu became president of Abako in 1955. In 1957 he was elected mayor of Leopoldville. In the pre-independence elections of May 1960, Abako polled strongly in areas where the Kongo people were dominant but weakly elsewhere and Kasavubu formed a rather tenuous coalition with Patrice Lumumba whereby he became president, with Lumumba as prime minister. The coalition broke down almost immediately as the new state descended into the chaos of civil war. In September Mobutu staged his first coup, but Kasavubu was reinstated as president. He remained in this position ruling over a fractured state until 1965, when he was ousted in a further coup by Mobutu. He died in 1969.

228   Francois-Xavier KATALI

Congo

Katali was a senior member of the ruling PCT and a leading figure in successive governments from the early 1970s to the late 1980s.

A member of the Bondjo ethnic group, he was born in the northern part of the country. He joined the army and was first appointed to the central committee of the PCT in 1972. The following year he became minister of agriculture in January and minister of water and forests in August. In 1977 he became minister of the interior, a position he held in successive governments until 1985. A member of the pro-Soviet faction within the PCT, he was a leading figure in its military committee. In 1985 he was downgraded to minister of agriculture and in 1986 to minister of rural development. In 1987 he lost his post in the cabinet.

229   Kenneth David KAUNDA

Zambia

Kaunda has dominated Zambian politics since independence in 1964 and has been president for the entire period. In recent years he has come under increasing pressure.

Born in 1924 in Lubwa to parents who had moved there from Malawi (then Nyasaland), he was educated at a mission school and later qualified as a teacher. He taught locally and in Tanzania and also worked as a welfare assistant on the Copperbelt. In 1951 he joined the Northern Rhodesian ANC and rose rapidly through its hierarchy becoming secretary general and second in command to the leader Harry Nkumbula in 1953. In 1955 he was imprisoned for two months for possessing 'subversive' literature. Relations between Nkumbula and Kaunda became strained as the latter favoured a more militant approach to the nationalist struggle and in 1958 he broke away from the ANC to form a new party, the ZNC, backed by his close friend Simon Kapwepwe. In March 1959 he was again imprisoned and on his release the following January he took over the leadership of UNIP, which had been formed during his imprisonment. The party rapidly emerged as the most popular in the country and, following victory in the pre-independence elections, Kaunda became prime minister and then president at independence in October 1964.

In the early post-independence period Kaunda's international image was extremely positive. Although his professed ideology of 'Zambian humanism' never rose above the level of platitudes he was seen as a popular democratic leader who was dedicated only to the uplifting of the Zambian people without undue concern for his own position. Gradually perceptions of his leadership have become more and more negative, although it would still be unfair to see him as one of Africa's out and out tyrants. However there is no doubt that his style of rule has become increasingly personalized and authoritarian as the very high level of personal legitimacy he enjoyed at independence has largely withered away. Although he had frequently stated that he would never introduce a single-party state in Zambia, when faced with a growth of opposition in 1972, led by his former colleague

Simon Kapwepwe, he moved rapidly to outlaw all opposition parties and make his own UNIP the only permitted party. Since then nobody has been allowed to challenge Kaunda, who has been regularly re-elected, most recently in 1988, as the sole candidate for the presidency. Prior to the 1988 election the secretary of state for defence and security, Alex Shapi, announced publicly that electors who voted 'no' to Kaunda in the presidential election would be 'found out and punished'.

Kaunda has established draconian control over the media, the trade unions, the university and indeed any group that might pose a threat. In 1989 he sought to consolidate his relationship with the army by appointing the army commander, General Malimba Masheke, as his prime minister. His position has been made more vulnerable by the continuing poor performance of the Zambian economy, especially the deprived agricultural sector. Until 1980 sympathetic observers blamed the failings of the economy on problems caused by the liberation war in neighbouring Zimbabwe, but a decade of Zimbabwean independence has resulted in no improvement. Rather the corruption and inefficiency of the regime's handling of economic matters have been identified as the major problems. During the 1980s there were increasing challenges to Kaunda's leadership, especially major riots in 1986 and an attempted coup in 1988. A major outbreak of anti-government riots in 1990 led Kaunda to promise a referendum on the question of a return to a multi-party system, although opponents were quick to express doubts as to whether this would be held fairly,

given the regime's control over all aspects of public life. By this time Kaunda looked like a man for whom staying in power was the overriding political goal. In July 1990 he postponed the referendum. This decision provoked an outburst of public opposition and in September he agreed to return to a multi-party system without a referendum on the issue. By 1991 several opposition parties had formed to challenge Kaunda and UNIP.

230   Rashidi Mfaume KAWAWA

Tanzania

Kawawa has occupied most of the top posts in government and is still secretary general of the ruling party.

Born in 1929 in the Songea district of southern Tanzania, he was educated to secondary level before joining the colonial administration. He became president of the Tanganyika African Civil Servants Association and in 1955 he became a full-time trade unionist when he formed and led the TFL. He cooperated closely with the TANU and entered a long-term partnership with Julius Nyerere. He was appointed minister of local government in the pre-independence government and temporarily took over as prime minister when Nyerere withdrew to reorganize the party. At independence in 1961 he became vice-president of the new state, but in 1964 he had to become second vice-president because the agreement to merge Tanganyika and Zanzibar to form Tanzania stipulated that a Zanzibari should be first vice-president. In 1972 he added the post of prime minister to his responsibilities. In 1977 he was demoted to minister of defence and in 1981 he lost his portfolio but remained in the cabinet. In 1982 he became secretary-general of the ruling CCM, a post he still holds. When Nyerere retired from the state presidency Kawawa was a leading contender to succeed him, but by that time his insistence on a highly statist form of socialism had lost support and the more pragmatic Ali Hassan Mwinyi took over instead. Kawawa remains an influential figure in Tanzanian politics.

231　Gregoire KAYIBANDA

Rwanda

Kayibanda was president of Rwanda from independence in 1962 until his overthrow in a coup in 1973.

Born in Tare in 1924 into the numerically dominant Hutu ethnic group, he was educated locally and qualified as a teacher. In 1959 he formed his PARMEHUTU to campaign successfully against Tutsi domination of the political system, which was by then in the final stages of collapse. In 1960 he became prime minister of the pre-independence government and in 1962 the first president of independent Rwanda. In 1965 he banned all political parties but his own. Periodic Hutu–Tutsi conflict punctuated his period in office, the most serious outburst coming in 1963 when 10 000 Tutsi were killed in communal violence. Kayibanda's rule also led to serious tensions between his own central Hutu and the northern Hutu, who were increasingly excluded from power. The economy also stagnated during this period. In 1973 he was overthrown in a coup led by Habyarimana, a northern Hutu. He was

initially sentenced to death but this judgement was commuted to imprisonment. He died of natural causes at the end of 1976 while still in detention.

232　Modibo KEITA

Mali

Keita was the first president of his country from independence in 1960 until he was overthrown in a coup in 1968.

Born in 1915 in Bamako into the clan which had ruled the ancient Mali empire, he trained as a teacher in Senegal and later worked as a schools inspector. After the war he became a senior figure in the nationalist movement in French West Africa, but his Marxist approach alienated many of the more conservative leaders like Houphouet-Boigny and Senghor and he became increasingly isolated. His own US party dominated domestic politics and he became Malian president in 1960.

Keita rapidly moved to a single-party state and banned all forms of opposition. During the 1960s the economy declined as a result of his policies. In 1962 he withdrew Mali from the Franc Zone, but this had such negative effects that by 1967 he was trying to rejoin. He also established stronger ties with the communist states, and was awarded the Lenin Peace Prize in 1963, but little material help was gained from this. Economic deterioration produced political unrest and in 1967 Keita launched a cultural revolution based on the Chinese model. In January 1968 he dissolved the parliament and placed all legislative power in his own hands. In November the same year the army, under Moussa Traore, seized power and he was imprisoned. Keita was finally released from prison in 1977 but died a few weeks later.

233 N'Famara KEITA

Guinea

Keita was a senior member of the government of Guinea from independence in 1958 until 1984.

Born in Kindia in 1924, he was educated in Dakar before joining the colonial administration at home. He was an active trade unionist and became closely associated with Sekou Toure and the PDG. In 1956 he was elected mayor of Kindia. In 1958 he joined the government and served in a variety of important ministerial roles for the next 24 years, including minister of the superministry of rural development. He was one of the few senior figures to survive at the top for the whole of the Sekou Toure period. Following the 1984 coup he was arrested and died in prison a short time later.

234 KENGO Wa Dondo

Zaire

Kengo was first state commissioner (the equivalent of prime minister) for most of the 1980s.

Born in 1935 in Libenge, he was educated locally before going to university in Belgium, where he obtained a doctorate in law before returning home to become legal adviser to the president. In 1968 he was appointed attorney-general and later became justice minister and head of the Judicial Council. He was a diligent supporter of President Mobutu and earned a deserved reputation for harassing judges who tried to support the notion of judicial autonomy. He finally lost this post in 1980 but was appointed ambassador to Belgium, where he was instructed to keep a close watch on Zairean opposition figures in exile. In 1982 he became first state commissioner, the second most important post in the government. He held this post until it was abolished in October 1986, but when it was reintroduced three months later he was not appointed. In November 1988 he was, once more, appointed to the post but was sacked again in April 1990 and dropped from the government completely. As with most members of the Zairean government, his rapid promotions and demotions have been largely dependent on the whim of President Mobutu.

235 Jomo KENYATTA

Kenya

Kenyatta was the dominant political figure in Kenya for nearly three decades covering the pre- and post-independence phases and can be regarded as the founding father of modern Kenya.

Born in 1890 in Gatundu into the Kikuyu ethnic group, his original name was Kamau Ngengi. After being educated at mission schools he worked for the Nairobi municipal government from 1921 to 1926. He became involved with the early developments of the nationalist movement, joining the East Africa Association (later the Kikuyu Central Association) in 1922. He became its general secretary and editor of its magazine, *Muigwithania*. In 1929 he led a delegation to England to press for African interests, especially over the issue of land alienation. In 1931 he returned to England and spent the next 15 years in Europe, mainly in the United Kingdom, but including a spell at Moscow University. During this period he was a student and a leading figure in the exile nationalist movement. In 1938 he published his book, *Facing Mount Kenya*, which remains one of the most important works on the impact of European influence in Africa from an African perspective.

In 1946 he returned to Kenya to assume the leadership of the KAU and was instrumental in expanding its support base. In 1952 he was arrested and charged with being a leading organizer of the Mau Mau movement. After a lengthy trial he was found guilty and was imprisoned, remaining in detention until 1961. As with other nationalist leaders, his status was enhanced by imprisonment. On his release he became the leader of the main nationalist party, KANU, which had chosen him as leader at its formation in 1960, despite the fact that he was still in jail. In 1962 he was elected to the legislative council and in 1963, following KANU's election victory, he became prime minister. He retained that position when Kenya became independent in December 1963 and with the creation of a republic the following year he became president.

Kenyatta remained president of Kenya and leader of KANU until his death in 1978. Over the period there was little significant challenge to him in either position and he became the totally dominant figure in Kenyan politics, earning the unofficial title 'Mzee' (a Kiswahili term meaning 'wise old man'). Over the years he developed a style that can only be described as monarchical. High government office became dependent on personal loyalty to Kenyatta. He was increasingly intolerant of any form of opposition and his rule was authoritarian but, for the most part, not especially repressive. He always retained great charisma and personal mass support, although the same cannot be said for some of his close associates or for some members of his family. The reputation of the latter was badly damaged by widespread suspicions of corruption and ivory smuggling.

Although he declared his dedication to socialist ideals he led Kenya very firmly down a capitalist path to development. Although this produced very significant gaps between the rich and the poor the Kenyan economy has proved to be one of the most successful in Africa, in spite of its agricultural base. Some progress has been made in developing an industrial sector and in terms of infrastructure Kenya has been better placed than most African states. In international affairs Kenyatta adopted a generally pro-Western stance, but he was not greatly interested in international relations and disliked travelling outside Kenya, leaving such matters to his subordinates.

The dominance of Kenyatta led many to fear that the political stability over which he presided was excessively dependent on his personal leadership and skilful political balancing of different groups in society. However, when he eventually died in August 1978, the political succession was conducted peacefully and constitutionally and did not appear to affect Kenya's political stability.

Benin

Since seizing power in a coup in 1972 Kerekou has proved, despite numerous attempts to oust him, to be much the most durable of Benin's post-independence heads of state, most of whom lasted only a short time in office.

Born into the Somba ethnic group in 1933, he completed his military training in France, transferring from the French to the Dahomean army in 1961. From 1961 to 1962 he served as an aide to President Maga. His progress through the army command structure was helped by the fact that he was the cousin of Colonel Kouandete, who acted as his patron. Kerekou assisted his cousin in staging the 1967 coup and was made president of the Revolutionary Military Committee. After a return to civilian rule in 1968, Kerekou went to France for further military training and was not involved in his cousin's second coup of 1969. In 1970 he was appointed deputy chief of staff of the army.

In October 1972 Kerekou led his own coup, which overthrew the government of Ahomadegbe. He then purged the army of officers senior to himself and became army chief of staff as well as head of state. Although Kerekou had previously exhibited little interest in political ideologies he suddenly announced, in 1974, that the country had been transformed into a Marxist–Leninist state. No preparations had preceded this announcement and it was not until the following year that the PRPB was established as the only legal party, with Kerekou as its leader. In 1975 he also changed the name of the state from Dahomey to Benin (an ancient African kingdom). The declaration of Marxism–Leninism was accompanied by large-scale nationalization of the economy and a massive expansion of the bureaucracy. At one stage bureaucratic salaries were taking 92 per cent of the state budget, even though they were paid in an erratic fashion.

In 1977 a new constitution was adopted which allowed for the creation of a Revolutionary National Assembly and in 1979 elections, for which only PRPB members were eligible, took place for the first time. In 1980 this body formally elected Kerekou as president. In theory Benin now had a civilian government, although it was not until 1987 that Kerekou officially resigned from the army, and military influence in government has remained strong.

In 1980, Kerekou converted to Islam whilst on a state visit to Libya, changing his first name from Mathieu to Ahmed. For a time Benin enjoyed very cordial relations with Libya as Kerekou sought to project his 'radical' international image. By the mid-1980s, however, he sought closer ties with western countries in an attempt to gain financial aid to help his bankrupt economy. In 1985 he announced to the PRPB congress that he had approached the IMF for assistance and since then the Marxist rhetoric of the regime has been considerably toned down. Some liberalization of the economy has taken place but this has been much resented by those with a vested interest in high levels of state control, leading to further tensions within the political system.

Through a mixture of political skill and oppressive force Kerekou has managed to engineer a precarious stability for his regime. He has proved to be a remarkable survivor, considering that before he took power the country had ten changes of ruler, mostly violent, in 12 years. Increased domestic political pressure on the regime brought an end to its formal adherence to Marxism–Leninism in December 1989 and, in February 1990, a re-introduction of a multi-party system. Kerekou remained as president but agreed to relinquish his defence portfolio. In February 1991 he announced that he would be a candidate in the presidential election scheduled for later in the year.

237   Edward Benyah KESSELLY

Liberia

Kesselly was a member of the government in the period before the 1980 coup and an opposition party leader in the 1985 election.

Born in 1937 in Lofa County, he was the son of a former commanding general in the Liberian army. He received higher education in the USA, Switzerland and in the United Kingdom, where he gained a doctorate in political science. He was brought into the TWP government in the 1970s as part of President Tolbert's policy of recruiting bright young men from the hinterland. He served in several ministerial roles including information (1973–8), posts and telecommunications (1978–9) and local government (1979–80). He was detained briefly following the 1980 coup.

In 1983 he was appointed chairman of the Constitutional Advisory Assembly. His proposal that soldiers should be barred from participation in the elections proved unacceptable to Doe and was dropped. For the 1985 election he formed his own UP and became its presidential candidate. He gained just over one-tenth of the votes and the UP captured three seats in the legislature. The election results were hotly disputed by the opposition and by neutral observers. Since 1986 he has been harassed by the government and has spent periods in detention.

238   Bennet Makalo KHAKETLA

Lesotho

Khaketla was a senior party leader in the 1960s and became a member of the post-coup government in 1986.

Born in 1913 in Qacha's Nek into a poor peasant family, he qualified as a teacher and taught in South Africa and in Basutoland. He also established himself as a writer of novels, plays and poetry in the Sesotho language. In the late 1950s he was a leading member of the BCP and became its deputy leader. In 1960 he broke away to form his own BFP, which later merged with the Marema-Tlou Party to form the MFP. This was strongly royalist but remained a minor actor in the political system.

From 1965 to 1970 he was a privy councillor to the king. Following the coup in 1970 he published a book on the event, *Lesotho 1970: An African Coup Under the Microscope*, which remains one of the best accounts of African politics from an insider's perspective. Following the 1986 coup he was appointed minister of justice in an attempt by the military to give their regime some intellectual credibility.

239 Seretse KHAMA

Botswana

A politician of immense skill and integrity, Khama was the founding father of modern Botswana.

He was born in 1921, the undisputed heir to the powerful Bamangwato chieftaincy and grandson of Khama the Great. When his father died in 1925, Seretse was only four years old and his uncle Tshekedi was recognized as regent until Seretse came of age and completed his education. Whilst reading law at the Inns of Court in London, Seretse married a white woman, Ruth Williams, in 1949. Although his marriage was accepted by the Bamangwato the British government, under pressure from the newly-elected National Party government in South Africa, with its policy of apartheid and racial dominance, reacted in a hostile fashion and banned Seretse and his wife from his homeland and stripped him of his hereditary rights to the chieftaincy. Although this action devastated Seretse at the time, it can be seen to have played an important part in his later political success. He maintained his enormous traditional prestige in the country (his people continued to regard him as their rightful leader, whatever the colonial authorities might decree) but he was never encumbered with the very considerable but essentially mundane day-to-day duties which went with chieftaincy. Out of this he was able to emerge as the modern well-educated leader who could gain widespread support in the country as a whole, rather than just from his own tribe. The BDP, which he was instrumental in founding in 1962, has won sweeping victories in every subsequent election and has proved itself a party of truly national support. Thus one can observe the twin paradox of Seretse Khama. He was the traditional leader who used his prestige to reduce the powers of the traditional chiefs and transfer their powers to the new democratically elected central government, and he was the leading Bamangwato who worked all along to reduce the old tribal animosities and to encourage the people to identify with the new nation-state rather than continue with parochial tribal loyalties.

Seretse Khama was president of Botswana from independence in 1966 until his death in 1980. Under his leadership this period was one of quite remarkable progress for Botswana. Economically the country was one of Africa's success stories: real national per capita income tripled as both agriculture and the new mineral extraction industries boomed. A unified, efficient and non-corrupt state structure was created virtually from scratch to replace the rather loose aggregation of tribes under a tenuous and half-hearted colonial administration, which existed until just before independence. The political system continued to be both stable and democratic, with a full range of civil liberties and regular free and fair elections. Seretse's personal abhorrence of racial discrimination and apartheid led him to pursue a successful policy of non-racialism within the country and relations between black and white Botswana were marked by an absence of tension.

He also emerged as an international statesman of great repute and, as a force for moderation among the Frontline

States, played an important role in achieving a solution to the Rhodesia/Zimbabwe crisis. His commitment to human rights did not extend just to attacks on white racism. He was one of the few African leaders who openly criticized the rule of Idi Amin in Uganda whilst the latter was still in power and refused to attend the OAU summit when it was held in Kampala as a protest against the atrocities of the Amin regime. Seretse Khama was always a skilful politician, never a tyrant. If politics is the art of the possible he always knew what was possible and was a natural conciliator. The extent of his success has to be seen in the context of Botswana's distinctly unfavourable location: a land-locked state in the heart of strife-torn southern Africa.

Seretse Khama's greatest legacy to Botswana was to have made himself dispensable and to have built a system that could survive his departure. Since his death from cancer in July 1980, Botswana has continued to be a well-run, democratic and prosperous state and has operated on the lines he set down.

240   Mwai KIBAKI

Kenya

Kibaki has been one of the leading political figures in Kenya's post-independence politics and has held most important positions in government, including a ten-year period as vice-president, although his career appeared to be in decline by the late 1980s.

Born in 1931 in Othaya into the Kikuyu ethnic group, he was educated at Makerere University, where he later lectured, and at the London School of Economics. In 1960 he returned to Kenya to help found KANU and became the national executive officer of the party. He was the main party organizer in the 1963 elections and in 1964 became assistant minister (to Tom Mboya) in the ministry of economic planning and development. In 1966 he became minister of commerce and industry and in 1969 finance minister. He retained this position after the succession of Moi to Kenyatta and was also made vice-president at the same time, partly in recognition of his role as unofficial leader of the Kikuyu.

Eventually Kibaki's role as Kikuyu leader led to tensions with the president and in 1988 he was dropped as vice-president and demoted to minister of health within the cabinet. He still retains this post and it remains to be seen if his demotion is permanent.

241   Edem KODJO

Togo

Kodjo was a leading government figure and also served as secretary-general of the OAU.

Born in 1938 in Sokode, he was educated locally before being trained as an economist in France. Following the Eyadema coup of 1967 he was brought into the government and in 1969 he became the first secretary-general of the RPT, the party established by Eyadema to give his military government a cloak of civilian respectability. In 1973 he was appointed finance minister and in 1976 foreign minister. Later that year he was chosen as the secretary-general of the OAU which is the most senior post in African diplomatic affairs. He remained in that post until 1983, but his independent way of operating caused conflict with his home government, to the extent that Togo threatened to withdraw from the OAU if he was reappointed. He stepped down but remained in Addis Ababa to work as an OAU bureaucrat.

242   Andre KOLINGBA

Central African Republic

Kolingba seized power in a coup in 1981 and is the current president of the CAR.

A member of the Yakoma ethnic group, he received military training in France and rose to become army chief of staff before seizing power in 1981 in a well organized and peaceful coup which overthrew President Dacko. He established a body entitled the Military Committee for National Recovery which included almost all the senior army officers and of which he was chairman. This lasted until 1985 when he declared himself president and appointed a cabinet containing a majority of civilians, mainly with a technocratic background.

Immediately after the coup he adopted a conciliatory approach towards the country's political leaders but a failed counter-coup, led by Ange Patasse, in 1982 produced a more hardline approach which resulted in the detention of most potential opponents. In 1986 a new single party, the RDC, was created, with Kolingba as leader, and he was elected to a six-year presidential term in an election in which no other candidates were permitted and most of the electorate did not bother to vote. Kolingba has added the defence portfolio to his presidential role. Lacking any significant basis of popular support, his hold on power is regarded by observers as tenuous.

243   Abraham Doward KOLLIE

Liberia

Kollie was a leading figure in the ruling military group following the 1980 coup and later served as deputy head of state.

Born in 1953 at Bazagazia in Lofa County, he received little formal education before joining the army. At the time of the 1980 coup he was a private, although he was subsequently promoted to brigadier-general.

He was a member of the initial ruling PRC and in 1981 became its secretary-general. In 1984 he became deputy head of state. His rapid promotions were due more to the desire of the head of state to achieve ethnic balance in the ruling military elite than to Kollie's personal abilities. He lost his government position following the 1985 elections.

244   Henri KONAN-BEDIE

Côte d'Ivoire (Ivory Coast)

Konan-Bedie has been a senior member of the Ivoirian government and ruling party since the mid-1960s and has been president of the national assembly since 1980.

Born in 1934 into the Baule ethnic group, he graduated in economics from the University of Poitiers and returned to work in the civil service. At independence in 1960 he switched to a diplomatic career and became ambassador to the United Nations. In 1966 he returned home to join the government as minister of economic and financial affairs, a post he held until 1977. In 1980 he became president of the national assembly and is viewed by many as a possible successor to Houphouet-Boigny.

245 Abdul Karim KOROMA

Sierra Leone

Koroma is a leading figure in the Sierra Leonean government and has been foreign minister since 1985.

Born in 1945, he was educated locally before going on to higher education in England, where he gained a postgraduate degree in international relations. He was first elected to parliament in 1977 and was soon appointed minister of education. He remained in this post until 1982, when he became resident minister in the Northern Province. Following the succession of Joseph Momoh to the presidency in 1985, he was promoted to the post of foreign minister, a position he has retained ever since. He is widely regarded as one of the most able and influential younger members of the regime.

246 Emmanuel Kwasi KOTOKA

Ghana

Kotoka was the leader of the coup which ousted Nkrumah in 1966 and a senior figure in the subsequent military regime until he was assassinated in a failed coup the following year.

Born in 1926 in the Volta Region into the Ewe ethnic group, he was educated locally before joining the army in 1947. He received officer training in England in the 1950s and later served in the UN peace-keeping force in the Congo. He continued to rise through the officer ranks and by 1965 he commanded the First Brigade of Infantry at Kumasi.

In 1966 he was the leading participant in the coup which overthrew Nkrumah and made the announcement of the coup on Radio Ghana. He became a senior figure in the NLC military regime, where he was minister of defence, health, labour and social welfare. In 1967 he was assassinated close to Accra Airport in an unsuccessful counter-coup. The airport was subsequently renamed after him.

247 Iropa Maurice KOUANDETE

Benin

A senior northern army officer, Kouandete led two successful coups in the 1960s and served briefly as prime minister.

Born in Gaba District, he joined the army in his late teens, receiving officer training at Saint-Cyr in France. From 1965 to 1966 he was commander of the Presidential Palace Guard and was then appointed head of security services. In December 1967 he led the coup which ousted President Soglo, but his support within the army was insufficient to gain the presidency and he became prime minister to President Alley. Following a return to civilian rule in 1968 he was appointed army chief of staff. In 1969 he led the coup which ousted President Zinsou but, again, failed in his bid to become head of state. In 1972 he attempted a further coup but this failed and he was sentenced to death for treason. Before the sentence could be carried out his cousin, Mathieu Kerekou, staged a successful coup and ordered his release. He was forced to retire from the army. Always unpopular amongst southerners within the army, Kouandete's arrogant attitudes had, by this time, alienated even his northern supporters.

248   Moro Naba KOUGRI

Burkina Faso

As emperor of the Mossi, Kougri ('the rock') was much the most important traditional leader in the country and an active participant in the political process.

Born in 1921 and named Moussa Congo, he acquired his formal name and title when he succeeded his father to the throne in 1957, after education in France. The Mossi empire, which dates back to the eleventh century, is much the most important traditional polity in the country and as emperor he wielded much influence and was deeply involved with several political parties in the 1950s. He opposed the first independence government of Maurice Yameogo and actively supported its overthrow by the military led by Sangoule Lamizana in 1966. In 1968 the latter appointed him Commander of the Voltaic National Order and continued to rely on his support and advice. On Kougri's death in 1981, the central market in Ouagadougou was closed by the government to prevent the looting which traditionally takes place on the death of the emperor.

249   Seyni KOUNTCHE

Niger

Kountche was president of Niger from 1974 until his death in 1987.

Born in 1931 in Fandou into the ruling family of the Gabda clan, he joined the French army in 1947 and received training in Senegal. In the 1950s he fought for the French in Indochina and in Algeria. From 1957 to 1959 he received officer training in France. After independence in 1960 he rose rapidly in the military hierarchy at home, becoming deputy chief of staff in 1966 and chief of staff in 1973. The following year he was involved in the coup which overthrew the regime of Hamani Diori and, as the senior military figure, became chairman of the Supreme Military Council and president of the republic.

Initially he was responsible for some liberalization of the political system and released most political prisoners, but subsequently he developed a harsher, more authoritarian, style of rule which resulted in a number of violent attempts to overthrow him. In economic terms he was fortunate that his coming to power coincided with the end of a serious drought and he later presided over the expansion of the uranium mining industry which strengthened Niger's fragile economy. In 1982 a start was made in reducing the military nature of the regime and more civilians were appointed to government posts. Proposals for adding an elected element progressed little before Kountche's death. In the final year of his life his health deteriorated badly and he took a less active role in political affairs. He died in a Paris hospital in November 1987.

250   Noe KUTUKLUI

Togo

Kutuklui was a government figure in the early post-independence period and later the major opponent of the Eyadema regime until his death in 1988.

Born in 1923 in Aneho, he was educated in Dakar and Paris, where he qualified as a lawyer. On his return to Togo in 1958 he joined the dominant party, the CUT, and in 1962 became its deputy secretary-general. Following the assassination of President Olympio in 1963 he assumed the leadership of the party and became minister of labour, but was arrested a few months later for plotting against the regime he had recently joined. He was released in 1965 but the following year was involved in a further coup plot and fled into exile in Benin. He remained in Benin until he was expelled in 1972, after being behind at least five further plots to topple the regime in Togo. He moved on to Senegal and later to Canada, where he continued to act as the main focus of opposition in exile and refused all offers of a political amnesty in Togo, claiming he could not trust President Eyadema. He died from natural causes in Montreal in April 1988.

L

251 Joseph LAGU

Sudan

Lagu has been a major military and political leader of southern peoples in Sudan.

Born in 1931 in Moli in Equatoria Province, he was educated locally before joining the Sudanese army in 1960. In 1963 he defected to join the southern rebellion against the northern-dominated government. By 1968 he was a commander in the Anya Nya rebel movement and in 1971 he united several southern groups to form the SSLM. He was the major southern leader at the talks which produced the Addis Ababa Agreement of 1972 which, for a time, ended the north–south conflict. He was appointed inspector-general of the Sudanese armed forces and, in 1974, the commanding officer of the army in the Southern Region. From 1978 to 1980 he was president of the High Executive Council of the Southern Region and national second vice-president. In 1983 he once again became second vice-president at the national level, but lost this position as a result of the 1985 coup. He remains one of the most influential southern politicians.

252 Sangoule LAMIZANA

Burkina Faso

Lamizana has thrice acceded to the presidency, twice through a coup and once through the ballot box, in the unusually unstable political system of this country.

Born in 1916 into the Samo ethnic group, Lamizana joined the French army in 1936 and fought in Algeria and Indochina, where he was awarded the Legion of Honour. At independence he became head of the army. In January 1966 he led the coup which overthrew President Yameogo and became head of state. He stayed in power for four years until in 1970 he organized elections in which Gerard Ouedraogo was elected premier although, under the constitution, the army still had a political role to play. In 1974, Lamizana overthrew Ouedraogo and imposed military rule once more.

In 1977 a new civilian constitution was approved and Lamizana made clear that he intended to contest the presidential elections the following year and, despite protestations from his opponents, refused to resign from the army first. In 1978 he won the presidential election with 56 per cent of the popular vote. In 1980 he was overthrown in yet another coup, led by Saye Zerbo, and placed under house arrest. In 1984 he was tried by the new Sankara government on charges of corruption, but was acquitted and later released. In 1987 he became chairman of the National Union of Burkinabe Elders, with his old enemy Yameogo as vice-chairman.

253 Emmanuel Odarquaye Obetsebi LAMPTEY

Ghana

Lamptey was a major figure in the Ghanaian nationalist movement and a major opposition leader after independence.

Born in Accra in 1902 into the Ga ethnic group, he graduated in law at London University in 1939 before returning home to practice. He was a founder-member of the UGCC and one of its most important leaders; he was arrested after the 1948 riots. In the late 1940s and early 1950s he was a major participant in the commission which drew up the new constitution. He became a leading figure in the opposition to Nkrumah in the NLM and UP. In 1961, fearing for his life, he went into exile in Togo but returned home when Nkrumah offered an amnesty to political opponents. In 1962 he was arrested and jailed. He died in prison in 1963.

254   Jonathan Kwesi LAMPTEY

Ghana

Lamptey was a senior figure in the CPP who later switched to the opposition. Subsequently he played a leading role in the government of the Second Republic.

Born in Sekondi in 1909, he was educated locally before graduating from Exeter and London universities. He returned home to work as a science teacher before joining the CPP in 1949. In 1950 he became deputy chairman of the party and in 1951 he was elected to the Legislative Assembly and was appointed junior minister of finance in the pre-independence administration. He soon broke with the CPP and was a prominent member of the major opposition parties of the first Republic. Following the 1966 coup he was appointed head of the State Gold Mining Corporation.

With the return to civilian rule in 1969 he was a leading figure in Busia's

PP and served as minister of defence and minister of parliamentary affairs in the latter's government. When Busia was out of the country Lamptey served as acting prime minister. Following the 1972 coup he retired to Sekondi to continue his legal work.

255   David LANSANA

Sierra Leone

Lansana was the leader of the first coup in 1967 and was involved in further coup attempts.

Born in 1922 in Baiima in Kailahun District, he joined the army in 1947 and later received officer training in England. He rose through the officer ranks and in 1965 was promoted to brigadier and appointed army commander, the first Sierra Leonean to hold this position. When the APC defeated the SLPP in the 1967 general election, he led the country's first coup to stop the APC coming to power. He was ousted a few days later by his own junior officers and was appointed to a minor diplomatic post in the USA. On his return to Sierra Leone in 1968 he was sentenced to five years in jail and was not released until 1973. In 1975 he was involved in a further coup plot and was tried and executed.

256   Justin Metsing LEKHANYA

Lesotho

Lekhanya has ruled Lesotho since seizing power in a military coup in 1986.

Born in 1938 he worked in the South African mines before joining the Basutoland police. By the time of the 1970 coup by Jonathan (to keep himself in power) Lekhanya was a platoon commander in the paramilitary PMU and strongly supported the coup, dealing ruthlessly with the prime minister's opponents. In 1974 he took command of the PMU and when the latter was transformed into the Royal Lesotho Defence Force he became head of the new army.

For the next decade he gained the reputation of the military hard man of the Jonathan regime, but in 1986 he led a coup against the latter. Although legislative and executive authority was in theory restored to the monarchy, real power lay with Lekhanya as chairman of the Military Council. The new regime restored friendly relationships with South Africa and expelled ANC refugees from the country. In 1988–9 Lekhanya was involved in a scandal over the murder of a student in a row over a woman and there was considerable evidence to suggest that he was personally guilty. At the same time he was involved in a corruption scandal involving a Taiwanese businessman. In 1990 he attempted to strengthen his position by downgrading the role of the monarchy.

257   Alice Mulenga LENSHINA

Zambia

Lenshina was a religious prophetess and leader of the Lumpa Church which was in very violent conflict with the government after independence.

Born around 1924 into the Bemba ethnic group, she had no formal education. In 1953 she claimed to have been visited by Christ who ordered her to found a new church, the Lumpa (a Bemba word meaning 'better than all the rest') Church. By 1960 it had attracted around 100 000 members and was a serious rival to the nationalist parties. The Lumpas were anarchists who rejected any state authority and after independence in 1964 they refused to pay taxes and fortified their villages to resist the new government of Kenneth Kaunda. The latter ordered the army and police to capture the villages and suicidal resistance by the Lumpas led to many hundreds of deaths. Lenshina was arrested and imprisoned until 1975 and the church was banned. In 1977 she was again arrested but was acquitted and released. She died in 1978.

258   Hilla LIMANN

Ghana

Limann was president of the Third Republic in Ghana from 1979 to 1981, when he was ousted in a coup.

Born in 1934 in the Sisala area of the Upper Region, he won degrees in economics and in history from London University before gaining a doctorate from the Sorbonne. In the First Republic he was a relatively minor figure in the CPP and continued to work as a teacher and in the diplomatic service. In 1969 he was a member of the commission which produced the constitution for the Second Republic. He steadily built a reputation as a competent and reliable public servant, but appeared to lack the flair necessary to make a dramatic impact on public affairs.

In 1979 he emerged from comparative obscurity when, owing largely to the influence of his uncle Imoru Egala, he was chosen as the presidential candidate of the PNP in the elections which marked the beginning of the Third Republic. Although the presidential election went to a second ballot, he emerged as a convincing victor and was installed as president in September 1979. Never a charismatic leader, he presided over a lacklustre regime which was gradually swamped by the problems facing Ghana, especially its bankrupt economy. He was generally regarded as being more honest than most of Ghana's previous rulers but his integrity was not matched by effectiveness. On the final day of 1981 the regime was overthrown by the second Rawlings coup. Limann was arrested but was finally released in 1983.

259   Mahamat Choua LOL

Chad

Lol was briefly head of state in 1979 and subsequently minister of transport in Habre's government.

Born in 1939 into the Kanembu ethnic group, he received higher education in France before joining the civil service at home. A rather obscure figure, he was catapulted to prominence in April 1979 when he became head of state of Chad, owing largely to the insistence of Nigeria at the Kano peace conference. He had no independent political or military power base and was accepted by the other GUNT leaders only as a temporary compromise candidate. In August 1979 he was ousted. After Habre's seizure of power in 1982 he was appointed to the latter's cabinet as minister of transport.

260   Mohamed Mahmoud Ould Ahmed LOULY

Mauritania

Louly was president of Mauritania from June 1979 to January 1980.

Born in 1943 in Tidjikja, he joined the army in 1960 and received military training at St-Cyr in France. He held mainly administrative posts within the army and became a member of the military government following the 1978 coup. He was minister of public services until June 1979 when he ousted Salek and became head of state. He failed in his main task of finally ending Mauritania's involvement in the war in the Western Sahara and was ousted in a further coup in January 1980.

261   Yusufu LULE

Uganda

Lule served, briefly, as the interim president following the overthrow of the Amin regime.

Born in 1912 in Kampala into the Baganda ethnic group, he was educated at universities in Uganda, South Africa, England and Scotland. On returning to Uganda he worked as a science teacher and then as a lecturer at Makerere. In 1954 he joined the colonial administration and from 1961 to 1963 was chairman of the Public Service Commission. In 1964 he became vice-chancellor of Makerere University but was sacked by President Obote in 1970 because the latter decided that the university had become too critical of the government. Lule went into exile and remained abroad until the overthrow of the Amin regime in 1979. In March 1979 he was elected chairman of the UNLF and in April became the interim president of the country. Although he was a man of great intelligence and ability he lacked the political skill to deal with the crisis which existed within the political system and in June 1979 he was ousted from the presidency. He returned to exile, where he died in 1985.

262   Patrice LUMUMBA

Zaire

Lumumba was the first prime minister of Zaire (then Congo Republic) until he was murdered in 1961.

Born in 1925 in Kasai province, he was educated locally before joining the colonial administration. He became assistant postmaster in Stanleyville (now Kisangani) but was later sacked for embezzlement and spent a year in prison. On leaving prison he moved to Leopoldville (now Kinshasha) where he became a brewery director. In 1958 he formed and led the MNC, which emerged as the party with the most widespread support, although lacking an overall majority. At independence in June 1960 he formed an uneasy coalition with Joseph Kasavubu and became prime minister with Kasavubu as president. The alliance rapidly broke down as the country descended into civil war and in September he was ousted as prime minister in a coup led by Mobutu. He spent some months under the protection of UN forces. When he left this protection he was captured by the Congolese army. In February 1961 he was murdered in circumstances which have never been fully explained.

263   Albert John LUTHULI

South Africa

Luthuli was the president of the ANC until his death in somewhat mysterious circumstances in 1967.

Born in 1898 in Rhodesia of South African parents, he was educated in mission schools in Natal and later spent 15 years teaching in the schools. In 1935 he inherited a relatively minor Zulu chiefship which entailed considerable mundane administrative duties. In 1946 he joined the ANC and soon became president of the Natal branch of the organization. In 1952 he was elected as the national president following the mass Defiance Campaign. From then on he was almost continuously banned, restricted or imprisoned by the government, which meant that his practical work with the ANC was limited. He was a staunch believer in non-violent passive resistance to apartheid, although it was during this period that the ANC began to reject such tactics as unproductive. In 1961 he was awarded the Nobel Peace Prize. In 1962 he published his autobiography, *Let My People Go*, which contained a moving call for a peaceful solution to South Africa's problems but which was, predictably, ignored by the government. In 1967 he was killed by a train while crossing a railway track in what may, or may not, have been a tragic accident.

M

264   Graca MACHEL

Mozambique

Machel is the widow of Samora Machel but has also been an important politician in her own right.

Born in 1945, she was a student of modern languages at Lisbon University when she secretly joined FRELIMO in 1972. She was quickly forced to flee to Tanzania where she undertook military training and actively participated in the armed struggle inside Mozambique. She was also appointed deputy director of the school established by FRELIMO at Bagamoyo in Tanzania. With the downfall of Portuguese colonialism in 1974, she was given responsibility for education in the transitional government and became minister of education at formal independence the following year. She held this post until 1989 and was responsible for the increase in literacy levels in the country, which had been very low under colonial rule. She has also been an active leader in the Mozambique Organization of Women and a leading campaigner for women's rights. Although she knew Samora Machel during the period of guerrilla struggle they married after independence in 1975. She was widowed when he was killed in a plane crash in 1986.

265   Samora Moises MACHEL

Mozambique

Machel was the leader of FRELIMO during the decisive phase of the anti-colonial struggle and the first president of post-independence Mozambique.

Born in 1933 in Gaza Province into a poor peasant family he left school part way through his secondary education to go and work as a nurse in Lourenco Marques (now Maputo). He was much influenced by the FRELIMO leader, Eduardo Mondlane, and in 1963 he joined the movement and was sent for guerrilla training in Algeria. He was involved in the armed struggle in Mozambique from the start of the campaign and was regarded as an important leader in the bush. In 1966 he became the movement's secretary for defence and by 1968 was the commander of the guerrilla forces operating in Mozambique. Following the assassination of Mondlane in 1969, Machel became one of a three-man council to succeed him and the next year he was elected as president of the movement. Under his leadership FRELIMO was successful in liberating much of the countryside from Portuguese control and establishing a new administration to replace the colonial one. The military success of FRELIMO, and of similar movements in the other Portuguese colonies, finally led to the 1974 coup by the Portuguese army and the end of Portuguese colonialism in Africa. Political power was transferred to FRELIMO and at independence in 1975 Machel became the first president of the post-colonial state.

During his period in office Mozambique was beset with myriad problems, many of which stemmed from its geopolitical location in the southern African region and, in particular, from its problematic relationship with South Africa. Machel's support for liberation movements in South Africa and in Zimbabwe (then Rhodesia) caused enormous security problems for the new state and attempts at destabilization by the white minority regimes. These problems were eased somewhat by the achievement of independence by Zimbabwe in 1980 and by the signing of the Nkomati Accord with South Africa in 1984, whereby Mozambique denied bases to the ANC in return for promises (arguably not kept at first) by South Africa to cease support for the RENAMO rebels in Mozambique. Initially Machel declared Mozambique to be a Marxist state aligned to the Soviet Union, although this stance was substantially modified over time and eventually abandoned after his death. In October 1986 he was returning from a meeting in Zambia when his plane crashed in the eastern Transvaal, killing all on board. Although there were strongly-voiced suspicions that the crash had been caused by the South Africans no conclusive explanation has ever been established.

266   Mario Fernandes Da Graca MACHUNGO

Mozambique

Machungo has been prime minister of Mozambique since 1986, as well as serving in several senior government posts.

Born in Inhambane, he was trained as an economist in Portugal and returned to Mozambique to work as an undercover agent for FRELIMO in Maputo. He was one of the few FRELIMO leaders not directly involved in the rural guerrilla movement. In 1974 he became econom-

ics minister in the transitional government and at independence the following year he was appointed industry minister. He has held a number of important departmental portfolios, including agriculture and economic planning. In 1986 he was appointed prime minister by Machel and continued in this post following the latter's death. He has also remained an important member of FRELIMO's political bureau. He has been extremely influential in Mozambique's movement from a state-dominated economy to one based more on free market principles.

267   MACIAS NGUEMA Biyogo Negue Ndong

Equatorial Guinea

Macias Nguema was president of Equatorial Guinea from independence in 1968 until he was overthrown in 1979. Under his rule the country became known as the 'Auschwitz of Africa' and any accurate assessment of him cannot avoid being entirely negative.

Born in 1924 in Nsegayong, a village on the mainland, he was a member of the numerically dominant Fang ethnic group. After a fairly rudimentary education he worked for the Spanish colonial service. In the 1960s he was a member of several political parties and rose to a leadership position in the IPGE which was Fang-dominated. In the 1968 pre-independence election he was narrowly elected president at the second ballot after forming several beneficial alliances. When the territory became independent later the same year he was president. He never held another election.

In 1969 he claimed a coup attempt had taken place and proceeded to arrest and kill all possible opponents. In 1972 he declared himself president for life, scrapped the constitution and ruled through presidential decree. Among the other official titles he awarded himself were 'the Unique Miracle' and 'Grand Master of Science, Education and Culture'. In 1976 he ordered all citizens to adopt African names, dropping his own, Francisco.

Macias Nguema maintained himself in power entirely through the use of terror. No reliable figures exist concerning the number of his victims, but they included almost all the educated elite, all political opponents, almost all who served in his governments and many who just happened to incur his displeasure for no particular reason. The nation's economy was shattered and most state revenue was diverted to building and maintaining his luxurious and heavily fortified palace and paying his numerous Fang bodyguards. It has been estimated that at least one-third of the entire population fled into exile. In an attempt to stop his citizens escaping he scrapped the fishing industry (selling all fishing rights to the USSR) because fishing boats were being used to escape.

In 1979 he was overthrown in a coup led by his nephew, Teodoro Obiang Nguema Mbasogo. He was quickly tried for a long list of crimes including genocide and was executed by firing squad.

268   Coutoucou Hubert MAGA

Benin

Maga was the most important of the politicians of the independence period, became the first president and had a second period as president in the 1970s.

A northerner, Maga was born in Parakou in 1916. After completing his education in Dakar he returned home to teach and later became a headmaster. He served as an elected member of the French National Assembly from 1951 to 1958 and served, briefly, in the French cabinet from late 1957 to early 1958. At home he switched party frequently in the 1950s but in 1960 joined with Apithy to form the PDU. At independence Maga became president. His period in office was marked by increasing authoritarianism, including the banning and imprisonment of political opponents, and unwise government spending, especially the construction of a multi-million pound presidential palace. Following large-scale public demonstrations against his rule, he was overthrown by a coup in 1963. After two years under house arrest he went into exile in France in 1965.

In 1970 he returned home and joined with Ahomadegbe and Apithy to participate in the scheme to rotate the presidency between them. In the elections his strong northern support resulted in his winning the first turn as president. His period in office lasted from 1970 to 1972, when he was replaced by Ahomadegbe, but both his period in office and the arrangement as a whole proved very unsuccessful in political and economic terms. It was brought to an end by the Kerekou coup of October 1972. Maga was imprisoned and was not released until 1981.

269   Moven MAHACHI

Zimbabwe

Mahachi has been a senior member of the government for most of the post-independence period and is currently minister of home affairs.

Born in 1948 in Rusape, he was educated locally before joining Cold Comfort Farm, a multi-racial farming cooperative on the outskirts of Salisbury (now Harare) which was funded by the World Council of Churches. In 1970 he became its chairman but shortly afterwards it was forced to close by the government. He became involved in underground nationalist activities and in 1975 was arrested and jailed until 1979. Following his release he became administrative secretary for ZANU in Manicaland and a member of the central committee of the party. In 1982 he joined the government in the key post of minister of lands, resettlement and rural development. In 1988 he was promoted to minister of home affairs.

270   Sadiq al-MAHDI

Sudan

Al-Mahdi was prime minister from 1966 to 1967 and again from 1986 to 1989.

Born in 1936 in Khartoum into one of the country's leading religious and political families, he was educated locally and at Oxford University. In 1961 he succeeded his father as leader of the UP and was prime minister from 1966 to 1967. Following the Numeiri coup in 1969 he was arrested and from then until 1985 he spent a high proportion of his time in detention or in exile. Following the overthrow of Numeiri in 1985, and the revival of multi-party civilian politics, he revived the UP, which won more seats than any other party in the elections of 1986, although not an overall majority. He formed a coalition government with himself as prime minister and minister of defence. In spite of his intellectual capability and political skill, his government failed to resolve the continuing civil war between the central government and southern rebels and in June 1989 he was overthrown in a coup led by Brigadier al-Bashir. Following the coup al-Mahdi went into hiding, but was captured a few days later and placed in jail. In January 1990 he was released from jail but was placed under house arrest.

271   Endalkatchew MAKONNEN

Ethiopia

Makonnen was a leading Ethiopian politician and diplomat and was briefly prime minister in 1974.

Born in 1926 into an aristocratic Amhara family which enjoyed close ties with Emperor Haile Selassie, he studied at Oxford University before returning home. He served in several ministerial and diplomatic posts, including ambassador to Britain, before being appointed Permanent Representative at the United Nations, where he was twice president of the Security Council. In 1971 he stood unsuccessfully as Africa's candidate for the post of UN secretary-general.

In February 1974, following unrest at home, he was appointed prime minister and embarked on a programme of rapid reform which came too late to save the regime of Haile Selassie. After the coup he was arrested and in November 1974 he was executed by the new government.

272 Magnus Andre de Merindol MALAN

South Africa

Malan is regarded as one of the most powerful figures in the government. He was previously chief of the SADF and since 1980 he has been minister of defence.

Born in 1930 in Pretoria, he started a degree course at Stellenbosch University but left to join the SADF and later completed a degree in military studies at Pretoria University. He rose rapidly through the officer ranks and in 1976 became chief of the SADF. In this role he forged close links with P.W. Botha, who was then defence minister, and in 1980 the latter, now prime minister, appointed Malan as minister of defence, the first serving soldier to be in the cabinet. The two men worked together very closely as the SADF became increasingly involved in the defence of apartheid through attacks on neighbouring states and in dealing with internal unrest. Malan kept his place in the government after F.W. de Klerk replaced Botha. He can be regarded as a pragmatic hardliner.

273 Wynand Charl MALAN

South Africa

Malan was a senior figure in the ruling NP until he defected and became co-leader of the liberal opposition Democratic Party. In July 1990 he resigned from the DP.

Born in 1943 in Port Elizabeth he graduated in law from the University of Pretoria. He worked in several important positions within the NP before be-

ing elected as MP for Randburg in 1977. In 1987 he resigned from the NP to form his own NDM, retaining his Randburg seat in the election of the same year when he stood as an independent. In 1989 he merged the NDM with the other liberal white opposition parties to form the DP and became one of its co-leaders. In the 1989 general election the DP won 33 seats and one-fifth of the votes. In July 1990 Malan resigned from the DP and from parliament following revelations that he was a member of the Broederbond, the secret Afrikaner society normally associated with the right of the political spectrum.

274 Timothee MALENDOMA

Central African Republic

Malendoma was the most able military figure in Bokassa's first cabinet and later served in Dacko's government.

Born in 1935, he joined the French army in 1953 and fought in Indochina. In 1966 he was appointed minister of national economy in the first cabinet formed by Bokassa after his seizure of power. In this post he was enormously successful in cracking down on the diamond smuggling which was so damaging to the economy of the country. Unfortunately for him the diamond smugglers proved to have more influence with the president than the minister who was attacking them and he was sacked by Bokassa. In the first post-Bokassa government of David Dacko he was appointed to head a large ministry which included transport, public works and the organization of the territory and environment. He served from 1979 to 1981, when he was again dismissed.

275 N'gakoutou Bey'ndi (Felix) MALLOUM

Chad

Malloum held most of the senior military and political posts in Chad, including commander of the armed forces and president, before he was forced into exile.

Born in 1932 to a southern father and northern mother, he had lengthy service in the French army which included two periods of officer training in France and active service in Indochina and Algeria. He returned to Chad in 1961 and rose through the officer corps, becoming army chief of staff in 1971 and overall commander of the armed forces in 1972. He also served as President Tombalbaye's minister of defence and saw action in the campaigns against rebel groups in several parts of the country. In 1973 he was arrested on charges of sorcery and remained in detention until the coup of 1975. Following the coup he was reinstated in his previous military role and became president and leader of the military government.

He attempted to unite the disparate armed groupings in the country, but with only partial success. In 1977 he formed a new government, in which he retained the presidency and Habre became prime minister. This alliance proved very fragile and in 1979 fierce fighting between supporters of the two leaders paved the way for the seizure of power by Goukouni in Ndjamena. Malloum fled into exile, first in Nigeria and later in France.

276 James MANCHAM

Seychelles

Mancham was the first post-independence president of the Seychelles; he was ousted in a coup in 1977.

Born in 1939 in Victoria on the island of Mahe, he studied law in France and England before qualifying as a barrister. In 1963 he formed and led the SDP, which was initially opposed to independence but which later reversed this policy. The SDP was the majority party in all pre-independence elections and Mancham served as chief minister from 1970 to 1975 and as prime minister from 1975 to 1976. He became the first president at independence in 1976. Although enjoying majority support in the legislature, he formed a coalition government with the SPUP, led by Albert Rene, who became his prime minister. Mancham was always a flamboyant politician but his political position was increasingly weakened by his deserved international playboy image. In June 1977 he was deposed in a coup by Rene while he was attending a Commonwealth Conference in London. Since then he has lived in exile and is strongly suspected of having been involved in several attempts at a counter-coup.

277 Nelson Rolihlahla MANDELA

South Africa

In spite of spending well over a quarter of a century in detention, Mandela is probably the best known and most highly regarded political leader in black Africa. Following his release from jail in February 1990 he returned to his struggle to bring an end to apartheid in South Africa in circumstances which were markedly changed.

Born in 1918 in Qunu, near Umtata, into the Thembu ruling family, he attended Fort Hare University but was expelled in 1940 for leading a student strike. He subsequently completed his degree through a correspondence course and qualified as a lawyer. In 1952, with Oliver Tambo, he opened the first black legal partnership in the country. In 1944 he was a founder-member of the Youth League of the ANC and went on to become its national president. During the 1950s he rose to the leadership of the ANC, but was subject to frequent arrest, detention and banning by the government.

Following the banning of the ANC in 1960 he went underground to organize its new military wing, Umkhonto we Sizwe (Spear of the Nation). In 1962 he was arrested and sentenced to five years' imprisonment. The following year, while still in detention, he was charged with treason and given life imprisonment. From 1964 to 1982 he was held in the notorious Robben Island prison and was then transferred to Pollsmoor prison in Cape Town. In 1985 he rejected the first of several offers from the government of release if he modified his opposition to apartheid. In 1988 he was moved to more comfortable detention in a house in the grounds of Victor Verster prison in Paarl.

Ironically his lengthy period in jail resulted in him becoming increasingly well known internationally as a powerful symbol of opposition to the apartheid system. Following a global campaign, the government eventually released him in February 1990, to scenes of joyous celebration in South Africa and around the world. At the same time the ANC and other anti-apartheid groups were unbanned.

Following his release he became deputy president of the ANC. Oliver Tambo was retained as president in spite of his ill health, but Mandela was universally recognized as the leading figure in the movement. In May he led the ANC into preliminary negotiations with the government, with the declared aim of creating a democratic and non-racial South Africa. He also toured extensively overseas, where he was often accorded the courtesies more normally reserved for a visiting head of state. In spite of his age and his lengthy period in detention he impressed observers with his intelligence and grasp of political realities. Perhaps most impressive was his lack of rancour towards the whites of his home country as he sought to assure them that they had a part to play in the future South Africa.

278 Nomzamo Winnie MANDELA

South Africa

Although Winnie Mandela is best known as the wife of Nelson Mandela, she has played a significant role in the anti-apartheid struggle in her own right.

Born in 1934 in Bizana, in Pondoland, she was the daughter of a Transkeian government minister. After school she qualified as a medical social worker and worked in the Baragwanath hospital. She met Nelson in 1957 and they married the following year. She shared her husband's work with the

ANC and was a member of its executive committee until it was banned in 1960. During Nelson's imprisonment from 1963 to 1990 she was banned and detained on numerous occasions and her home was attacked with fire bombs. In 1975 she founded the Black Women's Federation, but the organization was banned two years later. Her reputation suffered in 1989 when her 'bodyguards' were tried for the murder of a black youth and it was widely believed that she was implicated. The release of her husband in February 1990 restored her to a respected role in South African politics. In March 1991 she was brought to trial over the 1989 incident.

279 Lucas Manyane MANGOPE

South Africa (Bophuthatswana)

Mangope has been the president of the Tswana homeland since its 'independence' in 1977.

Born in 1923 in Motswedi into a chiefly family, he trained and worked as a teacher. On the death of his father in 1959 he became chief of the Motswedi-Barutshe-Boo-Manyane tribe. In 1961 he became vice-chairman of the Tswana Territorial Assembly and chief councillor in 1968. In 1972 he became chief minister of Bophuthatswana as the territory was prepared for independence under the Bantustan scheme. In 1974 he founded and led the BDP, which became the dominant party. When the territory was declared independent in 1977 he became president. No government apart from South Africa has ever recognized this independence. Although the Mangope regime has been less oppressive than those in the other homelands

and the territory has a viable economy (it is the world's largest producer of platinum), the fact that independence was part of the apartheid scheme has always caused problems and there has been considerable popular unrest. In February 1988, Mangope was overthrown in a coup, but South African forces intervened to restore him to power. More recently, in March 1990, a number of people were killed in demonstrations supporting reintegration with South Africa. Again the South African army provided Mangope with assistance. It is very much open to question how long the South Africans will be willing to prop up Mangope and it must be regarded as doubtful that he could survive without outside help.

280 Jacob Albertus MARAIS

South Africa

Marais is the leader of the far-right HNP.

Born in 1922 in Vryburg, Cape Province, to parents who had been interned in concentration camps by the British during the Boer War, he worked in the civil service after completing secondary school. He joined the NP in 1941 and was eventually elected to parliament in 1958. Always on the far right of the party, he was one of those who broke away in 1969 to form the HNP (the name means 'Purified National Party') which was opposed to any power sharing with non-Afrikaner whites, never mind non-whites. He lost his parliamentary seat in the 1970 election.

He became the leader of the HNP in 1977. Although the formation of the party was important in representing the first major split in Afrikaner political unity, the party has never enjoyed much success and has only ever won one parliamentary seat, in a by-election in 1985. Since the formation of the Conservative Party in 1982, the HNP has ceased to be the standard-bearer of the far right and in the 1989 election it won less than one per cent of the national vote. Although the release of Nelson Mandela and the unbanning of the ANC in 1990 may allow for some growth of support for the far-right white parties, it is difficult to see Marais and his party benefiting much. Marais represents a strand of political thinking in South Africa, but it is an increasingly anachronistic and marginal one.

281 Albert Michael MARGAI

Sierra Leone

Margai, brother of Milton Margai, was the second prime minister of Sierra Leone.

Born in 1910 in Gbangbatok into a wealthy Mende trading family, he worked as a nurse for 12 years after leaving school, before going to England in 1944 to study law and qualify as a barrister. In 1951 he joined his brother to form the SLPP, which won the election of that year. The election victory marked the political ascendancy of the people of the interior over the coastal elite and the Margai brothers were the main representatives of this new political force. In 1958, Albert split with his brother to form the PNP, but when the new party failed to gather much support he rejoined the SLPP and became minister of natural resources. At independence in 1961 he became finance minister in his brother's government. When

Milton died in 1964, Albert succeeded him as prime minister, but he never enjoyed the popular support within the party or within the country that his brother had done. In spite of his attempts to rig the 1967 election, Margai's SLPP still lost to the APC of Siaka Stevens, although military intervention was necessary before the APC came to power the following year. Margai went into exile in Britain, where he died from natural causes in 1980.

282 Milton Augustus MARGAI

Sierra Leone

Margai, brother of Albert Margai, was the first prime minister at independence.

Born in 1895 in Gbangbatok into a wealthy Mende merchant family, he was educated locally before going to England to study medicine. In 1926 he became the first person from the Protectorate to qualify as a doctor. He worked for the colonial medical service for over two decades, during which time he also published books on midwifery. In 1946 he formed the SLOS to campaign for better treatment of the local people under colonial rule and in 1950 retired from the medical service to undertake a full-time political career. In 1951 he merged the SLOS with the People's Party, which existed largely in the urban areas, to form the SLPP which, although a national party, also represented the growing influence of the people of the interior represented by the Margai brothers.

The SLPP rapidly emerged as the dominant party in the pre-independence legislature and, as party leader, Milton Margai became chief minister in the pre-independence government. At independence in 1961 he became the country's first prime minister. He continued to occupy this position until his death in 1964, when he was succeeded by his less able brother, Albert. Although cautious by nature, he was a highly skilled and honest politician and, if he had survived longer in power, Sierra Leone might well have avoided the political instability it experienced in the second half of the decade.

283   Jose MARTINEZ NVO BIKIE

Equatorial Guinea

Martinez was a senior figure in the government of Macias Nguema and was responsible for the killing of many of the latter's opponents until he himself was killed.

Born in 1933 in Ebebiyin district, he belonged to the Fang ethnic group. After completing primary education he worked as an office clerk. He was closely associated with Macias Nguema and became president of the Senate in 1972. In 1975 he was appointed minister of economic affairs. As well as his formal post he was a major participant in the murder of the president's enemies. Like most of those closely associated with Macias Nguema, he fell from favour and in 1976 he was murdered, burned alive in his house.

284   Jafta Kgalabi MASEMOLA

South Africa

Masemola was a leading figure within the PAC, although he spent much of his adult life in prison.

Born in 1932 in Marabastard, Pretoria, into a poor family, he was educated at mission schools and qualified as a teacher. As a teacher he was prominent within the Union of African Teachers and staunchly opposed the Bantu Education Act. In 1959 he was a founder-member of the PAC when it broke away from the African National Congress and became its regional organizer for Northern Transvaal. After the PAC was banned by the government in 1960 he went underground and organized its military wing, known as 'Poqo' (a Xhosa word meaning 'pure'). In 1963 he was arrested and sentenced to life imprisonment on the notorious Robben Island. He remained there until October 1989 and, with the exception of Nelson Mandela, was South Africa's longest-serving political prisoner. He was released at the same time as Walter Sisulu and immediately went back to working for the PAC. He was killed in a car crash in April 1990, just a few months after his release.

285   Quett Ketumile Joni MASIRE

Botswana

Masire has been president of Botswana since 1980 and was previously vice-president. He is also a major international statesman.

Born in Kanye in 1925, he was educated at Tiger Kloof in South Africa and worked as a farmer and journalist before entering politics. He also founded the first secondary school in his home village. In the pre-independence period he was a member of the Ngwaketse Tribal Council, the Legislative Council and the Executive Council. In 1962 he was instrumental, with his close friend and ally Seretse Khama, in founding the BDP, which became the ruling party at independence. He became the secretary of the BDP and editor of the party newspaper, *Therisanyo*. In the pre-independence elections of 1965 he was elected to parliament and the BDP won 28 out of the 31 seats, making it the first, and so far only, ruling party for the country. In 1965 he became deputy prime minister and, following independence in 1966, vice-president and minister of finance. His ministry was shortly after expanded to finance and development planning.

In the 1969 elections Masire suffered a political setback. Although the BDP achieved another resounding overall victory, he was defeated in his own constituency by ex-chief Bathoen Gaseitsiwe, representing the BNF. As the constituency composed a large part of the tribal capital, Kanye, it was universally recognized that anybody standing in opposition to the prestigious ex-chief would have been defeated. President Khama brought Masire back into parliament as a 'specially elected' member and he continued to occupy his senior government posts. For the 1974 elections Masire resisted the temptation of standing in a safe BDP constituency away from his tribal area and fought the more marginal Ngwaketse/Kgalagadi seat, which had also been won previously by the BNF. The gamble paid off and he won the seat for the BDP, retaining it in 1979.

Although he lacked the personal prestige of his close friend President Khama, Masire established himself through the 1970s as a popular and approachable politician and as an administrator of exceptional skill. After Seretse Khama's death in 1980, Masire was elected by the National Assembly to succeed him as president, with virtually unanimous support. Following his election Masire followed a policy of continuity with the Khama period: the major policy framework was maintained and the personnel of the government remained largely unaltered. In the 1984 and 1989 elections he led the BDP to victories which were only marginally less overwhelming than the previous ones. Some commentators had suggested that, without Khama's prestige, support for the party would wither away.

Since 1980, Botswana has continued to be a peaceful, democratic and prosperous state. Masire has also taken on the role of international statesman previously occupied by Khama. He has been prominent in the SADCC, an organization of economic cooperation formed by the black-ruled states of southern Africa to reduce dependence on South Africa, and was its president from 1981 to 1984. He has also been a significant contributor to the 'Frontline States' grouping and in spite of pressure from South Africa, which has included cross-border raids on Botswana, he has refused to sign any pact with the regime in Pretoria. In 1988 the aircraft in which he was travelling to a conference in Angola was mistakenly shot down by the Angolan air force, but he miraculously survived with only minor injuries.

Under Quett Masire's leadership Botswana has continued the pattern established by his predecessor of being one of black Africa's most successful and well-run states.

286 Alphonse MASSAMBA-DEBAT

Congo

Massamba-Debat was president of Congo from 1963 to 1968, before being ousted by the army.

A member of the Bakongo ethnic group, he was born in Nkolo in 1921. After completing his education he taught for a time in Chad and then returned home to become a headmaster in Brazzaville. From 1959 to 1961 he was president of the legislative assembly. He was then appointed to President Youlou's cabinet as minister of planning. Disagreements with the president lead to his dismissal, but, when Youlou was overthrown in 1963, Massamba-Debat replaced him as president with the support of the army. In 1964 he outlawed opposition parties and declared his own, newly-formed, MNR, the sole legal party with a commitment to Marxism–Leninism. Independent trade unions were also banned. Increasingly the real power in the country lay with the army and in 1968 the president was forced to resign in favour of Ngouabi, who was the candidate of the military. Although Massamba-Debat was brought to trial he was acquitted and released in 1969. He went into retirement in his home village and appeared to have left the political scene, but in 1977 he was accused of being involved in the assassination of Ngouabi and was quickly tried and executed. It has never been clear whether he was involved or whether he was used as a scapegoat.

287 Robert Stanley MATANO

Kenya

Matano has been a leading government and party figure in the post-independence period, although by the end of the 1980s his career appeared to be in serious decline.

Born in 1924 in Mazeras in Coast Province, he worked as a teacher before entering politics. He became a leading figure in KADU and was elected as one of its MPs in 1963. In 1964 he switched to the ruling KANU party and in 1965 he was brought into the government, where he served in a number of ministerial roles, including information (1973) and local government (1976). He was recognized as the leading Coast Province politician and from 1969 to 1979 was secretary-general of KANU. In the latter year he was appointed minister of housing and social services. In 1985 he was dropped from the cabinet in a reshuffle and in 1988 lost his seat in parliament.

288 Philip Parcel Goanwe MATANTE

Botswana

A highly flamboyant politician, Matante was one of the main figures of the opposition until his death in 1979.

Born in Serowe in 1912, he worked for many years in South Africa. He had a varied career as a businessman, evangelist speaker and political organizer and in the second world war fought for the Allies in the Bechuana troops, reaching the rank of sergeant-major, the highest open to him under the discriminatory promotion system then prevailing. He was a member of the ANC in South Africa but later switched his support to the PAC. In 1956 he was forced to flee South Africa and returned home.

In 1960 he was a founding member of the country's first significant political party, the BPP. The party suffered from extreme factionalism and at one time three different groupings claimed the BPP label, but by the time of the 1965 election Matante's BPP was the only one of significance. He was elected MP for the Francistown constituency, a victory he repeated in 1969 and 1974, but his party lacked widespread national support and won only three of the 31 seats available. The party never managed to improve on this in subsequent elections. As a great popular orator, with a taste for high living, Matante remained as the dominant figure on the opposition benches until 1979, when his health began to fail. He stood in the 1979 election but lost his Francistown seat and died a week after the election. At his funeral his political friends and opponents joined in paying tribute to this extremely colourful politician.

289   George Mzimvube MATANZIMA

South Africa (Transkei)

Matanzima was the prime minister of the 'independent' homeland until he was ousted in 1987.

Born in 1918 in Qamata, he was educated at Fort Hare University and became a lawyer. In 1963 he became a member of the Transkeian Territorial Authority and cooperated with South African government plans to grant independence under the Bantustan scheme. Transkei was the first of the territories to become independent in 1976 but, as with the others, this independence has never been recognized by any state but South Africa. Following independence, Matanzima became prime minister, with his elder brother Kaiser as the largely ceremonial president. Subsequently George banished his brother. In September 1987 the army sent Matanzima on 'sick leave' and replaced him as prime minister with Stella Sigcau. The latter might have been regarded as Africa's first woman prime minister had anybody recognized her state, but in any case she was overthrown by the military in December the same year. In 1988 Matanzima returned to Transkei but was arrested and charged with corruption. In 1989 he was sentenced to nine years' imprisonment.

290   Dick Tennyson MATENJE

Malawi

Matenje was a dominant figure in the government and ruling MCP until his death in mysterious circumstances in 1983.

Born in 1929 near Blantyre, he qualified and worked as a schoolteacher before going to Ottawa University, where he graduated. He became MP for Blantyre in 1971 and within a few weeks was appointed minister of education. Five weeks after that he became finance minister. One year later the portfolios of trade, industry and tourism were added to his responsibilities. In January 1982 he added the post of secretary-general of the ruling MCP to his government positions. His meteoric political rise resulted in the creation of powerful enemies, especially, it is widely believed, John Tembo. In May 1983 he was killed in circumstances which have never been adequately explained. It was officially announced that he had died in a car crash (with Aaron Gadama) but it was also reported that the men had been shot whilst trying to flee the country.

291   Gabriel Baccus MATTHEWS

Liberia

Matthews was a leading opponent of the TWP government and a leading figure in the post-coup government before returning to the ranks of the opposition.

Born in 1948 in Monrovia, he received higher education in the USA before working as a diplomat for the Liberian government. In 1976 he became chairman of the opposition movement, the PAL, and retained his position when the movement transformed itself into a political party, the PPP, in 1979. He was arrested in 1979, released a few months later and detained again in 1980 before the coup.

Following the coup he was released and appointed foreign minister in the new military-dominated government. Along with other radicals he was dismissed in 1981 but in 1982 he became director-general of the cabinet. In 1983 he resigned to form a political party, the UPP. The UPP was not recognized for the 1985 elections and Matthews was banned from participating in the presidential election. The following year the party was legalized, but its leaders have continued to suffer government harassment.

292   Leon M'BA

Gabon

M'Ba was the first post-independence president of Gabon and remained in office until he died of natural causes in 1967.

Born in 1902, the son of a Fang village chief, he was educated locally before joining the colonial civil service. He was a keen nationalist from the early 1920s and combined his job with part-time journalism. Criticisms of the French administration led to his exile in Oubangui-Chari (later to become the CAR) from 1933 to 1946. On returning home he became involved in politics and was elected to the Gabonese territorial assembly in 1952. In 1953 he founded a new party, the GDB, which he led until his death. In 1956 he was elected mayor of Libreville. Following the victory of his party in the elections of 1957 and 1958, he became head of the government and in 1961 the first president of the new republic following further elections.

In 1963 he forced opposition elements to join the GDB, thus creating a single-party state. This move created conflict and in February 1964 he was ousted by the Gabonese army. French troops rapidly intervened to restore him to power. In 1966 he became terminally ill and spent most of the final year of his life in hospital. He was re-elected president in March 1967 and managed to ensure that his chosen successor, Albert Bernard Bongo, took over at his death. He died in a Paris hospital in November 1967.

293 Serigne Abdoul Ahad M'BACKE

Senegal

M'Backe was the most important Islamic leader in Senegal and played a crucial role in politics.

Born in 1912, he was the seventh son of the founder of the powerful Mouride brotherhood, Amadu Bamba M'Backe. He became a prosperous large-scale farmer around the holy city of Touba and earned such luxuries as a Rolls-Royce car and his own private airstrip. In 1968 he became Khalifa-General of the Mourides, the most powerful of the Islamic brotherhoods in Senegal. He was a strong supporter of presidents Senghor and Diouf and, because of his unique authority amongst many of the Muslim peasants, was able to deliver crucial support for them at elections. The links between the government and the Mourides have been of crucial importance in Senegalese politics. M'Backe died in June 1989 and was greatly mourned.

294 Govan Archibald Mvuyelwa MBEKI

South Africa

Mbeki is a veteran leader of the ANC who was imprisoned from 1963 until 1987.

Born in 1910 in Nqamakwe district in Transkei, he was the son of a local chief who was subsequently deposed by the government. He graduated from Fort Hare University in 1937. In 1935, whilst a student, he joined the ANC and spent many years working for the organiza-tion, becoming its national chairman in 1956. Following the banning of the ANC in 1960 he went underground and joined its new military wing, Umkhonto we Sizwe (Spear of the Nation), serving as secretary of its high command. In 1963 he was arrested and sentenced to life imprisonment. He was released in 1987 but was served with a banning order and refused a passport. Following the legalization of the ANC in 1990 he once again became active in public life.

295 Thabo Mvuyelwa MBEKI

South Africa

Thabo Mbeki, who is the son of Govan Mbeki, is one of the leading younger figures within the ANC and head of its international affairs department.

Born in 1942 in Idutywa, Transkei, he joined the ANC Youth League in 1956 and was subsequently expelled from school for political activities. In 1961 he was a founder member of the African Students' Association and be-came its secretary, but the movement collapsed when most of its leaders were arrested. Following the banning of the ANC in 1960 he worked underground in South Africa until 1962, when he went into exile. He worked for the ANC in Britain, Botswana, Tanzania, Zambia and Nigeria, where he was the official representative of the movement. In 1985 he was appointed director of information and was subsequently given re-sponsibility for international affairs. Following the unbanning of the ANC in 1990 he returned to South Africa to be-come part of the ANC's negotiating team in talks with the white government.

296 Amadou Mokhtar M'BOW

Senegal

M'Bow was the controversial director-general of UNESCO from 1974 to 1987.

Born in 1921 in Dakar, he received higher education at the University of Paris before returning to teach in Senegal. He was minister of education in the pre-independence government from 1957 to 1958, but in the latter year he was sacked following a disagreement with Senghor. He returned to teaching but in 1966 he made peace with Senghor and again became minister of education. In 1968 he was appointed minister of culture. In 1970 he became assistant director-general of UNESCO and, in 1974, director. He was an extremely controversial figure in this post and was accused by his opponents of being arrogant, wasteful and inefficient. His supporters saw him as a defender of Third World interests. Several states, including the USA, Great Britain and Singapore, withdrew from membership of UNESCO in protest at his leadership. In 1986 he announced that he would not stand for a further term, but in 1987 he changed his mind. He withdrew part way through the election when it became obvious that he would lose following the withdrawal of Soviet support. He thus retired in 1987.

297 Thomas Joseph MBOYA

Kenya

Mboya was generally regarded as the most widely respected and able politician, trade unionist and government leader in Kenya until his tragic assassination in 1969.

Born in 1930 in Machakos district into the Luo ethnic group, he was educated locally before starting work as a sanitary inspector in Nairobi. In 1952 he founded and led the Kenya Local Government Workers' Union and from 1953 to 1963 led the Kenya Federation of Labour. Throughout the 1950s he became increasingly prominent both at home and abroad in trade union and political affairs. In 1958 he was elected to the executive of ICFTU and in the same year became chairman of the All-African Peoples' Conference in Ghana, reflecting his pan-Africanist beliefs. In 1957 he was one of the first group of Kenyan Africans elected to the legislative council and when KANU was formed in 1960 he became its secretary-general.

In the pre-independence government he served as minister of labour. In the 1963 election he was returned as KANU member for Nairobi and at independence later the same year he was appointed minister of justice and constitutional affairs. In 1964 he became minister of economic planning and development, a position in which he created the structures for Kenya's impressive record of economic development. In spite of his non-Kikuyu background he was universally regarded as the most able and popular of the younger generation of political leaders and was viewed as the most likely eventual successor to President Kenyatta, who was 40 years his senior. In July 1969, Mboya was murdered by a Kikuyu assassin. The precise details of the background of the assassination have never emerged publicly, but the event produced popular outbursts of discontent and has remained a topic of intense speculation in Kenya ever since.

298   Antoine Idrissou MEATCHI

Togo

Meatchi was a senior government figure and served as vice-president.

Born in 1925 in Sokode into the local royal family, he was educated in Mali and in France, where he trained in tropical agriculture. On his return to Togo in 1953 he was appointed deputy head of agricultural services. From 1956 to 1958 he served as minister of agriculture and then as minister of finance in the Grunitzky administration. When the latter went into exile following defeat in the 1958 elections, Meatchi became leader of their party, the UDPT, until 1961, when he too went into exile in Benin and Ghana. Following the 1963 coup he returned to Togo and tried to claim the presidency. The post eventually went to Grunitzky, but Meatchi became vice-president and held the finance, economy and planning portfolios. In 1966 he was purged from the government and the post of vice-president was abolished. Following the 1967 coup he was not appointed to the government but was appointed to the important post of director of agricultural services, which he held until 1978 when he went into private business. In 1982 he was charged with massive corruption during his period in agricultural services. He was found guilty and imprisoned. He was still in jail when he died in 1984.

299   Leon MEBIAME

Gabon

Mebiame has been prime minister of Gabon since the creation of the post in 1975.

Born in Libreville in 1934, he was educated locally and in Brazzaville. In 1959 he joined the civil service. He formed a close alliance with president Bongo and has benefited from the latter's patronage. In 1967 Bongo brought him into the cabinet, where he served in several ministerial roles. In 1972 he was made vice-president, but this post was abolished in 1975 and replaced with the new one of prime minister. Mebiame was immediately appointed to this new post and has held it ever since, in spite of frequent changes in government personnel by the president. He remains Bongo's most trusted ally, which, more than anything else, explains his lengthy tenure in office.

300   MENGISTU Haile Mariam

Ethiopia

Mengistu was a leading member of the group within the army which deposed Emperor Haile Selassie in 1974 and became Ethiopian head of state in 1977, following violent factional disputes within the new regime.

Born in 1935 into a poor family, he was raised in the household of the governor of Gojam province who helped him gain a place in the Holeta military academy. After graduating as a military officer he served in the emperor's palace staff and on the Somali border. When Haile Selassie was overthrown in September 1974, Mengistu became first vice-chairman of the new ruling group, the Provisional Military Administrative Committee, later known as the *Derg*. For three years this body was plagued by violent factional conflict which cost the lives of many of its initial leadership figures. By February 1977, Mengistu had emerged as the dominant figure in the regime and became head of state. He proceeded to crush remaining opposition to his leadership. Simultaneously he established close links with the Soviet Union and Cuba, who were later to provide him with extensive military support.

Mengistu declared his desire for the formation of a Marxist–Leninist party and several years were spent planning its organization. In 1984 the foundation of the WPE was announced, with Mengistu as its leader. The WPE is, in theory, the centre of political power, although the regime's major support base remains the army. Several attempts at a counter-coup have failed in recent years. More serious opposition to Mengistu and his regime have come from nationalist secession movements, especially those in Eritrea and Tigre. This has placed Ethiopia in a state of continuous civil war. The country has also been hit on several recent occasions by massive famines which have cost many thousands of innocent lives and which many blame, in part at least, on the policies of the government.

By the end of the 1980s Mengistu had established a highly personalized form of rule. Whilst it was more ruthless than that of his predecessors, in terms of style it seemed to many increasingly to resemble the old imperial style embedded in Ethiopian tradition.

301   Michel MICOMBERO

Burundi

President of Burundi from 1966 to 1976, Micombero is best remembered for the genocidal massacres of Hutus which occurred in 1972.

He was born in 1940 and joined the army in 1960, receiving training in Belgium. Although a soldier, he served in several civilian administrations as minister of defence. In 1966 King Ntare, the constitutional monarch of Burundi, appointed him as government leader, but a few months later Micombero ousted the king and declared a republic, with himself as president. He purged Hutus from the civil service and army, strengthening the dominance of his own Tutsi group. In 1972 he invited Ntare to return to Burundi, but then had him murdered while in government custody. Anti-government demonstrations by Hutu led Micombero to launch a military campaign against them and, in one of the most shameful developments ever seen in Africa, hundreds of thousands of Hutu were massacred by the army. The slaughter included the intentional annihilation of almost all the educated Hutu elite.

Micombero retreated into alcoholism and, in 1976, was ousted in a military coup led by Jean Baptiste Bagaza. He was arrested but later released to go into exile in Somalia, where he died of a heart attack in 1983.

302   Francis Misheck MINAH

Sierra Leone

Minah was a leading government figure over a long period, but was eventually executed for treason.

Born in 1929, he was educated in Freetown before proceeding to England, where he qualified as a lawyer. He was first elected to parliament in 1967 as a member of the SLPP, but in 1970 he defected to the ruling APC. He was first appointed to the government in 1973 as minister of trade and industry. He remained a senior government figure for nearly a decade and a half. In 1975 he was appointed foreign minister and in 1978 attorney-general and minister of justice. In 1980 he became finance minister, but the following year he was temporarily demoted to minister of health following financial scandals when Sierra Leone hosted the OAU summit. However by 1982 he was back as attorney-general and minister of justice. In 1984 he became second vice-president and in 1986 was promoted to first vice-president, the second most powerful position in the government. His long-term prominence in the government owed much to his close relationship with President Siaka Stevens and when the latter retired in 1985 his position became more tenuous. In 1987 President Momoh sacked Minah from the cabinet, along with other members of the Stevens old guard. Later the same year he was arrested and charged with plotting a coup. He was sentenced to death but a lengthy appeals procedure ensued. He was eventually hanged in October 1989.

303 Saydi MINGAS

Angola

Mingas was a leading member of the MPLA and minister of finance in the first post-independence government. He was assassinated in 1977 in the 'Alves' coup.

Mingas was born into a leading Cabindan family in 1943 and was educated in Portugal and, later, Cuba. He joined the MPLA in 1961 and served in important positions both as a guerrilla leader and as a diplomatic representa-

tive of the movement. In 1972 he was appointed as the MPLA representative for Scandinavia and was based in Stockholm for two years. In 1974 he returned to Angola and the following year became minister of finance at independence. Generally recognized as a man of outstanding ability, he was the most senior government figure to be killed in the abortive coup of May 1977.

304 Idriss MISKINE

Chad

In a relatively short time Miskine had established himself as one of Chad's major political figures before his premature death in 1984.

Born in 1948 in Ndjamena, he became a civil servant and first came to prominence in 1978 when he was appointed minister of communications and transport in the Malloum–Habre government. When this government was overthrown he stayed loyal to Habre and played a leading role in the latter's FAN guerrilla movement. He was one of the major commanders who put Habre back in power in 1982. He was appointed foreign minister and was very successful in gaining widespread international recognition for the regime. He was also the main negotiator in Habre's attempts to win the support of some of the government's internal opponents. In January 1984 he died of complications arising from malaria.

305 Peter Simako MMUSI

Botswana

Mmusi has been vice-president of Botswana since 1983 and has also held a series of key ministerial appointments.

141

Born in 1929 in Mmankgodi, he worked as a teacher and civil servant before entering politics. In the 1974 election he won the Kweneng South seat for the BDP and was appointed assistance minister of finance and development planning. He was subsequently minister of commerce and industry in 1977, home affairs from 1977 to 1979, and works and communications from 1979 to 1980. For the 1979 election he changed his constituency to Gaborone where he defeated Kenneth Koma, the leader of the BNF.

In 1980 he was appointed to the crucial post of minister of finance and development planning, succeeding Quett Masire, who had just become president. On the death of vice-president Lenyeletse Seretse in January 1983, Mmmusi was appointed vice-president by his long-time political ally, Masire. In the 1984 election he won the Gaborone seat again but the victory was quashed following evidence concerning a lost ballot box, and in the subsequent by-election he was defeated by Koma. He had to return to parliament as a specially elected member nominated by the president. He is widely regarded as an extremely able administrator, but is by nature a technocrat rather than populist politician and lacks a strong independent political base in the country.

306 MOBUTU Sese Seko Kuku Ngbendu Wa Za Banga

Zaire

Mobutu has totally dominated Zairean politics for over a quarter of a century, during which time he has ruled over one of the most corrupt, authoritarian and inefficient regimes in Africa.

Born in 1930 in Lisala in the north of the country into the Bengala ethnic group, he joined the colonial army straight from secondary school. He served for seven years, reaching the rank of sergeant before leaving to become a newspaper editor in Leopoldville (now Kinshasha). He joined Patrice Lumumba's MNC and became, for a time, a close ally of Lumumba. When the latter became prime minister at independence in June 1960, he appointed Mobutu army chief of staff. In September he was promoted to commander-in-chief and within a few days staged his first coup, ousting Lumumba who was murdered by Mobutu's soldiers a few months later. At this stage he did not wish to stay in power and reappointed President Kasavubu to run the government while he built up the army to deal with the various rebellions and secessionist movements. In 1965 he staged a further coup and installed himself as president of the country.

In the period from 1965 to 1970 he brought at least a partial end to the chaos which had existed since independence. To do this he created a highly personalized dictatorship in which all power was concentrated in his own hands and where political appointments were based solely on loyalty to the president. To a large extent this system has survived ever since, although in an increasingly decaying and degraded form. Only those state agencies which are designed to keep him in power have remained in real existence, whilst those concerned with social welfare have largely atrophied. In 1967 he created a notional political party, the MPR, to which all Zairean citizens automatically belonged.

Until very recently (see below) Mobutu was the leader of the party which has existed largely to glorify the president. In 1970 he began his programme of 'African authenticity', which started with the changing of the name of the country from Congo to Zaire and the dropping of his own christian name of Joseph. Over the years a personality cult has been established which rivals the most notorious examples in other parts of the world. Since 1974 Mobutuism has been the official state ideology, although its content changes on a regular basis to fit circumstances. Zaire has become possibly the most corruptly run state in the world and Mobutu himself is reputed to be one of the world's richest men. At the same time the potentially rich Zairean economy has moved from crisis to crisis.

Mobutu's rule has not been unopposed. There have been a number of coup attempts and unsuccessful invasions, most notably those of Shaba in 1977 and 1978. External help from France, the USA and China has played its part in keeping him in power, but the use of the army and police to coerce the population has probably been more significant. In 1990, in response to riots and mounting social pressure, Mobutu announced that reforms would take place within the political system. Chief amongst these was that Zaire would become a multi-party state 'after a transitional period'. At the same time he resigned as leader of the MPR, declaring that he was 'above party politics'. There was a certain amount of understandable cynicism as to whether real reform was possible under Mobutu.

307   Daniel Torotich Arap MOI

Kenya

Moi was always a significant figure in post-independence politics and in 1978 became president following the death of Jomo Kenyatta.

Born in 1924 in Baringo district into the Kalenjin ethnic group, he was educated locally before entering teaching. He progressed to become a headmaster and, later, vice-principal of a teacher training college from 1949 to 1954. In 1955 he left teaching after being nominated for the legislative council as representative for the Rift Valley Province by the colonial authorities. Two years later the first elections were held for the legislative council and he secured election, a fact which now makes him Kenya's longest-serving parliamentarian. In 1960 he became chairman of KADU, a party which was formed to represent the interests of non-Kikuyu Kenyan Africans. In the pre-independence government he was minister of education and then minister of local government.

In 1963 Kenya became independent, with KADU as the main opposition party and Moi opposition leader. In 1964, KADU merged with the ruling KANU party and he was appointed minister of home affairs, a post he retained until becoming president. He became closest of all the non-Kikuyu politicians to Kenyatta and in 1966 he became vice-president of the party. In 1967 he became vice-president of the country and leader of government business in parliament. On the death of Kenyatta in 1978, Moi became head of state in what was, to the surprise of

143

some, a peaceful succession. Constitutionally this was a correct procedure but, perhaps more importantly, he was able to get the backing of most of the heavyweight Kikuyu politicians who might otherwise have struggled amongst themselves for the presidency and thus endangered political stability. Two months later he strengthened his position when he was unanimously elected as leader of KANU.

Because he lacked Kenyatta's personal charisma, Moi projected himself, in the early years of his presidency, as simply following in the great man's footsteps. He pronounced his philosophy as *nyayo* (literally meaning 'footsteps') although more recently he has tended to reinterpret this as meaning that others should follow his footsteps (that is, accept his authority without question). He has strengthened his personal position by gradually easing out of positions of power the important Kikuyu politicians who might seek to rival him. At the same time the political system has become more authoritarian and the arrest and torture of political opponents has damaged Kenya's reputation on human rights which in the past had been relatively good. Because all legal opposition to the government is banned, opponents have been forced to use violent and subversive strategies. In 1982 an attempted coup, led by sections of the air force and supported by students and other disaffected groups, was put down with difficulty and followed by mass arrests, the disbanding of the air force and closure of the university. More recently there has been considerable evidence of the existence of a large-scale subversive organization known as Mwakenya (a Swahili acronym for the Union of Nationalists to Liberate Kenya) which appears to have widespread support, although this is impossible to measure. Because of the nature of the Kenyan political system, open opposition to Moi is impossible.

In foreign relations he has followed a generally pro-Western line, although sensitivity to western criticisms of his record on human rights has sometimes strained relations. Although not without problems, the Kenyan economy has continued under his leadership to be amongst the strongest in Africa, a factor which underlies the relative stability of the political system and the continuity of the leadership.

308   Ntsu MOKHEHLE

Lesotho

Mokhehle has been the major opposition leader in Lesotho since independence, spending most of his time in exile.

Born in 1918 in Tebetebeng, he was educated abroad in South Africa, where he became an active member of the ANC Youth League. In 1950 he returned home to teach and in 1952 he founded and led the Basutoland African Congress (later known as the Basutoland Congress Party, BCP). He was a member of the commission which worked out the independence constitution. In the pre-independence elections of 1965 the BCP narrowly lost to the rival BNP and at independence the following year he became leader of the opposition in parliament.

The BCP won the 1970 election but Mokhehle was prevented from taking power when Prime Minister Jonathan staged a coup to keep himself in power. Mokhehle was arrested and on his release he went into exile in Zambia. He rejected attempts by the Lesotho government to persuade him to join them, although some members of his party did join. In 1979 he launched the LLA to fight against the government. The LLA has received support from South Africa and has engaged in ineffectual acts of sabotage in Lesotho. In 1988 Mokhehle returned briefly to Lesotho for talks with the new military government but these produced no agreement and he soon left the country again to continue his opposition in exile.

309   Charles Dube MOLAPO

Lesotho

Molapo was a senior member of the ruling BNP and of the Jonathan government.

Born in 1818 in Hlotse Camp, he trained as a lawyer in South Africa and practised in Lesotho before entering politics. He became secretary-general of the BNP and ran its successful 1965 election campaign. At independence he was appointed minister of economic development. In 1970 he became minister of justice and in 1975 foreign minister. In the early 1980s he grew increasingly critical of regime policy and resigned in 1983. The following year he became president of the BDA, a small, rather conservative grouping. In view of his apparent hostility to the then prime minister, Leabua Jonathan (a cousin of his), it came as a surprise when, at the funeral of the deposed leader later in 1987, Molapo extolled his supposed virtues.

310   Joseph Saidu MOMOH

Sierra Leone

Momoh has been the president of Sierra Leone since he succeeded Siaka Stevens in 1985.

Born in 1937 in Binkolo in the north of the country, he was educated locally before joining the army. He received officer training in Nigeria and England and was appointed army commander in 1972. By this time he had formed a close alliance with President Siaka Stevens, which was to shape his political career. In 1974 he was nominated to parliament by the president and in 1975 he was brought into the cabinet as minister of state. For the next decade Momoh and Stevens enjoyed a symbiotic relationship. Having the army commander as a close ally offered Stevens some protection against a possible coup and in return he groomed Momoh to succeed him as president. When Stevens retired in 1985, Momoh replaced him in the presidency and as leader of the ruling APC. Momoh retained his military status but appointed a civilian cabinet. Initially there was considerable continuity in government personnel but President Momoh has since appointed new men of his own choosing. He also asserted his independence from his former patron and, until his death, Stevens complained bitterly that Momoh would not listen to his advice once he had gained the presidency. In 1986, Momoh added the defence portfolio to his duties. When he took over the presidency Momoh enjoyed a considerable amount of personal popularity but since then he has come under great pressure to end corruption, improve the sad state of the economy and allow the formation of opposition parties.

311   Eduardo Chivambo MONDLANE

Mozambique

Mondlane was the founder and first president of FRELIMO; he was assassinated in 1969.

Born in 1920 in Gaza Province, the son of a traditional chief, he received his education at a mission school. He proceeded to university in South Africa, but was expelled for political activities. After a similar experience in Portugal he went to the USA, where he eventually gained a doctorate in sociology at Northwestern University in Chicago. In 1957 he began work as an advisor to the United Nations, but in 1961 returned home to organize opposition to Portuguese colonial rule. In 1962, in Tanzania, he united several embryonic groups into FRELIMO, the movement which eventually defeated Portuguese colonialism and which has ruled Mozambique since independence. As leader of the movement he was responsible for the organization of the guerrilla campaign within the country. In February 1969 he was assassinated in Tanzania by a parcel bomb which many believed had been sent by the Portuguese secret police.

312   Suresh MOORBA

Mauritius

Moorba has been a significant figure in both government and opposition who has shown himself adept at frequent changes in party affiliation.

Born in 1941, he trained as a lawyer in England and was called to the bar in 1966. On his return home he joined the radical MMM and became one of its most important figures. Following clashes with the MMM leader, Berenger, he quit the party in 1971 to launch his own PPP. In 1975 he made peace with Berenger, abandoned the PPP and rejoined the MMM, for whom he was elected to parliament in 1976. Soon afterwards he clashed with Berenger again and defected to the ruling MLP. In 1980 he was appointed minister of information and held this post until the defeat of the governing party in the 1982 elections, when he lost office and his parliamentary seat.

313   King MOSHOESHOE the Second

Lesotho

Moshoeshoe has been king of Lesotho since independence in 1966, although his political fortunes have fluctuated.

Born in 1938, he was christened Constantine Bereng Seeiso and was the son of the paramount chief of the Basotho. He read philosophy, politics and economics at Oxford University and was installed as paramount chief in 1960. Under the independence constitution he became king in 1966 as a constitutional head of state. His relationship with Prime Minister Jonathan was poor and after the latter staged a coup to keep himself in power in 1970 the king was briefly detained and then spent a short time in exile in Holland. At the end of 1970 he returned home after agreeing to a ban on his participation in party politics. For the next decade and a half he remained as a largely ceremonial head of state. Following the 1986 coup the new military regime invested all legislative and executive authority in the monarchy, but real power was held by the military. In 1990 the military government stripped the king of his largely imaginery power. In 1991 he was deposed. In February one of his sons, Mohato Seeiso, was crowned King Letsie the Third.

314   Zephania Lekoane MOTHOPENG

South Africa

Mothopeng is a veteran of the nationalist movement and was the president of the PAC until his death in 1990.

Born in 1913 in Vrede, Orange Free State, he worked for an optician as a lens polisher before qualifying as a teacher. He was sacked from his teaching post for opposing the introduction of Bantu Education. In 1950 he became president of the Transvaal Teachers' Association. He was a member of the ANC from the 1940s, but was a supporter of the minority faction which opposed cooperation with non-blacks in the struggle against apartheid. In 1959 he was one of the leaders of this faction when it broke away from the ANC to form the PAC and was the chairman of its inaugural conference. Both the ANC and the PAC were banned in 1960, but Mothopeng continued to work underground for the PAC in South Africa. He was detained on a number of occasions and in 1978 was sentenced to 15 years in jail. He was elected president of the PAC in 1986, whilst still in detention. He was released from jail at the end of 1988 and in 1990 the PAC, along with other anti-apartheid groups, was legalized. Since the split in the nationalist movement the PAC has been rather overshadowed by the ANC, but the opposition of the former to any compromise with the white government and its rejection of cooperation with non-blacks has enabled it to generate a level of support in the townships. Mothopeng died from natural causes in October 1990.

315   Jason Ziyaphapha MOYO

Zimbabwe

Moyo was a leading figure in ZAPU and a major leader in the guerrilla war before he was assassinated in 1977.

Born in 1927 in Plumtree, he received only primary education before training as a carpenter. He became involved in trade unionism from the early 1950s and was secretary-general of the African Artisans Union. In 1961 he was a founder member of ZAPU and stayed loyal to Nkomo when the party split in 1963. He was the creator and leader of the military wing of the party, ZIPRA, and organized the guerrilla war from bases in Zambia and Botswana. He tried without success to unite the various elements in the nationalist movement. In January 1977 he was assassinated in Zambia by a letter bomb sent by the Rhodesian special branch.

316   Attati MPAKATI

Malawi

Mpakati was a leading figure in the exiled opposition movement until he was assassinated in 1983.

A committed Marxist, he received higher education in the Soviet Union and in Sweden, where he gained a doctorate in political science at the University of Stockholm. Before independence he was a significant figure in the nationalist movement, but he went into exile shortly after the end of colonial rule, spending most of his time in Sweden and in Mozambique. In 1974 he founded LESOMA, which, under his leadership, grew into the most important of the exiled opposition groups and established an organizational structure in Malawi. In Maputo, in 1979, he had his hands blown off by a letter bomb. In March 1983 he was assassinated in Zimbabwe while on a brief visit. Although no conclusive evidence has been presented, both events have been widely attributed to agents of the Malawian government.

317   Keyecwe Motsamai MPHO

Botswana

Mpho is the leader of BIP, one of the smaller opposition parties in the country.

A member of the Bayei ethnic group, he was born in Maun in 1921. During the late 1940s and the 1950s he worked in a number of jobs in South Africa, including employment as a clerk in the Christian Council of South Africa. In 1952 he joined the ANC and became active in anti-apartheid politics. He went on trial for treason in 1956 but was acquitted. In 1960 he was again arrested and held for four months before being deported to his home country. He joined Matante's BPP but later broke away to form his own party, the BIP, following disagreements with Matante. His party enjoyed a highly localized support base in the remote north west of the country.

In the 1969 and 1974 elections Mpho was elected to parliament for the Okavango constituency, but the party won no other seats. The seat was lost in the 1979 election and has never been recovered.

Whilst the BIP remained largely a one-man party, Mpho enjoyed a deserved reputation as a politician of great integrity who worked hard in the interests of his constituents. Ultimately, however, the respect he received from all sides in Botswana was insufficient to put him in a position of real power.

318   MPINGA Kasenda

Zaire

Mpinga was the first prime minister of the Mobutu regime and was later permanent secretary of the ruling party.

Born in 1937 in Tshilomba, he was educated locally before going to France for higher education, gaining a doctorate in social sciences. Returning to Zaire in 1966, he became a professor at the National University of Zaire and published a number of scholarly articles before turning to political work, when he became head of the party school. In 1977 the post of first state commissioner (the approximate equivalent of prime minister) was established and he became the first to hold it. He stayed in this post until 1980. In 1981 he became permanent secretary of the ruling party, the MPR, and held this position until 1985, when he returned to direct the party school. Few members of Mobutu's governments have exercised any significant autonomy, but Mpinga was more competent than most.

319   Cleopa David MSUYA

Tanzania

Msuya was prime minister from 1980 to 1983 and a leading government figure both before and since then.

Born in 1931 in Usangi in the north of the country into a poor peasant family, he was educated locally before earning a degree at Makerere in Uganda. He returned to work in government service and by 1970 was the top civil servant in the country. In 1972 he was appointed minister of finance and has held one or other of the senior economic portfolios ever since, apart from 1980 to 1983 when he served as prime minister. Since 1985 he has been minister of finance, planning and economic affairs. In many ways Msuya is more of a technocrat than a grass roots politician. In terms of economic policy orientation he is on the liberal wing of the party and the government.

320   King MSWATI the Third

Swaziland

Mswati, formerly Prince Makhosetive, has been King of Swaziland since his coronation in 1986.

Born in 1968, he was the second youngest of King Sobhuza's 70 sons. He was a pupil at an English public school, Sherborne in Dorset, when his father died in 1982. The death of the king produced intense factional conflict amongst the Swazi royals, but the group favouring Prince Makhosetive proved successful and he was brought home to be presented as the future king. He was crowned in 1986 and was confirmed in his kingship in 1989, when he reached

the age of 21. It is not clear to what extent he acts as an independent force or is manipulated by more politically experienced Swazi royals, but since his coronation a number of close relatives have been placed in positions of power.

321   Robert Gabriel MUGABE

Zimbabwe

Mugabe was a leader of the nationalist movement and has ruled Zimbabwe since independence.

Born in 1924 at Kutama Mission, he was educated locally before qualifying and working as a teacher. He then went to the University of Fort Hare in South Africa, where he graduated in 1951. He taught at home again and then for a period in Northern Rhodesia (now Zambia) and Ghana. He returned home in 1960 and the following year was a founder-member and deputy leader of ZAPU. In 1963 he split from the party and formed ZANU, becoming its secretary-general. In 1964 he was arrested and held in detention until 1974, when he was released under a government amnesty. He went into exile in Mozambique and by 1976 he was president of ZANU and commander-in-chief of its guerrilla army, ZANLA. In October the same year he formed the tactical political alliance between ZANU and ZAPU, known as the PF. At the end of 1979 he was a major figure at the Lancaster House Conference which resulted in the agreement for Zimbabwean independence under majority rule. Instead of fighting the 1980 independence election as part of a united PF, he chose to break with his erstwhile partner Nkomo and fight as ZANU–PF. His party won a majority of seats in the election and at independence in April 1980 he became prime minister. When the constitution changed in 1987 he became the country's first executive president, a post he still firmly holds.

Since independence ZANU–PF has continued as the dominant party in Zimbabwean politics, winning significant majorities in the elections of 1985 and 1990. At the end of 1987, Mugabe negotiated a merger (in practice a takeover) with Nkomo's PF, but subsequently other parties sprang up to oppose ZANU–PF. Mugabe has made clear for a long time that he would like to see a single-party state in Zimbabwe, with his own as the only party, and many expected this to be introduced following the 1990 election, but popular opposition to the move resulted in the decision being deferred. Although Mugabe personally continued to favour a move to a single-party, state support for the idea within his party evaporated. In August 1990 the ZANU politburo rejected the idea and in September it was also rejected by the party's central committee and was abandoned. Under Mugabe's leadership reconciliation with the white community has had considerable success, but for several years there was armed resistance to his rule in Matabeleland. This was put down with great brutality by the notorious Fifth Brigade who were often seen as acting against any opponents of the government whether they had any connection with the rebels or not. This was also seen by some as the majority Shona group (to which Mugabe belongs) attempting to subdue the Ndebele group (to which Nkomo belongs). To date

Mugabe's authoritarian inclinations have been constrained to some extent by the existence of constitutional checks and balances and a relatively independent judiciary and press, but this may not continue indefinitely. In 1988 and 1989 his government was rocked by a major corruption scandal involving several senior ministers, although Mugabe himself was not implicated. Although his speeches tend to be full of Marxist rhetoric the economy has retained a large free-market sector and is one of the more prosperous in Africa. The negative side to this is that control of farming land has remained very unequal despite promises made during the liberation struggle about redistribution of land. In both political and economic terms the results of Mugabe's period in power have to be viewed as rather mixed.

322   Murtala Ramat MUHAMMED

Nigeria

Muhammed was military head of state in Nigeria from July 1975 until he was assassinated during an abortive coup attempt in February 1976.

Born in 1938 in Kano into an aristocratic Hausa-Fulani family, he was educated locally before entering the army in 1957. He received officer training at Sandhurst in England and later fought with the UN peace-keeping forces in the Congo. In July 1966 he was an active participant in the coup which brought Gowon to power, although the two men always enjoyed a rather cool personal relationship. During the civil war he performed an active leadership role at the battlefront, where he led the recapture of Benin, Onitsha and Asaba.

In 1974 he was appointed federal commissioner for communications.

In July 1975 he led the relatively bloodless coup which overthrew the Gowon regime and became commander-in-chief of the armed forces and head of state. In the short period he was in power his regime earned a deserved reputation for decisive action in dealing with many problems which had built up in Nigeria since the end of the civil war. He conducted a major purge of public officials in which more than 10 000 were dismissed. He created seven more states in the federal structure and took the decision to move the capital from Lagos to Abuja. In international affairs he asserted a strongly nationalist position, including the recognition of the MPLA government in Angola, which displeased some western governments. Most importantly he set in motion the schedule for a return to civilian rule in 1979 which was adhered to in spite of subsequent events.

In February 1976 the failed Dimka coup took place and Muhammed was assassinated as he drove to work in Lagos. The coup was generally very unpopular and Muhammed was widely mourned. In his short time in office considerable progress had been made in many areas. However the huge personality cult which developed around him posthumously seemed at odds with the emphasis on collective decision making by the ruling military elite whilst he was alive. In some cases it was difficult to disentangle genuine grief over his death from attempts by individuals and groups to manipulate his memory for their own purposes. He is still regarded by many Nigerians as a national martyr.

323   Solomon Tandeng MUNA

Cameroon

Until his voluntary retirement in 1988, Muna was the leading Anglophone politician in Cameroon, with a career stretching back to the pre-independence period.

Born in 1912 in Ngyenmbo, he trained as a teacher in London and then taught in Southern Cameroons from 1932 to 1951. A supporter of unification with Francophone Cameroon, he joined Foncha's KNDP in 1957. He served in several ministerial roles in Foncha's government, including minister of finance. Following unification he became federal minister of transport under Ahidjo. In 1970 he was elected vice-president under Ahidjo and also became prime minister of Western Cameroon until a unitary state structure replaced federalism in 1972.

In 1973 he was made president of the National Assembly, a post he held until his retirement 15 years later. A constitutional change in 1983 officially made his post the second most important in the government hierarchy after the president. Muna was one of the few senior political figures to be unaffected by the mass dismissals which followed Ahidjo's replacement by Biya as president. A politician of integrity, Muna was trusted by both and tried hard, but unsuccessfully, to bridge the rift which developed between them. His retirement from public office in 1988 was only very reluctantly accepted by the president.

151

324 Nalumino MUNDIA

Zambia

Mundia was a leading figure in the ruling UNIP and government and was prime minister from 1981 to 1985.

Born in 1927 in Namanda, he was educated locally and at universities in India and the USA, where he trained as an economist. He was a founder-member of UNIP in 1959. After independence in 1964 he became minister of local government and, subsequently, of commerce and of labour. In 1969 he defected to the Zambian ANC and became its deputy president. When the party was banned in 1972 he rejoined UNIP and became a member of its central committee. In 1974 he rejoined the government as minister with special responsibility for North-Western Province. In 1981 he was promoted to prime minister. He was removed from the premiership in 1985, although he remained a member of the UNIP central committee.

325 Abubakar Balarabe MUSA

Nigeria

Musa was a major opposition leader of the Second Republic and was elected governor of Kaduna State.

Born in 1936 in Kaya, Kaduna State, he was educated locally and in England and qualified as a chartered accountant. With the lifting of the ban on political parties in 1978 he joined the PRP and rapidly emerged as one of its younger, more radical leaders. In the 1979 election he was elected as governor of Kaduna State but, in a situation which was unique in the Second Republic, his party was in the minority in the state legislature. This produced serious tensions and in 1981 he lost his position after being impeached. This was a highly partisan party political move. He remained a leader of the more radical faction of the PRP until all parties were banned following the 1983 coup. In 1989 he was arrested and detained by the military government for illegal political activity.

326 Yoweri Kaguta MUSEVENI

Uganda

Museveni has been president since coming to power in 1986 as leader of a popular rebellion.

Born in 1944 in Ntungamo into the Nyankole ethnic group, he was educated locally and at the University of Dar-es-Salaam before joining the civil service. He worked in the research section of the office of the president from 1970 to 1971, but went into exile in Tanzania when the Amin coup took place. Whilst in Tanzania he worked as a teacher and organized the exiled opposition to Amin. In 1979 he was one of the leaders of UNLA, a loosely-knit group of political exiles which supported the invasion of Uganda by the Tanzanian army and the ousting of the Amin regime. He served briefly as minister of defence in the interim government in 1979. In the 1980 elections he led the UPM, which consisted mainly of the younger, more radical elements who had fought with the Tanzanians and represented an attempt to move away from the older forms of ethnic and regional parties. The UPM won only one seat in the election but Museveni declared, with some justification, that the election had been rigged and returned to the bush to organize his NRA.

From 1981 to 1986 he led the NRA in a guerrilla war against the Obote regime and the ephemeral military administrations which succeeded it. The NRA proved to be the most disciplined force in the country as the national army and other groups fragmented into warring factions. It attracted considerable popular support from the population as the only grouping likely to bring some sort of order to the crumbling society. By January 1986 the NRA had gained control of Kampala and Museveni was sworn in as president. He announced the creation of a National Resistance Council (NRC) which included military and civilian elements and appointed a cabinet which included members of several political parties as well as members of his own NRA.

Most of Museveni's efforts have since been aimed at restoring law and order to Uganda by eliminating the numerous armed groups existing in the country, some of which claim political motivations but most of which are simply bandit gangs. In this he has had some success and Uganda is less lawless than when he came to power. In 1989 elections were held for some of the seats on the NRC, although political parties remained suspended. The rule of Museveni has improved the general situation in Uganda, but there is still a long way to go before the country returns to anything like normality.

327 Kebby Sililo Kambulu MUSOKOTWANE

Zambia

Musokotwane was a senior government figure and was prime minister from 1985 to 1989.

Born in 1946 in Musokotwane, in the Southern Region, he was the son of a chief and was educated locally before qualifying as a teacher. He taught for several years and became a headmaster. He was first elected to parliament in 1973 and joined the government as minister of water and natural resources. In 1977 he was appointed minister of youth and sports, but in 1979 was promoted to finance minister. He held this post until 1983, when he was demoted to the youth and sports portfolio. In 1985 he was again promoted, this time to the top position in the government, that of prime minister. His tenure in the premiership came to an end in 1989, when President Kaunda, in an attempt to secure his base within the military, replaced him as prime minister with the army commander, General Malimba Masheke. Musokotwane was demoted to the education, youth and sports portfolio. He regarded this as humiliating and successfully requested a transfer to the diplomatic service. He was appointed ambassador to Canada. His high-flying but erratic government career is a reflection of President Kaunda's use of government reshuffles as a device for sustaining the presidency.

328 Didymus MUTASA

Zimbabwe

Mutasa has been the speaker in Zimbabwe's parliament since independence in 1980.

Born in 1935 in Rusape, he was educated locally. On leaving school he joined a cooperative farming venture near St Faith's but this was closed down. He then became an administrative officer in the agriculture department and became involved in trade union activities, especially in relation to racial discrimination over pay. In 1964 he was one of the founders of Cold Comfort Farm, a multi-racial farming cooperative on the outskirts of Salisbury (now Harare). When this venture was crushed by the government in 1970, Mutasa was detained in solitary confinement for nine months. On his release he went to Britain to become a student, but also became involved in nationalist activities with ZANU. In 1977 he began to work for the party full-time in Mozambique, becoming a member of its central committee in 1978. He was elected to parliament in 1980 and was then chosen by the National Assembly to act as its speaker, a delicate role he has performed ever since. He remains one of the most highly regarded figures in public life.

329 King MUTESA the Second

Uganda

Mutesa was the last Kabaka of Buganda and the first president of post-colonial Uganda.

Born in 1924, the heir to the title of Kabaka (King) of the kingdom of Buganda, his initial name was Edward William Frederick David Luwangual Mutebi. He succeeded his father in 1939, although he was not formally crowned until 1942. He received higher education and some military training in England. In the colonial period Buganda had enjoyed a semi-autonomous status and Mutesa began campaigning for his kingdom to become a separate independent state and not part of Uganda. He was exiled for a time in Britain in

the 1950s because of his opposition to the inclusion of Buganda in Uganda, but eventually a compromise solution, whereby his kingdom would have a degree of autonomy in the independent state of Uganda, was agreed. In Uganda a royalist political party, the Kabaka Yekka (King Alone - KY) was formed to support the cause of Buganda. At independence in 1962 he became the first president, although this was a largely honorific position. Relations between Mutesa and the Ugandan government deteriorated and in 1966 he ordered the latter to withdraw from the territory of Buganda. The government brought in the army to storm the royal palace and Mutesa escaped to exile in Britain, where he died in 1969.

330 Paulo MUWANGA

Uganda

Muwanga was vice-president and minister of defence in the Second Republic from 1980 to 1985.

Born in 1925, he was educated locally and worked in the East African Posts and Telecommunications before entering politics. He was an early member of Obote's UPC, for whom he was elected to parliament in 1962. In the First Republic he remained a relatively minor figure but an ardent Obote supporter. He went into exile in Britain (where he ran a fish and chip shop) after the Amin coup. He was a leading figure in the UNLA, which supported the Tanzanians in the overthrow of the Amin regime in 1979. He became interior minister in the interim government and chairman of the military commission. His handling of the 1980 elections may have helped Obote to win, but it also did much to discredit the electoral process. He was appointed vice-president and minister of defence in Obote's government which was overthrown in 1985 after failing to restore any semblance of law and order to Uganda. He remained in detention until 1990. He was acquitted by a court in 1988, but was immediately re-arrested, and was finally released in October 1990.

331   Simon Vengai MUZENDA

Zimbabwe

Muzenda has occupied the second most important position in the government since independence.

Born in 1922 in Gutu, he trained as a carpenter after leaving school. In the 1950s he became involved in nationalist politics in Bulawayo and was one of the founders of the NDP in 1960, becoming its organizing secretary. When the party was banned the following year he joined its successor, ZAPU, as administrative secretary. In 1962 he was arrested and sentenced to 12 years in prison but he was released in 1964. He then joined ZANU, which had split away from ZAPU while he was in detention, and became its organizing secretary. He was detained again shortly afterwards and was not released until 1972, at the time of the Pearce Commission. In 1975 he moved to Mozambique and became a major figure in planning the guerrilla war. At independence in 1980 he became deputy prime minister and, when the constitution was changed in 1987, to allow for an executive presidency, he became vice-president. He has also continuously occupied the vice-presidency of the ruling

ZANU–PF party and is very much President Mugabe's right-hand man.

332   Abel Tendekayi MUZOREWA

Zimbabwe

Muzorewa was a leading political and religious leader, although he has now become much less prominent.

Born in 1925 in Old Mutare, he was educated locally. In 1953 he was ordained in the United Methodist Church and shortly afterwards left for further theological training in the USA. He was consecrated a bishop in 1968, but was banned by the government from working in the African communal lands because he was regarded as subversive. He rose to political prominence in 1972, when he led African opposition to the British–Rhodesian settlement at the time of the Pearce Commission. As the leader of the ANC, renamed UANC in 1976, he was able to persuade the Commission that the settlement was not acceptable to the black majority of the population. At this time his relationship with the guerrilla leaders of ZANU and ZAPU was very good, but it subsequently deteriorated and by 1976 was decidedly hostile.

In 1978, Muzorewa came to an agreement with the white prime minister, Ian Smith, to work out an internal settlement which excluded ZANU and ZAPU. Elections held later that year produced a UANC victory and Muzorewa became prime minister. His government lacked credibility and failed to gain international recognition or stop the civil war. At the end of 1979 he was a participant in the Lancaster House talks in London which did produce a settlement with wide support. In the pre-independence elections of 1980 the UANC performed poorly and won only three seats and in the 1985 elections it won none at all. Muzorewa was detained briefly on security charges in 1984, although it was not altogether clear how valid the charges were. Since 1985 he has more or less retired from politics and returned to his religious work. He lacked political acumen and his credibility was fatally undermined by his agreement with the Smith government.

333   Ali Hassan MWINYI

Tanzania

Mwinyi has been the president of Tanzania since succeeding Nyerere in 1985.

Born in 1925 in Zanzibar, he was educated locally and in England, where he qualified as a teacher. In 1964 he was appointed principal secretary in the ministry of education in Zanzibar. He joined the Tanzanian cabinet in 1970 and held a number of fairly senior posts, but he did not emerge as a major national figure until 1984, when he replaced Aboud Jumbe as president of Zanzibar and, automatically, vice-president of Tanzania. In the same year he became vice-chairman of the ruling party, Chama cha Mapinduzi (CCM – Party of the Revolution). When Nyerere retired from the state presidency in 1985, Mwinyi was chosen to succeed him. As a pragmatist occupying an ideological position near to the centre of the party, he was in some ways a compromise candidate in the struggle to re-evaluate the direction of government policy. Since coming to power he has liberalized the economy to some extent but continued to claim adherence to socialism. It is not likely that he will be able to exert the authority that his predecessor did.

N

334   Stephen NAIDOO

South Africa

Naidoo was the Roman Catholic Archbishop of Cape Town and a leading church campaigner against apartheid until his death in 1989.

Born in 1917 in Durban into the Indian community, he became a Roman Catholic priest and most of his early career was spent in the African townships and squatter camps. His work with the poor and oppressed earned him the nickname 'Mkhusele' (a Xhosa word meaning 'advocate'). In 1974 he was appointed auxiliary bishop of Cape Town and in 1984 he became archbishop. With Desmond Tutu and Alan Boesak he led the church campaigns against the apartheid system. On a number of occasions he was harassed and arrested, although his senior position in the church meant that he escaped the worst of treatment by the police. In 1989 he went to London for medical treatment but died there.

335   Lassimiau (Raymond) NAIMBAYE

Chad

Naimbaye has had a diverse career which has combined senior political and diplomatic appointments.

Born in 1940 in Tilo, he was educated in Chad and Mali before joining the civil service. He held the top bureaucratic posts in both the ministry of agriculture and ministry of foreign af-

fairs. In 1965 he was appointed ambassador to the Sudan. The following year he was brought home to become minister of agriculture. He held this post for five years and was one of the few non-Muslims to reach this level. In 1971 he became minister of public works. In 1974 he was appointed ambassador to China. When Habre came to power in 1982 he became one of his most important political advisors.

336   Claude NDALLA

Congo

Ndalla has been one of the leading ideologues of Congolese politics and has had a career which has alternated between positions of considerable power and long periods spent in detention. He has survived at least two death sentences.

Born in 1937 in Brazzaville, he gained a mathematics degree in the USA and then studied chemistry in the USSR. On his return home he became a leader of the youth wing of the ruling MNR and editor of its newspaper. In 1965 he was brought into the cabinet as minister of youth but the following year he was sacked after charges of embezzlement. He was then appointed director of Brazzaville radio and followed this by becoming ambassador to Peking. A convinced Maoist, he returned in 1969 and became secretary of the PCT politburo in charge of propaganda, being recognized as second only to President Ngouabi in terms of power. In 1971 he was purged and in 1972 led a failed revolt, for which he was sentenced to death. This sentence was commuted to life imprisonment and he was later released. In 1977 he was accused of being involved in the assassination of President Ngouabi and again received a life sentence. He was released once more, but in 1986 was charged with plotting bombings in the capital and was again sentenced to death. The sentence was commuted to imprisonment and he was released in 1988.

337 Atanasio NDONGO Miyone

Equatorial Guinea

Ndongo was one of the major nationalist leaders of Equatorial Guinea before independence and became foreign minister after independence. He was killed by President Macias Nguema following an alleged coup plot in 1969.

Born in Rio Benito and a member of the Fang ethnic group, he got into trouble at school for leading a student strike. He left to work in Gabon, where he married the daughter of Leon M'ba, later president of Gabon. In 1952 he joined the CNLGE, a movement formed in 1947 to campaign for the withdrawal of the Spanish colonial authorities. He devoted the next decade and a half of his life to the struggle for independence, spending much of the time in exile. In 1966 he returned to participate in the constitutional conferences leading to independence. In the 1968 pre-independence election he was a candidate for the presidency, but was placed third. At independence in September the same year he joined the government of Macias Nguema and was appointed foreign

minister, playing an important role in the ending of relief flights from Equatorial Guinea to Biafra. He was killed in confusing circumstances in 1969. The official version was that he went to the presidential palace to personally attack Macias Nguema in a coup attempt and that the latter threw him out of a window following a fight. Other reports suggest that it was the president who called him to the palace and then had him murdered. Given the subsequent record of Macias Nguema, the latter version is probably nearer the truth.

338 Agostinho Antonio NETO

Angola

Neto was the dominant figure in the Angolan liberation movement, the first president of the country after independence, and can be seen as the founder of modern Angola. He was also a qualified doctor and a significant poet.

The son of a Methodist minister, Neto was born in Kaxikane in 1922. In 1947 he went to Portugal to study medicine. During his student days he was involved in anti-colonial activity and was arrested on a number of occasions, but eventually qualified as a doctor in 1958. In 1956 he was a founder-member of the MPLA, which was the first significant nationalist movement in Angola and was eventually to form the post-independence government of the country. The MPLA began armed struggle against the Portuguese colonial authorities in 1961 and throughout the war was consistently the most effective of the Angolan liberation movements.

In 1959 Neto returned to Luanda and set up a private medical practice offering treatment to black Africans which was largely unavailable elsewhere in the capital. He continued with his political work and was arrested by the Portuguese in 1960. In 1962 he escaped detention and went into exile. Later that year he was elected president of the MPLA in place of Mario Pinto de Andrade and retained this position for the rest of his life. During the 1960s and early 1970s the Angolan nationalist movement remained badly split. Neto's MPLA was in conflict with two other significant nationalist movements, the FNLA of Holden Roberto and UNITA, led by Jonas Savimbi. In addition to this the MPLA was often riven with factional disputes. Neto exhibited considerable skill in maintaining his own position within the MPLA and in ensuring the eventual dominance of the movement over its rivals. Under Neto's leadership the MPLA built a mass base of political support within Angola and an increasingly effective military force dedicated to ending Portuguese colonialism. Ideologically attracted to Marxism, Neto opposed the class base of the colonial state but was as strongly opposed to any hint of anti-white racism: he himself had a white wife, Maria Eugenia.

During this period Neto expended considerable efforts in diplomatic work to build up international support for the MPLA. Close ties were established with the liberation movements of Mozambique and Guinea-Bissau and with the independent states of Africa. Neto also travelled widely outside Africa gaining considerable support from the Soviet Union and Cuba but making little headway with western governments. In 1972,

under the auspices of the OAU, Neto agreed to unification of the MPLA and the FNLA, but this agreement rapidly fell apart.

In 1974 the situation in Angola was transformed by the coup in Portugal which effectively signalled the end of Portuguese rule in Africa. In early 1975 Neto returned in triumph to Luanda, but the situation remained precarious, with continued fighting between the three nationalist movements and continued factionalism within the MPLA. Attempts by the OAU to help establish a government of national unity failed and outside powers were increasingly sucked into the conflict. In November 1975, Angola was declared independent with Neto as its president, but although the MPLA government received widespread, but not universal, recognition it became increasingly dependent on Cuban military support to defend itself against the South African-backed UNITA forces. The civil war in Angola which followed the end of Portuguese colonialism was a problem which Neto was never able to solve. The new president also inherited an economy and infrastructure devastated by the war against the Portuguese. In 1977 the MPLA government was further rocked by an attempted coup from the Nito Alves faction within the MPLA itself. Neto was able to defeat the coup, but it cost the lives of some of his most able lieutenants. In December of the same year the MPLA transformed itself into a Marxist–Leninist political party, the MPLA–PT, electing Neto as its president.

Internationally Neto retained very close relations with the Soviet Union and

Cuba but exhibited economic pragmatism by encouraging investment in Angola by western multinationals, especially the oil companies whose contributions were crucial to government revenue.

Ultimately Neto was never able to bring the Angolan civil war to an end. His health deteriorated rapidly and in September 1979 he died in Moscow, where he was undergoing treatment for cancer. The extremely smooth succession of Jose Eduardo dos Santos to the presidency was, however, an indication of the coherence and unity which Neto had brought to the MPLA.

339   Pierre NGENDANDUMWE

Burundi

Ngendandumwe was prime minister of Burundi in the early 1960s and, as such, was one of the few Hutus to have held senior office in the country.

Born in 1930, he was educated at the University of Lovanium in the Congo, where he graduated in political science. On returning to Burundi he worked for the colonial administration as an assistant territorial administrator. In the immediate post-independence governments he served as finance minister and, from 1962 to 1963 as deputy prime minister. In 1963, King Mwambutsa appointed him leader of the government. He formed an ethnically balanced government, a rare achievement in Burundi, but was sacked by the king in April 1964. In January 1965 the king again asked him to lead the government, but a few days later he was assassinated as he left a hospital where he had been visiting his newly-born son. His murder plunged Burundi into chaos.

340   Lamin NGOBEH

Sierra Leone

Ngobeh was one of the most important opposition leaders in the 1970s.

Born in 1934, he was educated locally and entered politics through the SLPP. He first entered parliament in 1967 as MP for Kailahun Central in an election which the SLPP lost to the opposition APC. Unlike many of his fellow-party members he refused numerous inducements to defect to the APC and for most of the 1970s was one of those who kept the official opposition alive in Sierra Leone. He was a leading opponent of moves towards the creation of a single-party state and stayed loyal to the SLPP until it was banned in 1978. He was the last SLPP MP to join, reluctantly, the APC and remained a critical voice within it. He died from natural causes in 1984.

341   Marien NGOUABI

Congo

Ngouabi was president of Congo from 1968 until 1977, when he was assassinated. A military leader, he claimed to have turned his country into a Marxist–Leninist state.

Born in 1938 in Ombele, he was a member of the Kouyou ethnic group. After secondary education he joined the army in 1960 and received officer training in France. He returned home in 1962 and the following year was given command of the newly-created paratroop battalion in Brazzaville. During this period he developed a commitment to Marxism–Leninism and organized a political support base within the army. His

160

relationship with President Massamba-Debat, who also proclaimed himself a Marxist, grew increasingly tense and, in July 1968, Ngouabi was arrested. This produced army unrest and he was released and appointed army chief of staff. By September Massamba-Debat had been forced to resign and Ngouabi gradually took control; by the end of the year he was confirmed as president.

In 1969 he created a new political party, the PCT, as the country's only legal party. The PCT was presented as an orthodox Marxist–Leninist vanguard party, but the real power base of the party remained, and still remains, within the army, rather than with the workers and peasants. In 1970 the name of the country was changed to the People's Republic of the Congo. As chairman of the central committee of the PCT, Ngouabi automatically continued to fill the presidency. His time in office was marked by severe conflicts involving a mixture of ideology, ethnicity and personal factors. There were several attempted coups and an almost constant purging of the army and civil service as he tried to keep himself in power. Labour unrest was dealt with equally harshly.

In March 1977, Ngouabi was assassinated in circumstances which are still very unclear and for which there are many conflicting official and unofficial versions of events. Cardinal Biayenda, the archbishop of Brazzaville, who many believe was a witness to the killing, was murdered the following day and there followed a series of purges and executions. By the time of his death Ngouabi had made so many enemies that the list of possible assassins was very long.

342 NGUZA Karl I. Bond

Zaire

Nguza has had an important but highly erratic political career. He has occupied all the senior government posts below the presidency but has alternated this with periods in prison (which included a death sentence) and in exile.

Born in 1938 in Musumba, in Shaba Province, he is a nephew of the late Moise Tshombe. He was educated locally and at university in Belgium. On returning home he worked as a radio announcer and in 1964 served briefly in his uncle's cabinet. From then until 1972 he worked in senior diplomatic posts in the USA and in Switzerland. He was foreign minister from 1972 to 1974 and from 1976 to 1977. In 1977 he was arrested and charged with treason, although many believed that his only crime was to have become identified as a possible successor to President Mobutu. He was tortured and sentenced to death, but the following year his sentence was commuted to life imprisonment. One year later, in 1979, he was rehabilitated in a quite remarkable fashion when he was released from jail and reappointed foreign minister.

In 1980 he was further promoted when he became first state commissioner, which is the equivalent of prime minister and is the second most important post in the ruling hierarchy. In 1981 he resigned and fled into exile in Belgium. For the next four years he was the major figure in the exiled opposition and testified to the cruelty and corruption of the Mobutu regime before several international tribunals. He also established a grouping called the Congolese Front for the Restoration of Democracy and there were reports of attempts to murder him. In 1985 he made peace with Mobutu and returned home, where he broadcast speeches lavishing praise on the president. In 1986 he was appointed ambassador to the USA. He held this post until 1988, when he was, once again, reappointed as foreign minister. In May 1990 he was sacked from his post and dismissed from the government. Nguza's erratic career presents an extreme example of the hazards and uncertainties of political life in a highly personalized dictatorship, where appointment and dismissal (or worse) are dependent on the fears and whims of the ruler.

343   Babacar NIANG

Senegal

Niang is an opposition party leader and was a presidential candidate in 1988.

Born in 1931 in Kaolack, he was educated locally before going to study law in Paris. He was much involved in student Marxism in France in the 1950s and on his return to Senegal he joined the communist PAI. After independence the party was banned and he was detained for a time. By the late 1960s he had become a wealthy Dakar lawyer and had abandoned Marxism. In 1973 he joined Diop in the RND, but the party was not legalized until 1981. In the 1983 election the party won one parliamentary seat which Niang occupied against the wishes of Diop, who called for a boycott. Following this disagreement Niang broke away to found the PLP, which he still leads. He stood in the 1988 presidential election but came a poor third.

344   Moustapha NIASSE

Senegal

Niasse was a major figure in the government and ruling party until 1984.

Born in 1939 in Keure Madiabel, he was educated at the universities of Dakar and Paris before returning home to join the civil service. He received rapid promotion and from 1970 to 1978 was the director of the cabinet. In 1978 he was brought into the government as minister of town planning and later the same year was promoted to foreign minister. He became a leading figure in the ruling party, the UPS, and was elected as its political secretary. In 1984 he fell from power as President Diouf began appointing his own men to senior positions. After reportedly becoming involved in a fist fight at a cabinet meeting he lost both his party and government posts.

345   Pierre Sarr N'JIE

The Gambia

N'Jie was a lawyer who was chief minister in the colonial period and leader of the opposition in the early post-colonial period.

Born in Bathurst (now Banjul) in 1909, he worked as a civil servant before training as a lawyer in Britain. In 1951 he formed the United Party (UP) which was supported by fellow Wollofs and other groups in the urban coastal areas. From 1961 to 1962 he was chief minister, but elections that year produced victory for the PPP and he became leader of the opposition. The inability of the UP to expand its support into the up-river rural areas, where most of the newly-enfranchized electorate lived, left it a dwindling political force. Until the creation of the NCP in 1975 the UP remained as the major opposition party, but thereafter it faded quickly and N'Jie retired from active politics. He retained some remnants of his political influence and newer opposition parties are still anxious for his support at election times.

346 Charles NJONJO

Kenya

Njonjo was one of the most senior and influential figures in the Kenyan government from independence until the mid-1980s, when he was ousted in some disgrace.

Born in 1920 in Kiambu into a Kikuyu chiefly family, he was educated locally and at universities in Britain before qualifying as a barrister at Gray's Inn in London. In 1962 he was appointed deputy public prosecutor in Nairobi. At independence in 1963 he became attorney-general, a post he held until 1980, when he became minister of constitutional affairs, which marked a downgrading of his position. Of greater importance than his official posts was his role as one of the top Kikuyu politicians who had extensive influence in the government and the KANU party. In 1978 he was influential in securing the presidency for Moi after Kenyatta's death. By 1983 the president had begun to feel threatened by Njonjo's influence and engineered his downfall. He lost his cabinet post and party membership and a public commission was established to investigate allegations of serious corruption. Njonjo was found guilty and,

although he was later pardoned, his political position was seriously undermined.

347 Enos Mzombi NKALA

Zimbabwe

Nkala was a senior member of the government until he was forced to resign following a scandal in 1989.

Born in 1932 in Filabusi into the Ndebele ethnic group, he was educated locally before starting work with an insurance company. In 1960 he was a founder member of the NDP and was its deputy secretary-general. In 1961 he was jailed and not released until 1963. He was a founder-member of ZANU in 1963, when it was formed at a meeting in his house, and became party treasurer. Shortly afterwards he was again arrested and was held in detention until 1979, thus missing the whole period of the guerrilla struggle. He was banned from participating in the 1980 independence elections by Lord Soames, following calls for violence if ZANU lost the election. In the event ZANU won a significant majority.

At independence Nkala joined the government as finance minister and was subsequently minister of local government (1982–85), home affairs (1985–88) and, in 1988, minister of defence. He continually failed to get the support of his own Ndebele people, who supported his rival Joshua Nkomo. This failure made him one of the most hardline members of the government in terms of relations with the opposition. He was finally elected to parliament in 1986 in a by-election, but this was in a Shona constituency, well away from his

Matabeleland home. In 1989 he was forced to resign from the government following a major corruption scandal. Relatively few regretted the political demise of the arrogant and abrasive Nkala.

348   Joshua Mqabuko NKOMO

Zimbabwe

Nkomo was the founding father of Zimbabwean nationalism and the leader of ZAPU. After independence he was the leading opposition figure and then a member of the government.

Born in 1917 in Semokwe into the Ndebele ethnic group, he was educated locally and in South Africa, where he gained a degree. He then worked as a social worker for Rhodesian Railways and became involved in trade union activities. In the 1950s he was the leader of the ANC (of Rhodesia) before it was banned. In 1960 he became the leader of the NDP, even though it was formed while he was abroad. When this was also banned the following year he formed ZAPU and became its long-term leader. For the next 15 years he spent most of his time in detention or in exile. From 1977 he was based in Zambia, from where he directed the ZAPU guerrilla forces in the civil war. In 1975 he was the co-founder, with Robert Mugabe, of the PF, a loose unification of ZAPU and Mugabe's ZANU. He was a major participant at the Lancaster House talks in 1979 which produced the agreement for Zimbabwe's independence. When Mugabe refused to fight the 1980 independence election as a united PF, Nkomo used the name of the movement in the election. The results of the election showed Nkomo's PF as the dominant party in Matabeleland, but in an overall minority in the new parliament.

At independence in April 1980, Nkomo refused the offer of the largely ceremonial post of president and became minister of home affairs in a coalition cabinet. Relations between him and Mugabe rapidly deteriorated again and in 1982 he was sacked from the cabinet. In 1983, claiming that his life was in danger because of government repression in Matabeleland, he fled into exile in Botswana and then Britain. While in exile he wrote his autobiography, *Nkomo: The Story of My Life*, in which he attacked the authoritarian nature of the government and its discrimination against Ndebeles in favour of the Shona. He returned home for the 1985 election and again his party dominated in Matabeleland but was in the minority on a national basis. Following continued government pressure Nkomo signed a unity agreement with Mugabe in December 1987 and was brought back into the government as senior minister (without portfolio) in the president's office, a post to which he was reappointed after the 1990 elections. The post is widely viewed as a sinecure given as a reward for dropping his opposition to the government, but by this time he had few alternatives open to him.

349   Kwame Francis Nwia Kofie NKRUMAH

Ghana

Nkrumah was the leading figure in the nationalist movement in the whole of Anglophone Africa (and, arguably, the

164

whole of Africa), the leading figure in the Pan-Africanist movement, and the first president of Ghana. Although he was overthrown by a coup in 1966 and died in exile in 1972, his memory still exerts a powerful force in many parts of Africa to this day.

Born the son of a goldsmith in Nkroful in south-western Ghana in 1909, into the small Nzima ethnic group, he was educated locally before moving to the USA for higher education. Here he received first and higher degrees in sociology, theology and education and was appointed as a lecturer at Lincoln University. He was also elected as president of the African Students Organization of the USA and Canada. During this time he was much influenced by the writings of Marx, Gandhi and, especially, Marcus Garvey, who was the major influence on his pan-Africanist beliefs. In 1945 he moved to England to study law, although he probably spent more time working for a variety of pan-Africanist organizations and editing a magazine entitled *New African*.

In 1947 he returned to Ghana to become general secretary of the recently-formed UGCC, a post to which he brought quite remarkable vigour. In 1948 he was arrested, along with other UGCC leaders, following major riots. Following their release major policy splits developed within the UGCC leadership, with Nkrumah favouring a much more radical and active approach to the demands for the end of colonial rule. In 1949 he broke away to form his own CPP, which rapidly developed as the major nationalist party in Ghana, forming close links with the trade unions and the urban working classes. In

the 1951 elections the CPP were the majority party and he became leader of government business and, in 1952, prime minister. Following repeated election victories he retained this position at independence in 1957 and became president with the creation of a republic in 1960.

After independence there were two distinct aspects of Nkrumah, the international and the domestic. On the international level he acted as an inspiration to those Africans still under colonial rule. He worked ceaselessly, but ultimately unsuccessfully, to bring about the political union of the newly emerging states of black Africa, spending large amounts of Ghanaian money in this quest. The creation of the OAU in 1963, which represented a bare minimum of real unity, was a disappointment for him, but he regarded it as a starting-point for more thorough unity in the future. On the world stage he was the most significant African leader of his generation.

In Ghana itself Nkrumah's period in office was marked by economic incompetence and a frightening build-up of political repression and corruption. As early as 1958 he introduced a preventive detention act which permitted arrest without charge and imprisonment without trial. Many opposition leaders were the victims of this act. Later he moved against all potential centres of opposition, including the trade unions, the judiciary, the universities and the traditional leaders. A rigid state censorship was introduced which resulted in the destruction of all parts of the mass media which were not totally supportive of the government. In 1964 all opposition parties were banned and he proclaimed himself 'president for life'. Throughout the period a massive personality cult was built up surrounding Nkrumah as he acquired such titles as 'star of Ghana', 'the redeemer' and 'initiator of the African personality'. Increasingly surrounded by sycophants, he became totally cut off from the reality of what was happening in Ghana as the country plunged into economic crisis and corruption mounted. Doubting the loyalty of the army, he built up a separate military force, the President's Own Guard Regiment, which was loyal only to him and was better equipped and paid than the regular armed forces.

In February 1966, with Nkrumah out of the country, the army staged a coup which met virtually no resistance and was popularly welcomed. Nkrumah went into exile in Guinea, where he was granted the honorary title of co-president by his friend and fellow pan-Africanist, President Sekou Toure. Whilst in exile he wrote a number of books, but his health began to fail and in 1972 he died of cancer in a Romanian hospital.

Kwame Nkrumah was an inspirational figure in the assertion of black African dignity but, for Ghana, his period of rule was an unqualified disaster.

350   Harry Mwaanga NKUMBULA

Zambia

Nkumbula was the most important of the early nationalist leaders and was a major opposition figure after independence in 1964.

Born in 1916 in Namwala, in the Southern Province, he qualified as a teacher and taught in Kitwe on the Copperbelt. In 1946 he went to the

London School of Economics (LSE) where he cooperated closely with other African nationalist leaders including Kwame Nkrumah and Jomo Kenyatta. After leaving the LSE he worked as a seashell salesman on the East African coast. In 1951 he returned home to take over the leadership of the (Northern Rhodesian) ANC, which was the main nationalist grouping. In 1958 several ANC members, led by Kenneth Kaunda, broke away from the party to found UNIP, which gradually replaced the ANC as the main nationalist party. Although UNIP became the dominant party at the national level, the ANC retained its position in the Southern Province and after independence in 1964 Nkumbula led the opposition in parliament. In the 1968 elections the ANC extended its support base by winning in Western Province. Nkumbula opposed the creation of the single-party state in Zambia but after his party had been banned in the process he joined UNIP in 1973. For the 1978 election he attempted to challenge Kaunda for the presidency, but was prevented from doing so. He died from natural causes in 1983.

351   King NTARE the Fifth (Charles NDIZEYE)

Burundi

Ntare was King of Burundi for a short period in the 1960s before he was ousted and the monarchy abolished.

Born in 1947, the son of King Mwambutsa, he was educated in Switzerland. He returned to Bujumbura in 1966 to succeed his father. He ascended to the throne in July 1966, at a time of great political confusion in Burundi, and appointed Captain Michel Micombero to head the new administration. The new king promised social and economic reforms but almost immediately fell out with the new government. In November 1966, whilst on an official visit to Zaire, he was deposed and the monarchy abolished. He remained in exile in Zaire until 1972, when he was invited back to Burundi by President Micombero. Almost as soon as he returned the ex-king was murdered by the military government.

352   Sam Daniel NUJOMA

Namibia

Nujoma is the founder and leader of SWAPO and, in March 1990, became the first post-independence president of Namibia.

Born in 1929 in Ogandjera into the Ovambo ethnic group, after an incomplete schooling he worked as a clerk and on the railways. In 1959 he established the OPO, but rapidly realized that to stand any chance of success in ending South African occupation of the territory a broader movement which could unite the various ethnic groups in the country was needed. The following year he established SWAPO and has remained its leader ever since. In 1961 he established SWAPO headquarters in Tanzania. Apart from a brief return home in 1966 when he was arrested, he remained in exile until his triumphal return at the end of 1989.

As the exiled leader of SWAPO he had considerable success in both the military and diplomatic fields. The waging of armed guerrilla struggle against the South Africans from bases in Angola was one of the factors which eventually persuaded the South African government to agree to Namibian independence. In the diplomatic field he succeeded in gaining recognition for SWAPO as the legitimate authority for Namibia by the OAU in 1968 and by the United Nations in 1973. Independence for Namibia was delayed for many years as the issue became entangled in the wider struggle in southern Africa, especially the refusal by the South Africans to grant independence to Namibia while Cuban troops remained in neighbouring Angola. In 1989 a deal was finally agreed by the participants in the conflict and UN-supervised elections were held. Nujoma returned home to lead SWAPO in the country and was given a hero's welcome. In the elections SWAPO won a narrow overall majority of seats in the assembly which was to draw up the new constitution. The constitution which emerged enjoyed broad consensual support amongst all the parties represented. In March 1990, Namibia became independent, with Nujoma as its first president. Although he had often used a great deal of Marxist rhetoric in the past he switched to support for a mixed economy and a democratic multi-party system as the reality of independence drew nearer.

353   Jafar Muhammed NUMEIRI

Sudan

Numeiri came to power in a coup in 1969 and was head of state until being ousted in a further coup in 1985.

Born in 1930 in a suburb of Omdurman into a poor family, he joined the army in 1949. As he rose through the ranks he frequently displayed political ambitions, for which he was suspended on several occasions. In 1958 he took an active part in the Abboud coup but was then sent for further military training in the USA. In 1969 he led his own coup and took over the government, although he did not formally adopt the presidential title until 1971.

In 1971 he survived a major coup attempt by communist officers within the army. In 1972 he established a political party, the SSU, as the only legal party. He remained its leader until his eventual overthrow, but it was never more than a front for what became an increasingly personalized form of rule. In 1972 he also secured what turned out to be a temporary cessation of the north–south civil war with the Addis Ababa Agreement, but he later reneged on important parts of the agreement, which caused further rebellion by southern forces – rebellion which still continues. In order to try and secure his power base in the north he turned increasingly to hardline Islamic ideals, including the mutilation of criminals, a move which further alienated the non-Muslim southerners and fanned the flames of revolt.

Apart from civil war, Numeiri's period in office was marked by more general political authoritarianism as well as by corruption and mismanagement which produced a chronic economic crisis. Talk of Sudan being the 'breadbasket' of the whole region was replaced by the reality of famine and starvation which eventually captured world attention and produced an international relief effort. Although he appeared to be a master of political survival, opposition to Numeiri's regime grew and by 1985 he faced a general strike and large-scale anti-government riots. In April of that year he left on a visit to the USA and was deposed by a coup while he was out of the country. Since then he has lived in exile and is strongly rumoured to have been behind attempts at a counter-coup.

354 Akwekwe Abyssinia NWAFOR-ORIZU

Nigeria

Nwafor-Orizu was a leading figure in the First Republic who officially handed power to the military after the January 1966 coup.

Born in 1920 in Onitsha, he was educated locally before going to the USA for higher education. Whilst in the USA he became heavily involved in the black political movement after joining the Marcus Garvey Movement in 1940. He was editor of the *Negro Digest* and succeeded Kwame Nkrumah as president of the African Students Association of the USA and Canada. He returned to Nigeria in 1949 and was briefly arrested for championing the cause of the Enugu mineworkers. He was first elected to parliament in 1951 as a representative of the NCNC. He functioned as party chief whip in both regional and national legislatures. In 1964 he was elected president of the senate and because of this position he was the person who officially handed power to the military after the first 1966 coup. He retired from public life, but with the lifting of the ban on political parties in 1978 he joined the NPN. Although the NPN emerged as the ruling party,

Nwafor-Orizu did not play a prominent role in the Second Republic.

355 Simon Sishayi NXUMALO

Swaziland

Nxumalo was a senior government figure and reputedly the second most powerful man in the country during the reign of King Sobhuza.

Born in 1936 in Nkambeni, he was educated locally and worked as a teacher and in the South African mines. In 1962 he founded and led the SDP, but after its defeat in the 1964 elections he defected to the dominant monarchist INM. In 1965 he was appointed as the king's envoy and was first elected to parliament in 1967. At independence in 1968 he was brought into the cabinet and remained a member until 1984. More important, however, was his post of director of Tibiyo Taka Ngwane, a monarchist institution which largely controls the economy of the country. In 1984 he became finance minister, but later the same year lost out in the succession struggle which had followed the death of King Sobhuza and was arrested and jailed on charges of corruption. At the end of 1985 he was given a royal pardon and released.

356 Maurice Tapfumaneyi NYAGUMBO

Zimbabwe

Nyagumbo was a senior figure in the government before committing suicide in April 1989, following a major financial scandal.

Born in 1924 in Nyagundi, he was educated locally before moving to South Africa, where he worked in a wide variety of menial jobs and became involved in nationalist politics. On his return to Rhodesia he was closely involved with ZAPU and then ZANU. His participation in the nationalist struggle was limited by the fact that he spent more time in prison for political activities than any other nationalist leader. After independence he served in the government as minister for mines and, later, political affairs. He was widely regarded as one of the senior figures in both government and ruling party. In 1989 his involvement in a major corruption scandal became known and he resigned from the government. Shortly afterwards his life came to a tragic end when he committed suicide because of the disgrace.

357 Julius Kambarage NYERERE

Tanzania

Nyerere has been one of Africa's most highly regarded statesmen in the post-independence period. He was head of state until retiring from the presidency in 1985.

Born in 1922 in Butiama into one of the smallest ethnic groups in the country, the Zanaki, he trained as a teacher in Uganda and taught for several years in Tabora. From 1949 to 1952 he was a student at Edinburgh University, where he became his country's first graduate. He returned home to teach and begin his political career. In 1954 he founded TANU, which was to become the ruling party, and became its president. In the 1958 and 1960 elections TANU won overwhelming majorities and became one of the very few nationalist parties to experience no serious opposition in the late colonial phase. Nyerere became chief minister in the pre-independence government and in December 1961 the country's first post-independence prime minister. Shortly afterwards he resigned the premiership for a few months to devote himself to reorganizing the party and with the creation of a republic in 1962 he became the country's first president.

There is little doubt that under Nyerere's leadership Tanzania has been amongst the more politically stable states in Africa, although there is considerable debate as to how far this is a result of leadership or how far it is due to an absence of significant ethnic and regional cleavages of the sort which have afflicted other African states. It is probably accurate to say that Tanzania has faced less intractable political difficulties than most states. Apart from an army mutiny in 1964, which was not a coup attempt and was dealt with easily by British forces, and a genuine but unsuccessful coup attempt in 1983, the regime has not been subjected to very serious challenge.

In 1964, Nyerere negotiated the union of mainland Tanganyika and the offshore island of Zanzibar to form a single state, although for many years the union was stronger on paper than in fact and still contains unresolved tensions. Before the 1965 elections he moved Tanzania to a single-party state, with TANU as the only party (excluding Zanzibar) but with some allowance for electoral competition between candidates of the same party. In 1977 a new party, Chama cha Mapinduzi (CCM – Party of the Revolution) was formed with the merger of TANU and the Zanzibari ASP. Nyerere

was continuously leader of TANU and CCM until he retired from the leadership of the latter in 1990. In 1967 the Arusha Declaration established a leadership code for party and government elites in an attempt to prevent single-party dominance leading to abuse of office, but it is generally agreed that this has been, at best, only partially successful. Although he was for many years the most articulate defender of the single-party state in Africa, by the late 1980s Nyerere was becoming increasingly critical of this form of government and was arguing that lack of opposition had produced complacency and neglect of the public interest in Tanzania. Some of his critics put it more strongly and claimed that the dominance of TANU and CCM had created a new elite who had used their undisputed control to further their own interests.

In terms of economic development the period produced extremely disappointing results. Following the adoption of 'African socialism' most significant sectors of the economy were nationalized and placed under the control of the state and the party, but performance standards have been extremely poor. In the 1970s a major attempt was made to restructure agricultural production with the creation of 'ujamaa' (communal) villages. At first this was done on a voluntary basis but, when the rural peasants failed to respond, compulsion, often involving high levels of coercion, was used. The whole scheme is now recognized as a failure. By the late 1980s Tanzania was moving slowly towards a more liberal form of economic policy.

In the international arena Nyerere has rightly been regarded as one of Africa's leading statesmen. Although Tanzania has received aid from a variety of sources, especially the USA, it has managed to follow a policy of genuine non-alignment. Nyerere has been amongst the leading critics of apartheid in South Africa but has also attacked abuses of human rights in black-ruled states. In 1979 it was the Tanzanian army which overthrew the despotic rule of Idi Amin in neighbouring Uganda. Nyerere has also been a leading supporter of economic cooperation between the black-ruled states of the southern African region. He has also emerged as the leading intellectual amongst Africa's political leaders and his numerous writings on 'African socialism' have been extremely influential, although by the 1990s they were viewed with increasing criticism. His literary achievements have included the translation of Shakespeare's plays into Swahili.

In 1985, Nyerere retired from the presidency, although he continued to lead the ruling party until 1990. Although the fruits of his period in power were not entirely positive nobody can doubt his integrity, personal humility and dedication to improving the lot of the Tanzanian people, who continued to respect 'Mwalimu' (Swahili for 'teacher') in spite of the problems that Tanzania still experienced.

358   Patrick Chukwuma Kaduna NZEOGWU

Nigeria

Nzeogwu was the leader of the first coup in Nigeria in January 1966.

Born in 1937 in Kaduna into the Ibo ethnic group, he joined the army in 1956 and received officer training at Sandhurst in England. By 1966 he had reached the rank of major. In January 1966 he led the first Nigerian coup which led to the death of many senior government and army figures. Nzeogwu claimed progressive ideological reasons for staging the coup, but as almost all the coup plotters were Ibos and almost all those killed were northerners the coup was perceived by many as an Ibo attempt at domination and was bitterly resented in non-Ibo areas. Because the coup plotters did not actually come to power it is difficult to judge their true motivations. Government leadership passed to Ironsi (himself an Ibo, but not involved in the coup) and Nzeogwu was arrested. He was released in 1967 by the Biafran leader, Ojukwu, and died later the same year on the battlefront in the civil war.

O

359 Olusegun OBASANJO

Nigeria

Obasanjo was military head of state from the assassination of Muhammed in 1976 until the return to civilian rule in 1979.

Born in 1937 in Abeokuta into the Yoruba ethnic group, he was educated locally and joined the army in 1958. He received officer training in England and later served in the UN peace-keeping forces in the Congo. He was an active military leader in the civil war and accepted the surrender of Biafra in 1970. Following further training in England he was appointed federal commissioner for works and housing in the Gowon regime.

He was a major participant in the coup which overthrew Gowon in July 1975 and became chief of staff supreme headquarters. In government he was second only to Murtala Muhammed. When the latter was assassinated in a failed coup attempt in February 1976, Obasanjo succeeded him as head of state, commander-in-chief of the armed forces and chairman of the Supreme Military Council. The fact that a Christian southerner had, quite innocently, replaced a northern Muslim did not provoke the violence that some had feared. Obasanjo strictly adhered to the established schedule for the return to civilian rule and handed over power to the politicians of the Second Republic in 1979. At the same time he retired from the army. Since then he has ostensibly been a farmer but for most of the time he has acted as an outspoken and controversial critic of subsequent political developments.

360 Teodoro OBIANG NGUEMA Mbasogo

Equatorial Guinea

Obiang became head of state in 1979, when he led a coup against his uncle, President Macias Nguema. He has remained in power since that time.

Born into the same Mongomo clan of the Fang ethnic group as his uncle, he grew in power during the latter's brutal period of rule. He received military training in Spain from 1963 to 1965 and became deputy minister of defence and military governor of the offshore part of the territory. By the late 1970s he effectively controlled the army and in August 1979 he ousted his dictatorial uncle, who was subsequently executed. On becoming president he promised to rectify all the defects in the governing of the state, but subsequent events have shown that the coup has made little difference and that Equatorial Guinea is still probably the worst-run state in the world. Whilst his style of rule is less bizarre and idiosyncratic than his deposed uncle's, it appears to be just as oppressive and corrupt. The regime has survived a number of coup attempts. In 1987, Obiang launched a new political party, the only one allowed, misleadingly entitled the Democratic Party of Equatorial Guinea (PDGE), with himself as leader. In July 1989 he was the only candidate in a

172

presidential election when he was, officially, endorsed by 99.9 per cent of the electorate. This figure may be regarded as indicating more about Obiang's control of the political system than about his popularity with the mass of the population of Equatorial Guinea.

361   Milton Apollo OBOTE

Uganda

Obote was the ruler of Uganda for two periods, from 1962 to 1971 and from 1971 to 1985.

Born in 1925 in Akoroko in the north of the country into the Lango ethnic group, he was educated at Makerere University, graduating in 1948. He worked for a time in Kenya before returning home in 1955 to organize the UNC in his home area. He was elected to the colonial legislature in 1958. When the UNC split in 1960 he formed the UPC. For the 1962 elections he formed an alliance with the royalist party, the Kabaka Yekka (King Alone–KY) and became prime minister at independence later the same year. In 1966 a new republican constitution was introduced and Obote became the executive president. As his rule became more authoritarian and his popular support dwindled he came to rely increasingly on his army commander, Idi Amin, to keep him in power. By the end of 1970 he had begun to fear Amin and planned to get rid of him, but in January 1971, with Obote abroad at a conference, Amin struck first and ousted him in a coup. Obote went into exile in Tanzania.

In 1972 he launched an unsuccessful invasion of Uganda but when it failed he returned to Tanzania. In 1979 the Tanzanian army invaded Uganda, ousted the Amin regime and the following year Obote returned to Uganda to participate in the elections. He re-formed his old UPC party and in the elections of December 1980 he emerged with a majority, although his opponents claimed, with some justification, that rigging had taken place. In spite of this he was once again installed in the presidency. His second period in office was even less successful than his first. He never really managed to establish any order from the chaos left by the Amin regime and lacked the control necessary to prevent the army pillaging the country. In 1985 he was ousted in a further coup. He fled to Kenya and later to exile in Zambia.

362   Ajuma Oginga ODINGA

Kenya

Odinga has been one of the most prominent politicians in Kenya, initially as a government figure but more latterly as a centre of opposition.

Born in 1911 in Central Nyanza into the Luo ethnic group, he became a teacher before entering politics. He organized a number of Luo self-help groups and was leader of the Luo Union from 1952 to 1957. In that year he became one of the first group of Africans to gain election to the legislative council. He joined KANU and was vice-president of the party from 1960 to 1966.

At independence he became home affairs minister and, in 1964, vice-president of Kenya. His relationship with other government figures was always stormy and in 1966 he resigned all his posts to form a new opposition party, KPU. In 1967 he published his influential book, *Not Yet Uhuru*. In 1969 the KPU was banned and he was arrested and detained. In 1971 he was released and rejoined KANU, although he did not play a prominent role. In 1979 he was partly rehabilitated and appointed chairman of the Cotton, Seed and Marketing Board. In 1982 he was expelled from KANU and was restricted to his home town after his son, Raila, had been charged with participation in the attempted coup of that year. Throughout the 1980s, Odinga continued as an outspoken public critic of the Moi administration, but, steering clear of illegal activities, he enjoyed some immunity from arrest on account of his status.

363   William Eugene Kwasi OFORI-ATTA

Ghana

Ofori-Atta, known ubiquitously as 'Pa Willie', was one of Ghana's most significant politicians from the 1940s to the 1980s, including several senior ministerial roles in his political career.

Born in 1910 into an aristocratic family at Kibi, he was educated locally and later graduated in economics from Cambridge University. On returning home he worked as a civil servant and headmaster. He was one of the founder members of the UGCC and, like most of its leaders, was jailed for a time following the 1948 riots. He was first elected to parliament in 1951 and was one of the major leaders of the opposition to Nkrumah in the First Republic, spending periods in detention. Following the 1966 coup he was a member of the constitutional commission and chairman of the Cocoa Marketing Board.

With the return to civilian rule in 1969 he was a leading member of Busia's PP and served in the latter's government as minister of education and, later, foreign minister. After the 1972 coup he was briefly detained. For the 1979 elections, which marked a further return to civilian rule, he led his own party, the UNC. The party performed only moderately in the election but he was later appointed chairman of the Council of State by President Limann. Because the Third Republic was overthrown in 1981 this was to be his last political office. In July 1988 he died of natural causes and was given a state funeral. Although he never quite reached the very top, he was one of Ghana's most popular politicians and was widely regarded as a man of great intelligence and integrity.

364   Babafemi Olatunde OGUNDIPE

Nigeria

Ogundipe was a very senior figure in the army at the time of the 1966 coups and came close to becoming head of state.

Born in 1924 into the Yoruba ethnic group, he joined the army in 1943 and fought for the British in Burma during the second world war. He later received officer training in England and was a member of the UN peace-keeping forces in the Congo. He later became commander of the Second Brigade of the Nigerian army. At the time of the July 1966 coup he had a strong claim, in terms of military hierarchy, to become head of state, but his Yoruba background told against him and he lacked popular support within the army, so that Yakubu

Gowon was preferred. The Biafran leader Ojukwu used the passing over of Ogundipe as an excuse for not recognizing the federal government, but in the circumstances the issue was not of real significance. Ogundipe was appointed Nigeria's high commissioner in London, where he died in 1971.

365 Adeniran OGUNSANYA

Nigeria

Ogunsanya was a major political figure in both the First and Second Republics.

Born in 1918 in Ikorodu, he was educated locally before qualifying as a lawyer in England. From 1956 to 1959 he was chairman of the Federal Government Industrial Board. In 1959 he joined the NCNC, subsequently becoming its secretary, and was elected to parliament for the party. In 1965 he was appointed federal minister of housing and surveys. In 1968 he became attorney-general in the military government and commissioner for education in Lagos State. With the lifting of the ban on party activity in 1978 he was a founder member of the NPP, which became one of the major opposition parties of the Second Republic. In 1979 he failed in his bid to become governor of Lagos State but subsequently became NPP chairman.

366 Chukwuemeka Odumegwu OJUKWU

Nigeria

Ojukwu was the leader of the Biafran secessionists in the civil war.

Born in 1933 in Zungeru into the Ibo ethnic group, he was educated locally and abroad before receiving university education in the USA and Britain. Returning to Nigeria in 1955, he worked in the civil service for two years before joining the army. He received officer training in England and served in the UN peace-keeping force in the Congo. He did not participate in the January 1966 coup and was subsequently appointed military governor of the Eastern Region by Ironsi. When the latter was assassinated in the July 1966 coup, Ojukwu refused to recognize the legitimacy of the Gowon administration. Relations between the Eastern Region and the federal government deteriorated badly and in May 1967 Ojukwu declared the region to be the new sovereign state of Biafra, with himself as head of the new state.

This action precipitated the civil war which was fought with extreme bitterness until the military defeat and surrender of Biafran forces in January 1970. With the defeat of Biafra, Ojukwu went into exile in Côte d'Ivoire, where he remained until 1982, when he was officially pardoned and returned to Nigeria to an ecstatic welcome. He joined the ruling NPN, but in the 1983 election, to the surprise of many, he failed to win a seat in the Anambra State senate. Following the 1983 coup he was detained but he was released in October 1984. Since then he has not been prominent in public life.

367 Michael Ibeonukara OKPARA

Nigeria

Okpara was a major political leader in the Eastern Region in the First Republic.

175

Born in 1920 in Yaba, he qualified as a medical doctor in Lagos and worked in several parts of the country before entering politics by joining the NCNC. He was first elected to parliament in 1953 and in 1959 became premier of the Eastern Region and president of the NCNC. After independence his party was initially in alliance with the ruling NPC, but when this broke down in 1964 he formed a coalition with other opposition groups. During the civil war he supported the Biafran cause and when Biafra was defeated he went into exile in Ireland for seven years. In 1982 he was appointed chancellor of the University of Benin. In 1983 he controversially joined the ruling NPN but he died a year later of natural causes.

368   Sylvanus Epiphanio OLYMPIO

Togo

Olympio was the first post-independence president; he was overthrown in a coup in 1963.

Born in 1902 in Lome into a wealthy family, he received his schooling locally before going on to universities in Vienna and London. After graduation he joined the United Africa Company as a manager and worked in Nigeria, Ghana and Togo. In 1941 he founded and led the CUT, which was later to emerge as the dominant political party. The CUT won the 1946 election and he became the leader of the territorial assembly. In the 1956 elections his party was defeated, but in further elections in 1958 he was again the victor and became prime minister in the pre-independence government. He retained this position

at independence in 1960 and in 1961, following a change in the constitution, he was elected to the presidency. His period in office saw the expansion of the phosphate industry which was to prove crucial to economic development. Towards the end of 1962 he embarked on a policy of reducing military expenditure, by cutting the size of the army, to release more funds for development projects. Retrospectively this would appear to have been a courageous but foolhardy decision. In January 1963 he was overthrown in the first post-independence coup to occur in the West African region. He was personally murdered by Gnassingbe Eyadema, who has ruled Togo since a further coup in 1967.

369   Victor Olabisi ONABANJO

Nigeria

Onabanjo was a major leader in the Second Republic and was governor of Ogun State.

Born in 1927 in Lagos, he was educated locally and in England before embarking on a journalistic career. He was editor of the *Nigerian Citizen* and in 1960 became editorial director of the Express Group of Newspapers. In 1964 he was elected to parliament as an AG MP but this phase of his career was brought to an end by the 1966 coup. He later served the military government as civil commissioner for home affairs and for economic planning. He was a member of the Constituent Assembly which finalized the constitution of the Second Republic. With the lifting of the ban on party politics in 1978, he joined the UPN and was elected governor of Ogun State in 1979. Following the 1983 coup he was charged with corruption and received a long prison sentence, but was subsequently released.

370 Bonifacio ONDO EDU

Equatorial Guinea

Ondo Edu was the leading figure in pre-independence politics and narrowly failed to become president. He was murdered shortly after independence.

Born in Evinayong into the Fang ethnic group, he worked as a planter before entering politics. In 1958 he created the UPLGE and in 1960 was elected mayor of his home town. In 1963 he created a new party, the MUNGE, which was well favoured by the Spanish colonial administration. In 1964 he became leader of the pre-independence government, but in the 1968 election he was placed second behind Macias Nguema. Fearing for his safety he moved to Gabon, but following promises from the president he returned home in November 1968. In January 1969 he was murdered by the government.

371 Aden Abdullah OSMAN

Somalia

Osman was the first president of Somalia, from independence in 1960 until he stood down in 1967.

Born in 1908 in Beledwin in the south of the country into a poor Hawiye family, he gained only a limited education before joining the colonial administration in 1929. He later worked as a private businessman. In 1944 he joined the SYL and became its leader in 1953. He retained this position and at independence in 1960 became the country's first president. He was re-elected for a further six-year term the following year, but retired shortly before this second term expired because of the growing factional conflict within the government, which he was unable to stop. Although he had retired he was arrested following the 1969 coup and remained in detention until his release in 1973 to continue his retirement.

372 Gerard Kango OUEDRAOGO

Burkina Faso

A major politician with close kinship connections with the Mossi royal family, Ouedraogo has alternated positions of considerable political power, including the premiership in the early 1970s, with abrupt cessations of power and imprisonment.

He was born into the Yatenga royal family in 1925. After completing his education in Bamako he joined the French colonial service in 1947 and became chief of the secretariat of the governor. He entered politics in 1952 and later became one of the leaders of the MDV. He was a member of the Territorial Assembly from 1952 to 1959 and of the French National Assembly from 1956 to 1960. In 1958 he was appointed minister of finance in the pre-independence cabinet of Yameogo. The latter, fearing Ouedraogo as a possible rival, removed him from the domestic political scene by appointing him Ambassador to the United Kingdom and he served in London from 1961 to 1966, when Yameogo's government was ousted in a coup.

He returned home, becoming an adviser on foreign affairs to the military government. In 1970 he became leader of the UDV on the legalization of civilian politics. His party won the December 1970 election and in February 1971 he was sworn in as prime minister. Plagued by drought and factional squabbling, his period in office was far from successful. In December 1973 the National Assembly passed a motion of no confidence in his leadership. He refused to resign but two months later was forced out of office by the military, who resumed control of the state. Under the next return to civilian rule in 1978, he achieved the lesser but still important position of president of the National Assembly. Following another coup in 1980, he was forced from office and arrested. After further coups he was eventually brought to trial by the Sankara government in 1984 and sentenced to imprisonment and property confiscation for corruption.

373   Victor OWUSU

Ghana

Owusu was a leading figure in the government of the Second Republic and the leader of the opposition in the Third Republic, as well as enjoying an outstanding legal career.

Born in 1923 in Agona-Asante, he qualified as a lawyer in the United Kingdom. In the first Republic he was not directly involved in politics but was president of the Ghana Bar Association. Following the 1966 coup, the military government appointed him attorney-general and commissioner of justice. In 1969 he was a major figure in Busia's PP, serving as national vice-chairman of the party. In the Second Republic he served as foreign minister and then as minister of justice and attorney-general.

Following the 1972 coup, he was detained for a time but later released. In 1978 he was again detained for opposing Acheampong's UNIGOV proposals but released when the latter was deposed. For the 1979 elections he formed and led the PFP, which was the second best supported party. In the presidential election he lost to Limann on a second ballot. During the Third Republic he was leader of the opposition and shortly before the Rawlings coup had succeeded in uniting most of the opposition in the All People's Party. In 1986 he was arrested by the Rawlings regime and charged with subversion but in 1987 the charges were dropped and he was released. He continued to campaign for the restoration of democracy in Ghana.

P

374 Aristides Maria PEREIRA

Cape Verde

A founder member, with Amilcar Cabral, of the African Party for the Independence of Guinea and Cape Verde (PAIGC), Pereira was the president of the Republic of Cape Verde until 1991.

Pereira was born in 1924, the son of a clergyman, on Boa Vista island in the archipelago which constitutes this state. He was trained as a radio-telegraph technician. He worked in Bissau, where he rose to become Chief of Telecommunications. In the late 1950s he became involved in the labour movement and led a strike. In 1960 he went into exile with Cabral and later became one of the major leaders of the PAIGC, a liberation movement which covered both the Portuguese colonies of Cape Verde and Guinea-Bissau. In 1964 he became joint secretary-general of the movement and was one of the major organizers of its guerrilla force. With the murder by the Portuguese of Cabral in 1973, Pereira became the senior political officer. Following the 1974 Portuguese coup, Cape Verde became an independent state in 1975 and Pereira was elected to the position of president of the new republic by the single-party National People's Assembly. He was re-elected president by this body in 1981 and 1986.

After independence it was planned that the two territories would amalgamate to form a unified state but the coup in Bissau in 1980 wrecked this plan and for a time relations between Cape Verde and mainland Bissau were very bad. Pereira formed a new party, the African Party for the Independence of Cape Verde (PAICV), which he has continued to lead ever since. Since then relations with Bissau have improved, but the two have not resumed attempts at unification. Pereira's leadership of his small state was not seriously challenged until 1990 and Cape Verde has enjoyed a high level of political stability without making much progress in the economic field. In late 1990, influenced partly by events in Eastern Europe, a multi-party system was introduced. In the legislative elections of January 1991 the PAICV was defeated by the new opposition Movement for Democracy (MPD) which won more than two-thirds of the seats in the National Assembly. In the presidential elections, held towards the end of February, Pereira was soundly defeated by the MPD candidate Antonio Mascarennas Monteiro, a former supreme court judge, and stood down.

375 Barend Jacobus du PLESSIS

South Africa

Du Plessis is one of the more reform-minded figures in the white minority government and has been finance minister since 1984.

Born in 1940 in Johannesburg, he was educated at Potchefstroom University and then trained as a teacher. After teaching he went to work for an international computer company and received further training in the USA. He was first elected to parliament for the NP in 1974. In 1983 he became minister of education and in this role he became much more involved in dialogue with black teachers and parents than his predecessors had been. In 1984 he was appointed finance minister, a post he has continued to hold. In 1989 he was a candidate to succeed P.W. Botha as party leader, but was narrowly defeated by F.W. de Klerk after three rounds of voting. He is regarded as being very much on the liberal wing of the party.

376   Jlatoh Nicholas PODIER

Liberia

Podier was a major participant in the 1980 coup and a key figure in the military government. He died in disputed circumstances in 1988.

Born in 1955 in Pleebo into the Kru ethnic group, he joined the army in 1974 and became a corporal in 1979. He was a significant participant in the 1980 coup and was subsequently promoted to the rank of brigadier-general. He was a leading figure in the PRC government, of which he was co-chairman. In 1981 he became the number two man in the government following the execution of his predecessor. He was implicated in a coup attempt in 1984 but was not arrested and in 1986 he was appointed speaker of the newly established National Assembly. Later the same year he fled into exile in Côte d'Ivoire. In 1988 he was killed in Liberia. The government announced that he had died leading an invasion but it was widely believed that he had been tricked into returning to the country and then murdered.

377   Radha POONOOSAMY

Mauritius

Poonoosamy was the first woman cabinet minister in the Mauritian political system.

Born in 1923 in Durban, South Africa, she was educated at Natal University and became involved in anti-government nationalist activities. She was the leader of the Women's League of the Natal Indian Congress and, later, a member of the executive committee of the South African ANC. She moved to Mauritius in 1952, after marrying a Mauritian doctor, and founded the women's section of the Indo-Mauritian Association. She joined the MLP in 1966 and became a member of the national executive three years later. In 1969 she became mayor of Quatre Bornes. In 1975 she became a member of parliament and was appointed minister of women's affairs, prices and consumer protection, making her the first woman to be a member of the government. In this post she was a pioneer of legislation against sexual discrimination. She resigned her post after 18 months.

Q

378 Percy QOBOZA

South Africa

Qoboza was the leading black anti-apartheid journalist until his death in 1988.

Born in 1938 in the Transvaal, he began his career in 1963 as an apprentice reporter on the *World and Weekend World*, becoming news editor in 1968 and editor in 1974. In 1976 he was the leading figure in the newspaper exposure of police violence at the time of the Soweto riots. In 1977 his newspaper was closed by the government and he was arrested and detained without trial. On his release he became editor of the *Post* and *Sunday Post* which had replaced his previous newspaper. In 1980 he went to the USA to become guest editor on the *Washington Post*, but while he was away his South African papers were closed by the government. In 1984 he returned home to become editor of another black opposition newspaper, the *City Press*. In spite of continued harassment by the authorities, Qoboza continued to preach black–white reconciliation whilst exposing the atrocities of the regime. He died in 1988 on his fiftieth birthday.

379 Thomas Gunkama QUIWONKPA

Liberia

Quiwonkpa was a leading figure in the post-coup government and the commander of the Liberian army. He went into exile in 1983 and was subsequently executed for attempting a coup.

Born in 1955 in Zurlay in Nimba County, he received little formal education before joining the army in 1971. By 1980 he had been promoted to staff sergeant, although he later became a general. He was a prominent figure in the 1980 coup and became a member of the ruling PRC. He also became army commander and was seen as the strongman of the regime.

His popularity with the rank and file in the army led head of state Samuel Doe to regard him as a dangerous rival and in 1983 he was stripped of his army leadership and offered the largely bureaucratic position of PRC secretary. He refused to accept this new post and fled the country. In 1985 he returned to lead a major coup attempt which almost succeeded in toppling the Doe regime. There was popular rejoicing when it appeared that the coup was successful, but Doe rallied enough of the army behind him to beat off the attempt. Quiwonkpa was killed or, according to some sources, committed suicide and his mutilated body was placed on public display.

R

380 Gabriel RAMANANTSOA

Madagascar

Ramanantsoa was military head of state of Madagascar from 1972 to 1975.

Born in 1906 in Tananarive to a wealthy family, he was educated locally and in France. He joined the French colonial army and received military training at Saint-Cyr, graduating in 1931. For the next three decades he was largely absent from his own country and fought for the French in Tunisia and Indochina. When Madagascar became independent in 1960 he returned to become commander-in-chief of the armed forces.

His coming to power in 1972 was not through a conventional military coup but rather through the total collapse of the government of Philibert Tsiranana following riots, a general strike and a breakdown of law and order. He restored order and began a programme of reforms in taxation and minimum wages. In October 1972 a referendum gave him a mandate to govern for five years. He was never a natural politician and found it difficult to handle political problems. In February 1975 he was persuaded to transfer power to Richard Ratsimandrava, but the latter was assassinated within a few days and replaced by Gilles Andriamahazo, who was himself replaced by Didier Ratsiraka four months later. Ramanantsoa died in Paris in 1979.

381 Matamela Cyril RAMAPHOSA

South Africa

Ramaphosa is a leading black trade unionist and is the general secretary of the NUM, the most important union in South Africa.

Born in 1952 in Johannesburg he was educated at the University of the North (Turfloop), where political activity led to his arrest in 1974. He subsequently qualified as a lawyer. He was active in Steve Biko's BPC and became involved in legal work with the black trade union movement. In 1982 he was a founder of the NUM and became its general secretary. He has been extremely successful in building up the membership of the union to around 400 000 and in 1987 led it in its first major strike. He is also an influential figure in the broader COSATU, which has close links with the ANC. The pivotal role of the mining industry in South Africa makes Ramaphosa a key figure in the political process.

382 Seewoosagur RAMGOOLAM

Mauritius

Ramgoolam was the dominant figure in Mauritian politics from the 1950s to the 1980s.

Born in 1900 in Belle Rive to a poor Hindu family, he was the first person from his community to receive higher education in Britain, where he qualified as a medical doctor. Whilst in Britain he was close to, and strongly influenced by, Mahatma Gandhi. Back in Mauritius he worked for Hindu interests and became a member of the legislative council. In 1948 he became an elected MP and in 1953 joined the MLP. He became leader of the MLP in 1958 and improved its organization. He was the leading figure in the demand for the end of British colonial rule. The MLP became the major party and at independence in 1968 Ramgoolam became the country's first independent prime minister, a position which he held until 1982. He was a supremely skilful politician who managed to bring together the different racial groups in a stable political system. He was also a committed democrat and the survival of a democratic system in Mauritius owes much to the foundations he built. In 1973 he was awarded the United Nations Prize for defence of human rights. He was also chairman of the OAU from 1976 to 1977.

In 1982 he became the first African leader to be voted out of office when his MLP lost the election. He accepted defeat with dignity and stepped down in favour of the victorious opposition. In 1983 he was appointed governor-general of Mauritius, a largely ceremonial position, as the representative of the British monarch, who remains titular head of state. He died of natural causes in December 1985.

383   Gerard Tlalinyane RAMOREBOLI

Lesotho

Ramoreboli was a leading figure in the opposition to Jonathan's government

and, later, a senior member of that government.

Born in 1913 in Likupa, he was educated at Roma College and became a teacher. He became involved in trade union affairs and was president of the Basutoland African National Teachers' Union from 1957 to 1964. He was an active member of the BCP representing it on the legislative council from 1960 to 1965 and in the national assembly from 1965 to 1970. In 1965 he became deputy leader of the party and the most significant opposition leader after Mokhehle. He was detained following Jonathan's 1970 coup. In 1973 he accepted Jonathan's offer to join the interim national assembly. This decision split the BCP into an exile wing led by Mokhehle and an internal wing led by Ramoreboli, although both continued to claim leadership of the party. In 1975 Ramoreboli joined the cabinet as minister of justice and retained this post until 1984.

384   Richard RATSIMANDRAVA

Madagascar

Ratsimandrava was military head of state in 1975 but only survived six days before being assassinated.

Born in 1931 in Tananarive, he was educated locally before undergoing military training in the French colonial army at Saint-Cyr. He served with the French in Morocco and Algeria before returning home at independence in 1960 to join the country's new gendarmerie. In 1968 he became the commander of the gendarmerie. With the establishment of military government in 1972, he was appointed minister of the interior. In this post he undertook the freeing of all political prisoners. In February 1975 he became head of state on the withdrawal from power of Gabriel Ramanantsoa. Six days later his car was ambushed by gunmen and he was assassinated.

385   Didier RATSIRAKA

Madagascar

Ratsiraka has been military head of state since 1975 and was previously foreign minister.

Born in 1936 in Vatomandry, near Tananarive, he received officer training in the French navy before moving to the Madagascar navy at independence. He was also a defence attache at Madagascar's embassy in Paris. Following the 1972 coup he was appointed foreign minister in the military government and was one of the most important men in the regime. As foreign minister he strengthened ties with socialist states whilst weakening those with the West. French military bases in Madagascar were closed down.

Following the assassination of Ratsimandrava in 1975, in which he was not implicated, Ratsiraka became head of state and head of government. Shortly afterwards he created the all-military Supreme Revolutionary Council, with himself as its president. He declared himself in favour of a 'scientific socialist' ideology and proceeded on a large-scale programme of nationalization. In 1975 he created the Vanguard of the Malagasy Revolution (AREMA), of which he was secretary-general, which has remained the dominant political grouping ever since. Small opposition groups have continued to exist and in spite of some government harassment have continued to have some representation in the National Assembly. Ratsiraka has been elected to the presidency three times, most recently in 1989.

In spite of several coup plots and periodic civil disturbances, Ratsiraka has not been seriously challenged as leader. During the 1980s, in spite of claiming continued adherence to socialism, he has moved back to a more mixed economy approach to development and has established closer ties with western states, especially France.

386   Georges RAWIRI

Gabon

Rawiri has been first deputy prime minister of Gabon since 1975 and has combined this with several important ministerial appointments.

Born in Lambarene in 1932, he was educated locally and in France. He joined the civil service in 1957 and in 1963 became the first director of the Gabonese television service. In 1964 he was brought into the government as minister of information. The following year he became ambassador to France. He returned in 1971 to become foreign minister and, in 1974, minister of finance. In 1975 he was appointed to the newly-created post of first deputy prime minister, the third most important position in the country, which he has held ever since, combining it with several other portfolios. He is widely regarded as one of President Bongo's most trusted political allies.

387   Jerry RAWLINGS

Ghana

Rawlings is one of Africa's most charismatic politicians and has been leader of Ghana for two separate periods.

Born in Accra in 1947 to a Scottish father and Ewe mother, he attended Achimota school and joined the military academy at Teshi in 1968. After flying training he became a flight-lieutenant in the Ghanaian air force in 1978. In May 1979 he led an unsuccessful coup against the Akuffo military regime and was imprisoned. The following month a group of his supporters launched another coup attempt and released him from jail. This time the coup succeeded and Rawlings came to power as chairman of the AFRC, which ruled Ghana until September 1979, when it handed over power to an elected civilian government. In its short time in power the AFRC regime exacted severe retribution against the leaders of previous regimes, including the execution of three former heads of state, Afrifa, Acheampong and Akuffo.

During the period of the Third Republic, Rawlings was forcibly retired from the armed forces but continued to be an influential figure. On the final day of 1981 he led another successful coup and returned to power as leader of the PNDC. This time he made no commitments concerning a restoration of civilian rule. In 1982 he replaced city and district councils with PDCs which in 1984 were redesignated CDRs. In 1988 and 1989 non-party elections were held for new district councils but they were severely controlled by the PNDC, who nominated a large minority of members.

The long-term nature of national government, however, remained uncertain.

Although the early stages of the regime were marked by a great deal of left-wing rhetoric, Rawlings gradually moved towards more orthodox economic policies, much to the approval of the IMF. Public austerity programmes were introduced and the national currency was significantly devalued. These measures resulted in an improvement within the Ghanaian economy, which before he came to power had been in a state of chaos. They also resulted in the alienation of much of his previous support base amongst the urban workers, students and radical intellectuals. The regime has become increasingly authoritarian and in March 1989 introduced heavy media censorship. Accusations of increasing corruption in the government have been made, although they have not usually been aimed at Rawlings personally. There have also been several failed attempts at a coup.

388   Albert RENE

Seychelles

Rene has been the president of the Seychelles since coming to power in a coup in 1977.

Born in 1935, he initially began training for the priesthood before moving to England to study law and qualify as a barrister. In 1963 he founded the SPUP, which changed its name to the SPPF in 1978. At independence in 1976 he became prime minister as the junior partner in a coalition government headed by President Mancham of the SDP. In 1977, Rene ousted Mancham in a coup backed by Tanzania and became president. Since coming to power he has created a single-party state, with his own SPPF claiming a Marxist–Leninist vanguard role. State intervention in the economy increased significantly and the pro-Western stance of his predecessor was abandoned. In recent years there has been a marked softening of the official line in these matters. Rene's period in office has been marked by several violent attempts to oust him, including one, in 1981, which was led by South Africa-based mercenaries. He was last elected unopposed to the presidency in 1989. He is also secretary-general of the SPPF, commander-in-chief of the armed forces and holds the portfolios of defence, finance, planning, legal affairs and external relations.

389   Muhamadu RIBADU

Nigeria

Ribadu was, arguably, the second most important government figure in the First Republic.

Born in 1910 in Balala, he was educated locally and worked for a time as a schoolteacher. He later worked as a civil servant in the colonial administration. He was a founder member of the NPC in 1951 and rose rapidly within the party, which was to govern Nigeria, becoming its second vice-president. He was first elected to parliament in 1951 and later served as federal minister of land, mines and power (1954–7) and minister of Lagos affairs (1957–60) in the pre-independence government. At independence in 1960 he became minister of defence, a post he continued to hold until the time of his death. He was regarded as the most influential figure in the re-

gime after Ahmadu Bello. He died of natural causes in 1965.

390   Mohammed Abubakar RIMI

Nigeria

Rimi was a leading opposition figure in the Second Republic and governor of Kano State.

Born in 1940 in Kano, he was educated locally before going on to higher education in England. Before entering politics he worked as an academic, a diplomat and a civil servant. In 1977 he was a member of the Constituent Assembly which finalized the constitution of the Second Republic. With the lifting of the ban on political parties in 1978 he joined the PRP. In 1979 he was elected PRP governor in Kano State, the main support base of the party. He was involved in serious clashes with the emir of Kano, which led to mass violence. In 1983, following rifts within the PRP, he defected to the NPP, but failed in the 1983 election. Following the coup he was given a long prison sentence for corruption but was subsequently released.

391   Holden Alvaro ROBERTO

Angola

Roberto is an Angolan nationalist leader who has spent almost all of his life outside the country. His movement, the FNLA, is now almost certainly defunct. He is the brother-in-law of President Mobutu of Zaire.

Born in Angola in 1923, he left at the age of two to live in the Belgian Congo. After completing his education he worked as a clerk in the Belgian colonial administration. In 1958 with other Angolan exiles he formed the UPA and in 1960 became its president. In 1962 he merged the UPA with other exile nationalist groups to form the FNLA, which he led from the start. Although FNLA guerrillas participated in the liberation war against the Portuguese, Roberto himself continued to reside in Kinshasha, Zaire, where he was well supported by his brother-in-law. At other times he received support from China, Romania and the USA. The FNLA gained early diplomatic success, including recognition by the OAU as the 'government-in-exile' in 1963. In 1969 this recognition was withdrawn following diplomatic efforts by Neto's MPLA.

In ideological terms Roberto has consistently adopted a strongly anti-Marxist stance, but this is largely to be explained as an attempt to gain support from opponents of the pro-Soviet MPLA rather than as a firmly-held philosophical position. In 1972 Roberto agreed to merge the FNLA with the MPLA, but this agreement rapidly proved abortive. Following the 1974 coup in Portugal further attempts at creating unity between the Angolan liberation movements failed and the MPLA emerged as the dominant group, albeit with outside support. In 1975 the FNLA split into various factions but Roberto, still based in Kinshasha, was still widely recognized as the leader. Armed conflict with the forces of the MPLA government continued, but with decreasing intensity. The agreement between the governments of Angola and Zaire in 1979 forced Roberto to leave Zaire and he went into exile in Senegal, Gabon and then France. In 1986 Roberto appeared before a congressional panel in the USA in an attempt to secure funding to revive the FNLA which was, by this time, largely defunct. This attempt failed and it would appear to be the case that future involvement in Angolan politics by Roberto and his movement is unlikely.

S

392 Ali SAIBOU

Niger

Saibou has been president of Niger since he came to power on the death of his predecessor in November 1987.

Born in 1940 into the Djerma ethnic group, he joined the army and was a participant in the 1974 coup which brought his cousin, Seyni Kountche, to power. By 1987 he had risen to the position of chief of staff of the armed forces. During Kountche's last illness he often performed the duties of head of state. When his cousin died in 1987, Saibou became chairman of the ruling Higher Council for National Orientation and president of the republic. He also took the defence and interior portfolios.

He announced the release of all political prisoners, while promising a policy of continuity. In 1988 he moved in the direction of more civilian participation and announced the formation of a new political party, the MNSD, of which he became chairman. He also appointed a civilian majority to his cabinet. In December 1989 he was elected to the presidency for a seven-year term in an election in which he was the only candidate.

393 George SAITOTI

Kenya

Saitoti was an academic and technocrat before gaining political prominence with rapid promotion to finance minister and vice-president.

Born in 1940 to a Masai father and Kikuyu mother, he received university education in the USA and Britain before returning to an academic post at Nairobi University teaching mathematics. He also became chairman of the Kenya Commercial Bank and chairman of the Mumias Sugar Company. His involvement in politics was minimal until 1983, when he was nominated to parliament and appointed minister of finance. In 1988 he was elected chairman of the Kajiado branch of the ruling KANU party. In May 1989 he was catapulted to greater prominence when he became vice-president at the same time as retaining the finance portfolio. The following month he also became vice-president of KANU. Although his intellectual ability is undisputed, his meteoric rise in government owes more to President Moi's preference for technocrats with no independent power base over established political heavyweights in top political positions.

394 Moustapha Ould Mohamed SALEK

Mauritania

Salek was head of state after leading a coup in 1978 but was himself overthrown in 1979.

Born in 1936, he was educated locally before joining the army and receiving military training in France. He rose rapidly through the ranks of the Mauritanian army and by 1978 he was chief of staff. In July 1978 he led the first coup to take place in the country and became head of state and prime minister. His position was never secure and in April 1979 he relinquished the post of prime minister. In June the same year he was finally ousted in a bloodless coup. In 1982 he was implicated in a further coup attempt and sentenced to ten years in jail, but was released following a general political amnesty at the end of 1984.

395   Salim Ahmed SALIM

Tanzania

Salim has been a leading government figure and is currently secretary-general of the OAU.

Born in 1942 in Zanzibar, he was educated locally and at the University of Delhi. Before independence he was a leading figure in the UP. Since independence his career has been largely concerned with foreign relations, both as a diplomat and as a member of the government. His ambassadorial postings have included India, China, Korea, Cuba and extensive work with the United Nations. From 1980 to 1984 he was foreign minister. In 1984 he became prime minister and was a leading candidate to succeed Nyerere in the presidency. Ideologically to the right of the ruling elite, he failed to become president and in 1985 became deputy prime minister and minister of defence. He was also vice-chairman of the ruling party, Chama cha Mapinduzi (CCM – Party of the Revolution). In July 1989 he was elected secretary general of the OAU, which is the most important position in African international relations. He is thought by many to be a likely future contender for the presidency, despite his lack of success in 1985.

396   Jorge Isaac SANGUMBA

Angola

Sangumba is a leading member of Jonas Savimbi's UNITA.

An Ovimbundu, Sangumba was born in 1944 and as a teenager worked for the MPLA in Angola. At the age of 18 he went into exile in Tanzania, where he met the Mozambican nationalist Eduardo Mondlane. The latter arranged a scholarship for Sangumba in the USA, where he graduated with a degree in political science in 1968. After graduation he joined UNITA and became its foreign affairs spokesman. He is one of Savimbi's closest advisors and a leading propagandist of the movement abroad.

397   Thomas SANKARA

Burkina Faso

Without doubt the young and charismatic Sankara was one of the most notable and popular military political leaders of post-independence Africa, despite the fact that he was only in power for four years before being assassinated in 1987.

He was born in 1949 into a low-status family descended from former slaves. He entered the army in 1966 and received extra training in Madagascar and France. He made rapid progress and was appointed commander of the commando training centre in Po in 1976. In 1978, whilst on a parachute training course in Morocco, he met Blaise Compaore for the first time; as events turned out this was a fateful meeting.

In 1981, following initial hesitation, Sankara joined the military government of Saye Zerbo as secretary to the president in charge of information. In 1982 the government decided to ban strikes and Sankara resigned in protest at the anti-union legislation. He was arrested and imprisoned to await court-martial. In November 1982 the Zerbo government was overthrown and replaced by one led by Commander Jean Baptiste Ouedraogo, who appointed Sankara to the post of prime minister. Once again Sankara's relationship with the military government of which he was a member became strained and in May 1983 he was arrested. He had become, by this time, a leader of the more radical grouping of junior officers within the army and had also established considerable popular support amongst the wider civilian population, especially in the urban areas. In August 1983 a military force led by Compaore released Sankara from prison and he was installed as the leader of the new military government designated as the National Council of the Revolution. The new government appeared to enjoy considerable mass support.

For the next four years Sankara followed a radical populist path which was markedly different from those of previous governments. His style had considerable popular appeal but also made him important enemies. He abolished most of the powers of the traditional chiefs, including their right to tribute payment and obligatory labour, transferring most of their functions to newly established CDRs. He abolished the head tax which had weighed heavily on the rural population and forced top civil servants and army officers to contribute one month's salary per year to help fund development projects. People's Revolutionary Courts were established to investigate members of previous governments and anti-corruption campaigns were launched. A number of ambitious mass literacy campaigns were established. A determined attempt was made to bring basic health care to the rural population, with massive vaccination programmes and an assault on the terrible problem of river blindness which received financial support from the United Nations.

In 1984 Sankara changed the name of the state from Upper Volta (the old colonial name) to Burkina Faso (meaning 'the land of people of integrity'). All land and mineral wealth were nationalized, although the country has little of the latter and most of the former is of very poor quality. One of Sankara's most controversial campaigns, but one to which he exhibited a passionate personal commitment, was that of the extension of women's rights. In this rather backward and conservative country, female emancipation was not an issue which had been raised by previous political leaders. Sankara established the UFB to mobilize women and encourage them to demand equality with men. He practised what he preached in appointing more women to official positions than had hitherto been the case, but even he recognized that this was not a battle which could be won overnight, given the patriarchal nature of indigenous society and custom.

Sankara travelled widely and frequently throughout the world establishing particularly close links with other

Third World Marxist states such as Cuba, Nicaragua and Angola. With the exception of Jerry Rawlings's Ghana, relationships with Burkina Faso's neighbours were less cordial and a short border war was fought with Mali at the end of 1985.

Sankara's inspirational leadership, the influence of which extended well beyond the borders of Burkina Faso, marked something very new in the political history of the country. His downfall, however, followed a pattern only too familiar to observers of that state. By 1987 he seemed to be firmly established in power: an attempted counter-coup in 1984 had been put down with little difficulty. The overthrow and murder of Sankara came from a most unexpected source. In October 1987 his closest and most trusted friend and colleague, Blaise Compaore, led a coup against him in which Thomas Sankara was assassinated and his body dumped in an unmarked grave. His official death certificate claimed that he died of 'natural causes', a statement which absolutely nobody believed. A popular outburst against his death was only controlled by the new government with considerable difficulty.

In retrospect, Sankara may have attempted to do too much too quickly, but his death was deeply lamented. Only time will tell whether Sankara's period of rule will prove to be merely a brief interlude or of truly lasting influence.

398 Abubakar Sola SARAKI

Nigeria

Saraki was a major political leader during the period of the Second Republic.

Born in 1933 in Ilorin, he was educated in Lagos and later qualified as a doctor in England. He returned to Nigeria in 1962 and enjoyed a successful medical career before entering politics. In 1977 he became a member of the Constituent Assembly which finalized the constitution of the Second Republic. With the lifting of the ban on party politics in 1978 he became a founder member of the NPN, which was to become the ruling party. He was elected national vice-chairman of the party and its chairman in Kwara State. In 1979 he was elected to the senate, where he was chosen as NPN leader. He was arrested after the 1983 coup but was released in 1985.

399 Denis SASSOU-NGUESSO

Congo

Sassou-Nguesso has been president of the Congo since 1979, his most recent re-election being in July 1989. Under his leadership the political system has become less unstable than it was previously and he has recently played a more significant role in international affairs.

Born in Edou in 1943, he joined the army after completing his secondary education and received officer training in France in the early 1960s. He was a supporter of President Ngouabi and a leading figure in the PCT from its formation. In 1975 he was appointed minister of defence and in 1977 added the role of vice-president of the PCT military committee. Following Ngouabi's assassination in 1977, Sassou-Nguesso was defeated in his attempt to succeed him by his arch rival Yhombi-Opango. By 1979 the latter had lost the support of most of the leading military figures in the PCT and Sassou-Nguesso was chosen as the new head of state and leader of the party.

Although maintaining a strong rhetorical commitment to the regime's Marxist–Leninist ideology, he has vastly improved relations with Western states, especially France, and increased the role of the private sector within the economy. He has released a number of political prisoners and has had some success in balancing the various ethnic and ideological factions within the army. However, although he has survived longer than any of his predecessors as Congolese head of state, internal opposition has manifested itself in the form of several, poorly organized, attempts at a coup.

His international role has expanded since he was chairman of the OAU in 1986–7. He played an important part in the securing of a cease-fire between Chad and Libya in 1987 and in late 1988 was a key mediator in the talks which led to the agreement on Namibian independence.

In late 1990 he reluctantly gave in to pressure from within the PCT and from striking workers to allow a multi-party system. In January 1991 opposition parties were legalized.

400   Landing SAVANE

Senegal

Savane is a Maoist opposition leader and was a presidential candidate in 1988.

Born in 1942 in Casamance, he was educated locally before going on to higher education in France. He became the leader of the Senegalese student organization in France and was much in-volved in the 1968 student uprising there. As a result of this experience he became a Maoist and back in Senegal in 1974 he launched a clandestine Maoist group called And-Jef ('to act together'). He was arrested and spent a year in jail from 1975 to 1976. In 1981, with the total lifting of the restrictions on political parties, the movement was reconstituted as the AJ-MRDN. In the 1988 presidential election Savane stood as a candidate but came a bad fourth and bottom of the poll. The party had no candidates in the parliamentary elections on the grounds that, if the party leader won the presidency, he would immediately dissolve the parliament and establish a revolutionary government. Savane must be regarded as marginal to the real struggle for power in Senegal and yet he is also typical of the leadership of the small far-left parties which proliferate in the urban areas.

401   Jonas Malheiros SAVIMBI

Angola

Savimbi is one of Africa's most controversial political leaders. In the war of liberation against Portuguese colonial rule he led one of the most important nationalist movements, UNITA. Following independence he continued to lead his movement against the MPLA government.

An Ovimbundu, Savimbi was born in 1934. Following university education in Portugal and Switzerland he returned to Africa in 1961 and joined Holden Roberto's UPA, becoming its general secretary. In 1962 he became foreign minister of the government-in-exile. He worked closely with Roberto in the creation of the FNLA. In 1964, Savimbi and his Ovimbundu supporters broke with the FNLA and in 1966 created UNITA. During the war of liberation UNITA fought against the Portuguese, but there is evidence to suggest that on occasion Savimbi cooperated with the Portuguese to attack the MPLA. Following Portuguese decolonization, Savimbi entered into abortive agreements with both the MPLA and the FNLA. When these agreements broke down Savimbi continued to lead UNITA in rebellion against the government. For much of the late 1970s and the 1980s his movement controlled large areas of Angola, although these were always contested by the forces of the MPLA and its Cuban backers. Savimbi lost the support he had once enjoyed amongst many black African leaders as a result of the massive financial and military assistance he received from the South African government and army. Because of his opposition to the Cuban forces Savimbi also received considerable support from the USA and on a visit there in 1986 he was received in a way normally reserved for visiting heads of state. In spite of earlier claims to be a Maoist, he presented himself as a bastion of anti-communism in Southern Africa. In 1988 the UNITA cause was undermined by a peace agreement between Angola, South Africa and Cuba which had the backing of the USA, and in 1989 Savimbi entered into a peace agreement with the MPLA government at a conference held in Zaire.

Savimbi has shown himself to be a fine orator and a charismatic leader with widespread popular support. His experience as a guerrilla leader fighting in the bush is second to none, but he has also acquired a reputation for considerable brutality in dealing with his opponents and, at times, his own supporters.

402   Amos SAWYER

Liberia

Sawyer is a leading member of the radical opposition who has recently been operating in exile.

Born in 1945 in Greenville, Sinoe County, he received higher education in the USA where he received a doctorate in political science. He returned to Liberia to work as an academic in the University of Liberia. In the 1970s he was a leading figure in the radical opposition MOJA, which was harassed by the TWP government. In 1979 he challenged the government by standing as an independent candidate in elections for the mayor of Monrovia and proved so popular that the government postponed the election.

Following the 1980 coup he was appointed chairman of the Constitution Drafting Committee in 1981 but, like all the radicals who had worked with the Doe regime, he was rapidly denied any political influence. In 1984 he was detained for a time on trumped-up charges of plotting a coup. He formed the LPP, which consisted largely of MOJA members, but the party and Sawyer himself were banned from participating in the 1985 elections. Shortly after he went into exile in the USA, where he is the director of ACDL, the main opposition in exile. Following the overthrow of the Doe regime in 1990 he was named as interim president by a group of other West African states who were attempting to mediate in the Liberian conflict but, with at least four other candidates laying claim to that title, the situation remained very confused.

403   Lennox Leslie Wongama SEBE

South Africa (Ciskei)

Sebe was the president of the 'independent' South African homeland of Ciskei until he was overthrown by a coup in March 1990.

Born in 1926 into a family of commoners of the Tshwane lineage, he qualified as a teacher before becoming adviser to the paramount chief of the Ciskei reserve. In 1973 he became chief minister and awarded himself the title of a chief. He subsequently formed the CNIP, which became in practice the only permitted party. In 1981 he opted for independence from South Africa under the infamous Bantustan scheme and became president. As with the other homelands, Ciskeian independence was not recognized by any state but South Africa. Under Sebe's inept, corrupt and coercive rule, Ciskei became an embarrassment even to the South Africans. In 1983 he had himself declared president for life. All opposition was ruthlessly crushed and there were numerous attempts to overthrow him, including one by his brother. Relations with the other Xhosa homeland, Transkei, were very poor and there were many border conflicts and abductions. Large-scale corruption became rife in Ciskei. Trade unions were banned, as was the ANC, even after it had been legalized in South Africa. In March 1990, Sebe was overthrown in a coup while he was out of the country, to the delight of most of the population.

404   Assane SECK

Senegal

Seck was a leader of the Casamance separatist movement who later occupied senior government posts for nearly two decades after independence.

Born in 1919 in Inor in the Casamance region, he received higher education at Paris University and after returning to Senegal in 1952 became the first black African lecturer at the University of Dakar. In 1954 he founded and led the MAC and, although he later abandoned the separatist cause, the region remained his support base. In 1957 he merged the MAC with Senghor's BDS to form the BPS, but throughout the late 1950s and early 1960s he had a fluctuating political relationship with Senghor which included periods of hostility. In 1966 he finally made peace with Senghor and joined the government as minister of culture. He remained in the government throughout the rest of the Senghor period and into the Diouf period. From 1968 to 1973 he was minister of education and from 1973 to 1978 he was foreign minister. In 1978 his government career began a slow decline and he was demoted to minister of culture. He held this post until 1982, when he became minister of state for supplies. In 1983 he was finally dropped from the cabinet.

405   Joseph Ibrahim SEID

Chad

Seid was the leading intellectual in the post-independence politics of Chad, serving in key government and diplomatic positions.

Born in Fort Lamy (Ndjamena) in 1927, he became Chad's first university graduate in 1949 before pursuing postgraduate legal studies in Paris. He became an internationally respected lawyer and legal scholar. He was, briefly, public prosecutor in Mandou before being appointed as Chad's ambassador to France in 1960. He served in this key diplomatic post until 1966, when he was brought home to be minister of justice in Tombalbaye's cabinet. He survived in this post until the 1975 coup, managing to stand above the factional squabbling within the regime and distancing himself from its more repugnant aspects. Because of this he was retained by the successor military government and served as attorney-general from 1975 until 1978, when he retired. He died of natural causes in 1980.

406   Kam SELEM

Nigeria

Selem was a major figure in the Gowon regime and a less prominent figure in the Second Republic.

Born in 1924 in Dikwa, Borno State, he was educated locally before joining the police in 1942. He rose through the ranks and in 1962 he became commissioner of police for the Northern Region. In 1965 he became deputy inspector-general of police and the following year was promoted to inspector-general, the top position in the Nigerian police. This earned him a place in Gowon's military government and in 1967 he also became commissioner for internal affairs. He was one of the most powerful men in the government. In 1975, after Gowon had been overthrown, he was purged and went into private business. In 1978 he was a founder member of the NPN, which was to become the ruling party of the Second Republic. In the 1979 elections he was the NPN candidate for the governorship of Burno State, but lost. He was subsequently appointed chairman of the Nigerian National Shipping Line. He died of natural causes in 1981.

407   Leopold Sedar SENGHOR

Senegal

Senghor was one of Africa's most important political leaders before and after the end of colonial rule. He occupied the presidency from independence in 1960 until he retired at the end of 1980.

Born in 1906 in Joal into the Serer ethnic group, he was educated at Catholic mission schools before going on to higher education at the Sorbonne in France. He was a brilliant intellectual and later emerged as a major poet in the French language. In the 1930s he developed the notion of 'negritude' which asserted the value of black African culture and, as a precursor of black consciousness philosophy, had a very significant influence throughout Francophone Africa. When the second world war broke out he joined the French army and was taken prisoner by the Germans. On his release he joined the French resistance, with which he worked until the end of the war.

After the war he was a member of the French Constituent Assembly which drew up the constitution of the Fourth Republic. He was a deputy of the French National Assembly from 1946 to 1958

195

and a member of the French cabinet from 1955 to 1956. In 1948 he formed and led a political party, the BDS, which changed its name to BPS following a merger with the MCA in 1957. This emerged as the major party and, after changing its name to the UPS in 1958, became the ruling party at independence in 1960. Senghor became the first post-independence president of Senegal.

Senghor was a man of many paradoxes. He was at the same time a lofty intellectual and a highly skilled grass roots politician. Although he is a Roman Catholic in a predominantly Muslim country he was able to establish strong links with the Islamic leaders in the rural areas who provided vital support for his leadership of the country. Between 1960 and 1974 Senegal gradually became a *de facto* single-party state, but in the latter year Senghor began the process of restoring multi-party democracy. This was a partial development at first which placed restrictions on the number of parties permitted but gradually these restrictions were lifted. In spite of this renewed electoral competition Senghor's party, renamed the PS in 1976, continued to win substantial majorities at the polls. In international relations he remained a pro-western, and especially pro-French, leader who was at the same time a determined Senegalese nationalist.

At the end of 1980 he announced his decision to retire from public life and so became the first civilian president in post-independence Africa to retire voluntarily. He left behind a stable and relatively prosperous state. Since retirement he has not sought to determine government decisions but is thought to retain a level of influence.

408 Shehu Aliyu Usman SHAGARI

Nigeria

Shagari was a major government figure in the First Republic and was President of Nigeria in the Second Republic.

Born in 1924 in Shagari village, Sokoto State, he qualified as a teacher and taught science for a number of years. In 1951 he joined the newly-formed NPC and became secretary of the Sokoto branch. He was first elected to parliament in 1954. In 1958 he became parliamentary secretary to the prime minister, Balewa, and in 1959 he was minister of commerce and industry and, later, minister of economic development in the pre-independence government. After independence he served in a number of important ministerial posts, including internal affairs and works and communications. He was one of the few major NPC leaders to survive the coup of January 1966 and retired to work as a farmer.

He later served in several top posts in the Gowon regime, including federal commissioner for economic development, rehabilitation and reconstruction following the civil war and federal commissioner for finance from 1971 to 1975, when the Gowon regime was ousted. Once again he briefly retired to farming. In 1977 he was elected to the Constituent Assembly which finalized the constitution of the Second Republic.

With the lifting of the ban on party politics in 1978, he was a founder-member of the NPN and was chosen as its leader and presidential candidate. In the 1979 election he secured election to the presidency, a victory he repeated in the 1983 election. He was thus the first, and so far only, directly elected executive president of Nigeria. During his period of rule he was a conciliatory if somewhat conservative leader who maintained a reputation for personal integrity. However, as time went on, his government gained a justified reputation for large-scale corruption and doubtful competence. The dramatic decline in oil revenue from 1982 had catastrophic effects on the economy. The 1983 elections were marred by malpractice and violence involving all the parties, although most observers agree that Shagari and the NPN would have won anyway.

At the end of 1983 the Second Republic was overthrown by a coup led by Buhari. Shagari was arrested and kept in detention until 1986, when it was decided that there was no evidence of wrongdoing against him personally. He was released but restricted to his home village until 1988 when all restrictions on his movements were lifted. Shagari was a leader of great honesty and intelligence but in the end was unable to cope with the massive problems and conflicts within the Nigerian political system.

409 Nathan SHAMUYARIRA

Zimbabwe

Shamuyarira has been a major government figure since independence and has been foreign minister since 1987.

Born in 1930, he was educated locally before working as a teacher and as a journalist. He was a leading member of ZAPU and in 1963 a founder-member of ZANU. In 1964 he left for higher education in the USA and later obtained a doctorate at Oxford University. He worked for a time as a lecturer in political science at the University of Dar-es-Salaam and continued as a rather critical member of ZANU. In 1977 he dropped his criticisms and went to Mozambique to work as ZANU's administrative secretary. After independence he joined the government as minister for information and posts and telecommunications. In 1987 he became foreign minister and was reappointed to this post following the 1990 election. He is generally regarded as one of the most able members of the government.

410 Alex Kaunda SHAPI

Zambia

Shapi is a leading figure in the ruling UNIP and has been secretary of state for defence and security since 1985.

Born in 1932 in Samfya, he was educated locally and at Oxford University. He was first elected to parliament in the pre-independence elections of 1964. In 1973 he joined the central committee of UNIP and has been a leading figure on it since then. In 1985 he joined the government in the crucial post of secretary of state for defence and security. He is regarded as a party hardliner and earned a level of notoriety at the time of the 1988 elections, when he warned the electorate that they would be 'found out and punished' if they voted against Kenneth Kaunda in the presidential election.

411 Abdirashid Ali SHERMARKE

Somalia

Shermarke was prime minister from 1960 to 1964 and president from 1967 until his assassination in 1969.

197

Born in 1919 in Haradere in the north of the country into a wealthy family of the Darod ethnic group, he was educated in local schools before joining the civil service as a clerk. He joined the SYL in 1944 and went on to become a leading member. From 1950 to 1958 he worked to expand his education and finally earned a doctorate in political science from the University of Rome. He returned to Somalia and was elected to the legislative assembly in 1959. At independence in 1960 he became prime minister and acted as a moderating force in the growing pan-Somali nationalist demand for incorporation of neighbouring territory where Somalis formed a majority ethnic group. In 1964, following factional conflict within the SYL, he was dropped as prime minister. In 1967 his political career revived when he was elected president of the republic by the legislature. In October 1969 he was assassinated while on a tour of the north of the country. His death produced a crisis which led to the intervention of the military a few days later.

412   Andreas SHIPANGA

Namibia

Shipanga was a founder-member and leading figure in SWAPO before defecting to form his own movement.

Born in Ovamboland he was a founder-member of OPO in 1959. When the movement decided to enlarge its ethnic base in 1960 with the formation of SWAPO he was again a founder and became secretary for information. He went into exile at SWAPO's base in Zambia, but in 1976 quarrelled with other leaders of the movement and was held in jail for two years. On his release in 1978 he returned home and established a rival movement called SWAPO-Democrats. Although he was appointed minister of mines by the South Africa-backed 'transitional government', his movement gained little popular support. In the UN-supervised pre-independence elections of 1989 his party failed to win a single seat.

413   Gertrude SHOPE

South Africa

Shope is a leading figure in the black nationalist movement and since 1981 has been head of the Women's Section of the ANC.

Born in 1925 in Johannesburg, she trained and worked as a teacher. She joined the ANC in 1954 and also became a leading figure in the Federation of South African Women which provided assistance and advice to the families of those arrested for anti-apartheid activities. She went into exile in 1966, she and her husband, Mark Shope, working for the ANC in Zambia, Tanzania and Nigeria. In 1981 she became head of the Women's Section of the ANC and a member of its executive committee. Following the legalization of the ANC in 1990 she returned to South Africa.

414   Abdurrahman Darman SHUGABA

Nigeria

Shugaba was an opposition leader in the Second Republic and the central figure in a celebrated court case.

Born in 1931 in Maiduguri into the Kanuri ethnic group, he was a leader of the youth wing of the ruling NPC in the First Republic. In 1989 he was elected to the Borno State House of Assembly as a member of the GNPP and became majority leader in the House. He came to national prominence in 1980 when he was deported by the government on the grounds that he was not a Nigerian citizen. This move was interpreted as a government attack on the opposition and a major court case ensued. The courts decided in favour of Shugaba and against the government. He was declared to be a Nigerian citizen and substantial costs and damages were awarded against the government, which accepted the verdict. This was seen as an important test of judicial autonomy and of the willingness of the government to be bound by legal decisions that went against it.

415 Mohammed SIAD BARRE

Somalia

Siad Barre was head of state in Somalia, having come to power in a coup in 1969, until his violent overthrow in 1991.

Born in 1919 in Lugh District in the north of the country into a family of Darod herdsmen, he was orphaned at the age of ten. He received only elementary education and joined the police force in 1941, making excellent progress through the ranks. By 1950 he was a chief inspector, the highest position held by a Somali at the time. During the 1950s he received higher police training in Italy and continued to expand his education, largely on a self-help basis. Just before independence in 1960 he transferred from the police to

the army and by 1965 he was its commander. Although he showed no interest in the party politics of the period he developed an interest in political ideologies, especially Marxism. In October 1969 he led a coup against the civilian government of Egal and established the SRC, with himself as its president, as the government. Somalia was proclaimed a socialist state which would combine Marxism with Islam.

In more than two decades in power the Siad Barre regime has exhibited far more negative aspects than positive ones. It was always a thoroughly authoritarian regime, but by the end of the 1980s it gained a deserved reputation as one of the most oppressive on the continent. Although it was always based on military support an attempt was made in 1976 to give it a civilian gloss through the creation of the SRSP, with Siad Barre as leader. The SRSP was the only legal party, although by 1990 the government was making promises to allow opposition parties to form in the future. However Somali politics has been based much more on clan than on party and the government looked increasingly nepotistic and dynastic, with positions of real power given mainly to close relatives of the president as internal and external opposition built up. The regime's record on human rights was viewed as one of the poorest in Africa.

In terms of international relations the regime has gone through dramatic changes. In its early years Somalia was the major recipient of Soviet aid in Africa, but following the decision of the Soviet Union to support the arch-enemy Ethiopia following the 1974 coup there the country has become a major recipient of US aid. Government support for pan-Somali nationalism (the view that the Somali state should include parts of neighbouring states which contain an ethnic Somali majority) has produced difficult relations with surrounding states. The outstanding example of this was the 1977–8 Ogaden war, which was a disaster for Somalia, but smaller-scale conflicts have continued ever since.

In economic terms Siad Barre's rule was disastrous. The government followed a plan of nationalization throughout the 1970s, although this was modified in the 1980s. In reality there is not much to nationalize in Somalia, apart from the land, and that is generally of poor quality and subject to frequent drought. A combination of war, drought, corruption and mismanagement have produced destitution for a sizeable proportion of the population. Siad Barre developed a highly personalized system of rule but by 1990 he was struggling to survive. His health was known to be poor, especially since he had been involved in a serious car crash in 1986. The long-term survival of Siad Barre's leadership did not appear to be a likely prospect and in January 1991 he was ousted by a military revolt. He fled the country leaving behind a bitterly divided and confused political system.

416   Abba SIDDICK

Chad

Siddick has been a senior member of several Chadian governments and was also the at times disputed leader of the FROLINAT guerrilla forces.

He was born in the CAR in 1924 of a Chadian father and CAR mother. A member of the pre-independence government in which he served as minister of education, he was sacked by Tombalbaye shortly before independence. He spent the next eight years in France, where he qualified as a doctor and was involved in exile opposition politics, rising to a leadership position within the FROLINAT movement. Following the death of Abatcha in 1968, Siddick became the secretary-general of the movement. Under him the movement began to fragment and his leadership was widely criticized. His opponents censured him for spending all his time in Libya rather than becoming directly involved in the armed struggle in Chad. In 1977 he was ousted but continued to lead a small group of supporters which adopted the name 'FROLINAT Originel'.

In 1979 Goukouni included him in his coalition GUNT government and made him minister of education. In 1981, when it appeared that Goukouni was losing the conflict with Habre, Siddick switched sides and began to support the latter. In 1982 he retained the education portfolio in Habre's new government. He held this until 1986, when he was dropped by Habre.

417   Sheriff SISAY

The Gambia

Sisay was a founder-member of the ruling PPP and one of the country's most important politicians. He was finance minister from 1962 to 1968 and 1982 to 1989.

Born in 1935 in Niamina District, he was the son of a chief. After completing his education he joined the colonial civil service. In 1959 he founded the PPP with Dawda Jawara and became its secretary-general. He was elected to the House of Assembly in 1960 and was appointed finance minister in 1962. In 1968 he came into conflict with Dawda Jawara and left the party and government to found an opposition party, the PPA. The PPA enjoyed little success and for most of the 1970s he was little involved in politics.

In the early 1980s a reconciliation between Sisay and Jawara took place and in 1982 the president appointed him minister of finance. He remained in this post, performing with considerable skill, until ill health forced him to retire in February 1989. He died a few weeks later.

418 Nontsikelelo Albertina SISULU

South Africa

Albertina Sisulu (who is the wife of Walter Sisulu) has been a major figure in the anti-apartheid movement and is a president of the UDF.

Born in 1918 in the Tsomo district of the Transkei, she originally trained as a nurse. In the 1940s she became active in the ANC, especially its Youth League. She married her husband, who was later to become secretary-general of the ANC, in 1944. She was an active leader of the ANC Women's League, which later became affiliated to the FEDSAW, becoming president of FEDSAW in 1983. From the 1950s until the end of the 1980s she was frequently detained by the police and was subject to restriction and banning orders which made it impossible to live a normal life. When the

UDF was established in 1983 as a broad-based multi-racial organization in opposition to apartheid, she became one of its presidents. Her husband was finally released from jail in October 1989. For nearly half a century she has been the leading black woman campaigner against the apartheid system and enjoys enormous status which is related to but also largely independent of her husband.

419 Walter Max Ulyate SISULU

South Africa

Sisulu has been one of the leading figures in the ANC since the 1940s. He was imprisoned from 1963 until 1989.

Born in 1912 in the Encobo area of the Transkei, he was raised by his uncle, who was a headman. In 1929 he began work on the gold mines but was subsequently a domestic worker and was also employed in a number of factories. Of necessity his education was largely through private study. In 1940 he was sacked from a bakery for organizing a strike. In the same year he joined the ANC and later became treasurer of its militant Youth League. In 1949 he was elected secretary-general of the ANC. Throughout the 1950s he was a leading figure in the ANC struggle against apartheid and a close colleague of Nelson Mandela. During this time he was subject to frequent arrest and imprisonment. He was arrested in 1963 and in 1964 he was sentenced to life imprisonment. He was finally released in October 1989, after more than a quarter of a century in jail. When the ANC was unbanned in February 1990, Sisulu was appointed chairman of its Interim Leadership Committee and was a leading participant in the subsequent talks between the movement and the government. With the exception of Nelson Mandela, Sisulu is arguably the most important of the older generation of ANC leaders, most of whom have spent lengthy periods of their lives in detention in South African jails.

420 Edson Furatidzayi Chisingaitwi SITHOLE

Zimbabwe

Sithole was a leading figure in the nationalist movement until he was murdered in 1975.

Born in 1935 in Gazaland, he was educated locally before becoming involved in nationalist politics after leaving school. He was a founder-member of the Rhodesian ANC in 1957, but spent most of the next few years in prison. In 1964 he was appointed publicity secretary of the newly-formed ZANU, but was soon back in prison. Whilst in detention he qualified as a lawyer through a correspondence course and managed to obtain a doctorate in law. In October 1975 he was abducted from an hotel in Salisbury (now Harare) by men believed to be government special branch agents and, although his body has never been found, it is presumed that he was murdered.

421 Ndabaningi SITHOLE

Zimbabwe

Sithole was one of the major nationalist leaders but lost support after participating in the internal settlement and faded from significance in the 1980s.

Born in 1920 in Nyamandhlovu, he was educated locally and was ordained a minister in the Congregationalist Church in 1958. He was an important figure in the NDP until it was banned and was then a founder-member of ZAPU in 1961, becoming its chairman. In 1963, together with Robert Mugabe, he broke away to form ZANU, of which he became president. Shortly afterwards he was imprisoned. He spent much of the next decade in jail, during which time he was ousted from the leadership of ZANU. In 1978 he participated in the internal settlement with Ian Smith and became a minister in the ensuing government which failed to gain recognition. For the 1980 elections he formed his own rump party, known as ZANU-Sithole, but won no seats. In the 1985 election the party managed to win one seat, but by then Sithole was living in exile, having left for the USA in 1983. Since then he is rumoured to have been behind several embryonic coup plots but nothing significant has come of this. In 1989 he declared that he might return to Zimbabwe to join the opposition to Mugabe but he did not do so. Although he was extremely important in the development of the nationalist movement in the 1960s, a major political comeback now looks unlikely.

422 Frederik van Zyl SLABBERT

South Africa

Slabbert has been one of the leading white opponents of apartheid and was the leader of the PFP from 1979 to 1986.

Born in 1940 in Pretoria, he was educated at the universities of Witwatersrand and Stellenbosch, gaining a doctorate at the latter in 1967. He held a number of academic posts at the universities of Stellenbosch, Cape Town and Witwatersrand, becoming a full professor and head of the Department of Sociology at the latter in 1973. In 1974 he was elected to parliament for the PP – later PFP – and became party leader and parliamentary leader of the official opposition in 1979. In 1986 he resigned, having decided that, at that time, parliamentary opposition to apartheid had a very limited value. He then established an organization called the IDASA to act as a forum and think-tank for peaceful opposition to apartheid. In the late 1980s he was influential in arranging meetings abroad between the ANC and leaders of the Afrikaner community, especially businessmen and academics. At the time this was regarded by the South African authorities as a dangerously subversive path to follow, but with the unbanning of the ANC in February 1990 it was seen as having prepared the ground for later dialogue. Slabbert is regarded as the most important white politician outside of the government.

423 Joe SLOVO

South Africa

Slovo is the general secretary of SACP and has for many years been the leading white figure in the ANC.

Born in Lithuania in 1926, he moved to South Africa with his parents in 1935. He qualified as a lawyer at the University of Witwatersrand and later specialized as a defence lawyer in political trials. He was an active member of the SACP from the 1940s and was one of the first arrested under the Suppression of Communism Act in 1950. In terms of the race question the SACP has a very progressive record of opposing apartheid. It has always had a multi-racial membership and has enjoyed a close relationship with the ANC with many individuals, including Slovo, being members of both organizations. Until very recently it was also among the most Stalinist of the world's communist parties. (It was not until late 1988 that Slovo admitted the horrendous excesses of the Stalin era.) Slovo rose to be an influential figure within the ANC and in 1963 he went into exile. He continued to work for the movement and became chief of staff of its military wing, Umkhonto we Sizwe (Spear of the Nation). He resigned from this position in 1988, when he became general secretary of the SACP, but retained his post on the ANC executive committee. Following the legalization of the ANC and the SACP in 1990, he returned to South Africa to participate in talks with the government as part of the ANC negotiating team. His wife, Ruth First, who was also a leading communist, was assassinated by a parcel bomb in 1982.

424 Ian Douglas SMITH

Zimbabwe

Smith was the prime minister of Rhodesia from 1964 to 1979 and led the settler rebellion against British colonial rule. He remained in politics after independence but has since faded from importance.

Born in 1919 in Selukwe, he was the son of Scottish immigrants. He served with the British RAF in the second world war and later graduated from Rhodes University in South Africa. He first entered the legislature in 1948, switching parties on several occasions in the 1950s. In 1962 he was a founder-member of the RF, which aimed at preserving minority rule in Rhodesia. In 1964 he became party leader and prime minister. The following year he announced UDI under which the settler community attempted to achieve independence with minority rule by the whites. This move never gained international recognition and led to the development of a guerrilla struggle against his government which was eventually successful. In 1978 he managed to patch up an internal settlement, which excluded the guerrilla leaders, with Bishop Muzorewa, but this also failed to gain recognition and in 1979 he was a major participant at the Lancaster House Conference in London which did produce a recognized settlement.

In the 1980 election his party, now renamed the Republican Front, won all 20 parliamentary seats reserved for whites. By the time of the 1985 election Smith's party, by now renamed the CAZ, had lost its monolithic white support but managed to win 15 of the reserved seats (reserved seats were abandoned in 1987). An increasing number of whites were now turning away from Smith's dated approach to politics and he was looking an anachronistic figure. In 1987 he resigned from politics and went back to farming. Retrospectively Smith's attempts to preserve minority rule can be seen as futile, but he did delay full independence by at least 15 years and also produced a civil war.

425   King SOBHUZA the Second

Swaziland

Sobhuza was King of Swaziland from independence in 1968 until his death in 1982.

Born in 1899 at almost the same time as his father Bhunu died, he was proclaimed king of the Swazi nation almost immediately, although his grandmother Gwamile acted as regent until his coronation in 1921. He was educated locally and in South Africa. He remained a very powerful figure throughout the colonial period, maintaining the traditional Swazi system but making subtle adaptions to reflect changing realities. Towards the end of the colonial period his position appeared to be threatened from a number of different directions. The British colonial forces made it clear that they wished to see a democratic parliamentary system replace the traditional monarchy at independence. European settlers in Swaziland wished to see a politically privileged position for themselves and there were also more modern African nationalist groups who resented . the power of the traditional monarchy. Exhibiting a very high level of political skill, Sobhuza outmanoeuvred all his opponents. Crucial in this was the creation of a political party, the INM, which acted as the political wing of the Swazi traditionalists and which generated overwhelming support amongst the Swazi people. In the pre-independence election the INM won all the seats in parliament. At independence in 1968,

Sobhuza was legally a constitutional monarch but in reality had almost total control of the political system.

In 1973 he scrapped the constitution and ruled by decree as an absolute monarch. Although a new constitution was introduced in 1978, it reflected the traditional power structure and did little to limit the power of the king. Under Sobhuza's rule Swaziland enjoyed a large measure of political stability and economic prosperity. At the time of his death in 1982 he was the longest-reigning monarch in the world, and the preservation of the traditional political system, more or less intact, was a unique achievement in black Africa. It is probably unlikely that any future monarch in Swaziland (including the current King Mswati) will ever enjoy the personal power and authority of Sobhuza.

426   Robert Mangaliso SOBUKWE

South Africa

Sobukwe was the founder and first president of PAC.

Born in 1924 in Graaff-Reinet, in the Cape, he was educated at mission schools before qualifying as a teacher. From 1952 to 1960 he taught African languages at the University of Witwatersrand. He was an active member of the ANC, where he was closely associated with its 'Africanist' wing which rejected alliances with whites in the struggle against apartheid. He became the editor of *The Africanist*, which was the newspaper of this group. In 1958 he left the ANC and the following year he founded the PAC, becoming its first president. In 1960 he was the organizer of the Sharpeville protest which led to the massacre of unarmed demonstrators by the police. Following this he was arrested. At his trial he refused to testify, arguing that he did not recognize the legal system of the apartheid state. He was jailed until 1969, when he was released but placed under a restriction order. He died of cancer in 1977.

427   Christophe SOGLO

Benin

Soglo was army chief of staff and led three coups, the last of which resulted in him becoming president from 1965 to 1967.

A Fon, born in Abomey in 1912 into a family of traditional rulers, Soglo joined the French army in 1931 and saw action on numerous occasions, including fighting for the allied forces in the second world war and in Indochina in the 1950s. In 1960 he returned home as army chief of staff and military advisor to President Maga. In 1963 he led a coup against Maga and replaced him with Apithy as president. In 1965 he led further coups in November and December and became president himself. He proved an inept government leader and increasing factionalism within the army led to a further coup and his ousting by Kouandete in 1967. He went into exile in France with his French wife, returning to Benin shortly before he died in 1984.

428   Ali SOILIH

Comoros

Soilih led the coup which ousted his predecessor, Ahmed Abdallah, in 1975 and became president of Comoros, before being overthrown in a counter-coup led by Abdallah in 1978.

Born in 1936, he trained as an agronomist in France before entering politics at home where he served in the pre-independence government as minister of public works. In August 1975, just one month after independence, he led a mercenary-backed coup which overthrew the government of Abdallah. He became minister of defence and of the interior before becoming president in 1976. His period of rule, guided by a bizarre mixture of Maoism, Islam and anarchism, included the dismantling of the civil service and the burning of government records and archives. Following several failed coup attempts, Soilih was overthrown by a mercenary-led coup in May 1978 which restored Abdallah to power. Many of the mercenaries involved in ousting him were the same ones who had brought him to power nearly three years earlier. Soilih was killed two weeks later while attempting to escape from detention.

429 Edward Moringe SOKOINE

Tanzania

Sokoine was a leading government figure who was prime minister at the time of his death in a car crash in 1984.

Born in 1938 in Monduli, he was educated locally and pursued local government studies abroad before working for the Masai District Council. He was first elected to parliament in 1965 and served in minor government posts. Following the 1970 election he joined the cabinet as minister of state in the vice-president's office and in 1972 was pro-moted to minister of defence. In 1978 he became prime minister, a position which he held until 1981 and to which he was restored in 1983. In March 1984, President Nyerere announced his decision to retire in the near future and Sokoine was widely regarded as the most likely successor. However the following month he was killed in a car crash.

430 Wole SOYINKA

Nigeria

Soyinka is a Nobel laureate and a major social critic of successive Nigerian governments.

Born in 1934 in Abeokuta into the Yoruba ethnic group, he graduated from both Ibadan and Leeds universities and has subsequently held a large number of distinguished academic posts at home and abroad. He has emerged as an internationally renowned writer of novels including *The Interpreters* (1964) and *Season of Anomy* (1973), plays including *The Lion and the Jewel* (1963) and *Death and the King's Horsemen* (1978) and poetry. He was awarded the Nobel prize for literature in 1986, the first black African to be honoured in this way. Although not a politician in the conventional sense of the term, he has had considerable political influence as a vocal critic of Nigeria's leaders since independence. He was jailed from 1967 to 1969 for public dissent. Following his release he published his prison memoirs, *The Man Died*. More recently he incurred death threats from the Muslim community for his public defence of Salman Rushdie's *The Satanic Verses*.

431 Siaka Probyn STEVENS

Sierra Leone

Stevens dominated the politics of Sierra Leone from 1968 until his retirement in 1985 and was one of Africa's most important and durable politicians.

Born in 1905 in Tolobu in the north of the country to a Christian Limba father and Muslim Gallinas mother, his later marriage to a woman of Temne/Susu origins enhanced his ability to act as an ethnic chameleon which was an important factor in his political career. He received his schooling in Freetown, which added a further dimension to his ethnic/regional persona. In 1923 he joined the colonial police force and served for seven years, rising to the rank of sergeant. After leaving the police he had a number of jobs including work as a clerk, a telephone operator and as station master on the Marampa–Pepel railway. From the late 1930s he was involved in trade union activities, becoming a full-time trade unionist in 1943 and then founding the United Mine Workers Union in 1945. In 1947 he spent a year at Ruskin College in England on a trade union scholarship.

The early 1950s marked the rise in influence of the people of the interior in a system which had previously been dominated by the coastal elites, and in 1951 Stevens was one of the founders, with the Margai brothers, of the SLPP. During the 1950s the SLPP emerged as the dominant party and gained an overall majority in the 1957 elections. Stevens was included in the pre-independence government, but later fell out with the SLPP leader, Milton Margai, and was dropped from the government.

In 1958 he left the SLPP and, with Albert Margai, founded the PNP, becoming its general secretary. In 1960 the PNP was allied with some minor parties to form the APC, which Stevens came to lead. At independence in 1961 Stevens became the leader of the opposition.

In the 1967 elections the APC defeated the SLPP but the military intervened to stop Stevens taking over the government and it was not until the following year, following further military intervention, that he became prime minister. In 1971, Sierra Leone became a republic, with Stevens as its first president. His long period in power was marked by political unrest, including further coup attempts, a growth of government corruption and serious economic decline, but Stevens was a master of the art of political survival. In spite of the difficult circumstances he did enjoy a level of popular support which earned him the affectionate nickname of 'Pa' amongst large sections of the population. In 1978 he moved to the creation of a single-party state, with the APC as the only legal party, in spite of previous support for a multi-party system, especially when he led the opposition. Although his rule was authoritarian it never degenerated into total repression and he preferred coopting opponents to eliminating them. During his later years in power he worked hard to build up his chosen successor, the army commander Joseph Momoh. In 1985 he retired from active politics to be replaced by Momoh. He wrote his autobiography, *What Life Has Taught Me*, which unfortunately gave little away concerning his time in office, although it did provide fascinating insights into his earlier career. Stevens died from natural causes in May 1988 and was given a state funeral, but his legacy to Sierra Leone was, at best, very mixed.

432   Helen SUZMAN

South Africa

Suzman was the leading parliamentary opponent of apartheid for over three decades until her retirement from political life in 1989.

Born in 1917 in Germiston, in the Transvaal, to Jewish immigrants from Lithuania, she was educated at the University of Witwatersrand and later became a lecturer in economic history there. In 1949 she joined the UP, which was then the major opposition party. She was elected to parliament for the UP in 1953. In 1959 the party split and its more progressive members, including Suzman, broke away to found the PP. In the 1961 general election she was the only PP candidate to win a seat and for the next 13 years she remained as the only representative of the party in parliament. During this time she was the only MP who consistently opposed the expansion of the oppressive legislation of the apartheid state. She later admitted that she came close to abandoning her lonely opposition role in parliamentary politics, but the party increased its representation in 1974 and by 1977, after changing its name to the PFP, it became the official opposition. In 1989 the PFP merged with other liberal parties to form the DP. Although Suzman remained a liberal she enjoyed excellent relations with many of the more radical black nationalist leaders who recognized her integrity and courage in the struggle against apartheid and the numerous practical ways in which she helped the victims of the system. She finally retired from parliament in 1989.

T

433 Oliver Reginald TAMBO

South Africa

Tambo is a veteran nationalist leader and has been the president of the ANC since 1967, living in exile.

Born in 1917 in Bizana, in Pondoland, into a peasant family, he was educated at Fore Hare University and later qualified as a lawyer. In 1944 he was a founder-member of the Youth League of the ANC. In 1952 he and Nelson Mandela opened the first black legal partnership in South Africa. He was subject to frequent arrest and, following the banning of the ANC, went into exile in 1960. He was elected president of the ANC in 1967. For 30 years he was the leading figure in the exiled ANC and did more than anyone to keep the apartheid issue alive in the world community. When Nelson Mandela was released in February 1990, Tambo retained the presidency of the movement, with Mandela becoming deputy president, in recognition of his decades of work in exile, although it was Mandela who was recognized as the senior spokesman. By the time of the legalization of the ANC in 1990, Tambo's ill health prevented him from taking a very active part in its activities.

434 Joseph Sarwuan TARKA

Nigeria

Tarka was an opposition party leader in the First Republic, a senior figure in Gowon's military regime and a major politician of the Second Republic.

Born in 1932 in Igbor, Benue State, into the Tiv ethnic group, he trained and worked as a teacher before entering politics. In 1955 he founded and led the UMBC, a party formed to support the interests of the minority ethnic groups of the central parts of the country. When elected to parliament he allied himself and his party with Awolowo's AG. He remained in opposition throughout the First Republic and was detained for a few months in 1962.

After Gowon came to power he became a member of the Federal Executive Council and served as commissioner for transport and for communications. In 1974 he was forced to resign following allegations of corruption. He went into private business and, when the ban on political parties was lifted in 1978, he joined the NPN, which was to become the ruling party of the Second Republic. In the 1979 election he won a senate seat. In 1980 he died of cancer.

435 Maawiya Ould Sid'Ahmed TAYA

Mauritania

Taya has been president of Mauritania since coming to power in a coup in 1984.

Born in 1943 in a remote village in the north of the country, he joined the army and served in the war in Western Sahara. Following the 1978 coup, in which he was a major participant, he was appointed minister of defence in the new military government. In 1979 he became commander of the national gendarmerie and, in 1980, army chief of staff. The following year he became prime minister and also regained the defence portfolio. In 1984 he led the coup against Haidalla and became chairman of the Military Committee for National Salvation, prime minister and president of the republic. He also retained the defence portfolio, thus uniting all the top positions of state in his own hands.

In 1986 he embarked on a partial liberalization of the political system by allowing competitive multi-party elections at the level of local government. Elections were held in the urban areas in 1986 and in the rural areas in 1989. Unrelated to this development there was an outbreak of communal violence between black and Moorish communities in 1987 and 1988 which Taya dealt with severely and not very even-handedly, purging many black soldiers from the army. In 1989 there was a serious deterioration in relations with neighbouring Senegal which resulted in mass deportations from both sides, accompanied by considerable violence. Again a racial element was present in the conflict and Taya's handling of racial issues appears very suspect. As a Moor himself he appears guilty of political favouritism.

436   Vroumsia TCHINAYE

Cameroon

Until his premature death, Tchinaye was one of the leading northern politicians in Cameroon and one of the most educated.

Born in 1932 he gained his doctorate in France before returning to work as an educationalist in Cameroon. He rapidly became principal of the Higher Teachers College in Yaounde. In 1964 he was appointed secretary of state for rural development and in 1965 secretary of state for finance. His first ministerial appointment came in 1970, when he gained the information portfolio, and in 1974 he became minister of public service. For many years he was a leading figure within the ruling UNC and was a member of its central committee. He died of natural causes in 1982.

437   Edgar Zivania TEKERE

Zimbabwe

Tekere was a leading figure in the government and in the ruling ZANU until he was sacked. He was the main opposition leader in the 1990 election.

Born in 1937 in Rusape, he was educated locally and became involved in nationalist politics on leaving school. He was a member of several groupings, including the NDP and ZAPU. In 1963 he was a founder-member and chairman of ZANU. From 1964 until 1974 he spent most of the time in political detention. On his release he became secretary-general of ZANU and was a major participant in the 1979 Lancaster House Conference, at which an independence settlement was agreed. In the first post-independence government in 1980 he was appointed minister of manpower planning and development.

Shortly afterwards he was acquitted on a murder charge but lost his government post. In 1982 he was demoted within the party but was appointed party leader in Manicaland. He became increasingly critical of the party and government, opposing proposals to create a single-party state and attacking corruption by government ministers. In 1988, following student riots in support of his criticisms of government, he was sacked from the party, just at the time when evidence of government corruption was coming to light. In April 1989 he launched a new opposition party, ZUM, promising clean government if elected. In the campaign for the March 1990 election ZUM was subjected to considerable government harassment but still won nearly 20 per cent of the votes cast, although only two seats. Tekere claimed considerable ballot rigging, but vowed to continue the fight for democracy in Zimbabwe. He remains a volatile and rather unpredictable political figure.

438   John Zenas Ungapake TEMBO

Malawi

Tembo has been a senior figure in the government and ruling MCP since independence.

Born in 1932 in Dedza into the Chewa ethnic group, he qualified and worked as a teacher before entering politics. He was first elected MP for Dedza in 1961. After independence in 1964 he became minister of finance, a post he held until 1969. He stayed loyal to Banda when many other cabinet members resigned or were dismissed in 1964. From 1969 to 1971 he was minister of trade and industry. In 1971 he was appointed governor of the Reserve Bank of Malawi, a position he held until 1984.

Tembo has always been a leading figure in the national executive committee of the MCP and in July 1987 became its treasurer. He is also the uncle of President Banda's influential 'hostess', Cecilia Kadzamira. He is widely viewed as one of the most powerful political figures in Malawi. Although President Banda has always refused to allow any discussion of a possible successor, Tembo is widely seen as the most likely candidate in the present ruling elite.

439   Eugene Ney TERRE BLANCHE

South Africa

Terre Blanche is the leader of the far-right AWB.

Born in 1941 in Ventersdorp, in the Transvaal, he joined the police after leaving school, but later became a farmer. Always on the far right of South African politics, he was an active member of the HNP, for which he stood as a parliamentary candidate. In 1973 he was the founding leader of the AWB, which is committed to retaining white Afrikaner dominance in South Africa by whatever means are believed necessary. The AWB is not a political party and does not put up candidates in elections, although it enjoys an overlapping membership with the CP. It projects a neo-Nazi image which is an accurate reflection of many of its policies. Terre Blanche is a powerful speaker and enjoys strong support amongst those whites who reject any changes in the apartheid system. He survived as leader of the AWB following a sex scandal in 1989, although a splinter group broke away in protest. Under his leadership the AWB presents a potentially violent obstacle to peaceful change in South Africa, although it is uncertain how many whites would be willing to take up arms to defend apartheid.

440   Jean-Pierre THYSTERE-TCHICAYA

Congo

Thystere-Tchicaya was, until the mid-1980s, the most important of the civilian politicians in a series of military Marxist governments.

Born in 1936 into the ruling family of the Loango kingdom of the Vili ethnic group, he received higher education in France before returning to the Congo and becoming a headmaster. In 1971 he was brought into the government and appointed minister of technical and higher education. A leading Marxist theorist, he became president of the central committee of the ruling PCT in 1974. He was a senior member of all the organs of party and state and by the time Sassou-Nguesso came to power in 1979 he had become the second most powerful man in the political system. His status as a civilian enabled him to stand above the murderous factional squabbling in the army. In 1983 he also became the president of the Congolese Commercial Bank.

Increasingly, however, his hardline ideological approach to politics caused a deterioration in his relationship with the more pragmatic President Sassou-Nguesso and in 1984 he was purged from the party. In 1986 he was imprisoned in connection with bomb explosions in the capital. In 1988 he was pardoned and released.

441   Togba Nah TIPOTEH

Liberia

Tipoteh was a leading opposition figure in the 1970s and a senior member of the government following the 1980 coup, before returning to an oppositional role.

Born in 1941 in Monrovia into the Kru ethnic group, he received higher education in the USA, where he gained a doctorate in economics. He returned home to work as a professor at the University of Liberia. In 1973 he was instrumental in the founding of MOJA, a radical opposition group which he has led ever since. The movement was harassed by the government throughout the 1970s, with frequent arrests of its leaders.

Following the 1980 coup he became minister of planning and economic affairs. Like all the radical intellectuals in the government he rapidly quarrelled with head of state Samuel Doe and in August 1981 he resigned from the government. He returned to the role of an opposition leader and in 1985 was jailed for a short time. Following his release he went into exile to continue opposition to the government through MOJA.

442   Reginald Stephen Garfield TODD

Zimbabwe

Todd was prime minister of Southern Rhodesia from 1953 to 1958 but later became one of the most outspoken critics of white minority rule.

Born in 1908 in New Zealand, he moved to Southern Rhodesia in 1934 to work as a missionary. He was elected to the legislature in 1946 as a member of the UP and in 1953 became prime minister. In 1958 he was ousted from the premiership when his cabinet resigned in protest at his leadership. During his time in office there were significant advances in black education. During the 1960s and 1970s he was one of the strongest white critics of the minority government and was arrested and imprisoned on several occasions. He also acted as an adviser to the nationalist leader Joshua Nkomo. At independence in 1980 he became a senator and he finally retired from politics in 1986.

443 Andimba (Herman) TOIVO JA TOIVO

Namibia

Toivo ja Toivo was a founder and leading member of SWAPO despite spending around 18 years in prison.

Born in 1924 in Omungundu in Ovamboland, he was educated at a mission school and served in the South African army during the second world war. He then worked on the South African gold mines until he was deported for political activities in 1957. In 1960 he was, with Sam Nujoma, a founder-member of SWAPO and became northern region secretary of the movement. Unlike other SWAPO leaders, he remained in the territory and he was arrested for nationalist activities in 1966. In 1968 he was sentenced to 20 years' imprisonment in the infamous Robben Island prison. He was eventually released in 1984 and was then elected secretary-general of SWAPO. When Namibia gained independence in March 1990, he became minister of mines, a vital post in this mineral-rich country.

444 William Richard TOLBERT

Liberia

Tolbert was the last of the TWP presidents of Liberia before he was executed following a coup in 1980.

Born in 1913 in Bensonville, Montserado County, into a wealthy Americo-Liberian family, he gained a degree at Liberia College before entering the civil service. Like all aspirant Americo-Liberian politicians he joined the TWP, which had been in power since 1877, and he was elected to parliament in 1943. In 1951 he became vice-president under William Tubman and served in this largely ceremonial role for 20 years.

In 1971, following the death of Tubman, he became the twentieth president of Liberia, a position to which he was re-elected in 1975. In power Tolbert sought to lessen the overwhelming dominance of his own Americo-Liberian elite by bringing more hinterland people into the government and bureaucracy, but his reforms in this matter were really too little and too late. With a deteriorating economy political opposition, which was both ideological and ethnic, became more pronounced as the 1970s wore on, culminating in massive anti-government riots in 1979. Tolbert's response to opposition fluctuated erratically between oppression and conciliation but neither approach proved effective.

In 1979, Liberia hosted the OAU summit and Tolbert was elected chairman of the organization, but government expenditure on the proceedings further weakened the economy. In April 1980 the government was toppled in a coup led by Samuel Doe and other low-ranking soldiers. Tolbert was killed by the rebels, along with many other members of his government, in scenes of horrific barbarity. The killing of the incumbent chairman of the OAU raised problems of international recognition by other African states for the new regime which took some time to overcome. In many ways Tolbert was unfortunate in being the final leader of a regime which, after over a century in power, was in the last stages of inevitable decline.

445   Ngartha (François) TOMBALBAYE

Chad

Tombalbaye was president of Chad from independence in 1960 until he was overthrown in a coup in 1975. His leadership was always coercive and authoritarian and in later years became increasingly idiosyncratic.

Born in southern Chad in 1918, he received secondary education in Brazzaville and then worked as a teacher before being sacked for political reasons by the French. He was involved in the trade union movement and was a founder-member of the PPT in 1946. He displayed considerable organizational ability and became one of the major PPT leaders. In 1957 he was elected to the territorial assembly and in 1959 took over the leadership of the party, which was by then the major party in the country. He became prime minister in the pre-independence government and president at independence in 1960.

In 1962 he banned all the opposition parties, forcing his opponents to rely on armed struggle to replace him. This rapidly developed into a civil war between the Tombalbaye government and a variety of guerrilla movements fighting for his overthrow. Initially he received military assistance from the French and then, in 1972, the Libyans became his main supplier of armed support.

During this period he lost not only the popular support he had once had in the country but also, more crucially, the backing of senior figures in his own army. In the early 1970s there were several coup attempts which resulted in the imprisonment of many senior officers. In 1973, in an attempt to shore up his position, he launched a cultural revolution. The ruling PPT was replaced by the MNRCS and a policy of 'authenticity' was announced. Some aspects of this, like the dropping of French personal and place names, were relatively uncontroversial but others were bitterly resented. All adult males were forced to undergo ritual initiation rites based on those of Tombalbaye's own Sara ethnic group. Those who refused, whether for religious or political reasons, were executed.

In March 1975, in a last desperate attempt to cling to power, the increasingly insecure Tombalbaye purged his army leadership and arrested most of its senior figures. One month later he was assassinated as the army staged a coup. Although no single individual can be held responsible for the political turmoil which has existed in Chad for most of the post-independence period, Tombalbaye's inept and brutal rule must be seen as a major contributory factor.

446 Josiah Magama TONGOGARA

Zimbabwe

Tongogara was the most important of the nationalist guerrilla leaders in the struggle against minority rule, but died in a car crash shortly before independence.

Born in 1940 in Shurugwi, he spent all of his adult life in the nationalist campaign. In 1963 he joined ZANU in exile and was sent for military training in China. On his return he worked in Tanzania and Mozambique and was responsible for the cooperation between Zimbabwean and Mozambican nationalist guerrillas, personally fighting alongside the latter. In 1972 he was appointed military commander of ZANLA, the military wing of ZANU, and became the main organizer of the guerrilla campaign. He was a major participant at the Lancaster House Conference in 1979 which drew up the independence agreement. He died on Boxing Day, 1979, in a car crash in Mozambique. His death gave rise to intense speculation that he had been murdered by rivals within the nationalist movement, but no proof ever emerged.

447 Ahmed Sekou TOURE

Guinea

Toure was the leading radical African nationalist leader in Francophone Africa and president of Guinea from independence in 1958 until his death in 1984.

Born in 1922 at Faranah into the Malinke ethnic group, he exhibited his radicalism early on when he was expelled from primary school for leading a strike. He later worked as a clerk in the colonial administration and became an active trade-unionist, leading a strike in 1945. In 1946 he became a full-time trade union official and the following year became secretary-general of the PDG, which he was to lead for the rest of his life. He was first elected to the territorial assembly in 1952.

During the 1950s he emerged as the most radical of the nationalist leaders in Francophone Africa. As a strong supporter of pan-Africanism he enjoyed poor relations with the more moderate and conservative leaders of most of the other Francophone states. He was a close friend and supporter of Kwame Nkrumah of Ghana and together they led the ultimately unsuccessful movement for African political unity at the time of independence. In 1958 he organized opposition in Guinea to de Gaulle's constitutional plans for Francophone Africa and led the country to immediate independence, with himself as president and the PDG as the sole legal party. Relations with France were marked by hostility in both directions and deteriorated even further when Guinea opted out of the Franc Zone in 1960, a move which asserted Guinean independence but had negative effects for the economy.

Throughout the more than quarter of a century he ruled Guinea, Toure's PDG regime was highly personalized, consistently authoritarian and frequently coercive. All opposition, real or imagined, was ruthlessly crushed. He has been accused of 'ruling by coup' as throughout the period there were numerous attempted coups, some of them genuine but many invented by the president. Each was met with a fresh round of purges, jailings and executions of opponents. Constant paranoia was a major feature of the regime. Any expression of mass discontent was violently crushed. The outstanding example of this came in 1977, when a demonstration in the capital, Conakry, by market women who had hitherto been Toure's most ardent supporters, was brutally repressed by the army. Dozens of women protestors were shot dead and several soldiers were executed for refusing to fire on unarmed female demonstrators. Toure survived through repression and the careful selection of political subordinates for positions of power. Personal loyalty to the president became the major criterion for political office and the regime was packed with his relatives and co-ethnics. This produced a highly corrupt and inefficient administration which harmed attempts at economic development.

In the late 1970s Toure embarked on a policy of reconciliation with France and other western powers. He abandoned much of his left-wing rhetoric and argued for cooperation with capitalism. This brought some liberalization of the Guinean economy but was not accompanied by any political liberalization in the domestic political system. In March 1984, Toure suffered a heart attack and was flown to the USA for medical treatment, but died a few days later. Almost immediately the Guinean military staged a coup which was joyfully welcomed by the people and the PDG era was brought to an end. The speed and ease with which this happened gives a clear indication of the extent to which the overthrown regime was dependent on Sekou Toure himself.

448   Ismael TOURE

Guinea

Toure was the half-brother of Sekou Toure and a senior figure in his regime.

Born in 1925 to the same father but a different mother from that of his more famous kinsman, he trained as an electrician before entering politics. He was first elected to the territorial assembly in 1956. After independence he served in his kinsman's government in a variety of senior positions, including minister of finance and minister of economic development. He was briefly dropped from the cabinet in 1979 but was soon rehabilitated. His long-term membership of the government was the most outstanding case of nepotism within the regime and he became one of its most widely detested members. Following the 1984 coup he was arrested and charged with murder, torture and massive corruption and was subsequently executed.

449   Diarra TRAORE

Guinea

Traore was a leader of the 1984 coup and became prime minister before leading a failed coup the following year.

Born into the Malinke ethnic group, he was an unknown army colonel until 1984. In that year he was the joint leader of the coup which brought Lansana Conte to power in April. Traore became prime minister in the CMRN military government. A flamboyant and eloquent man, he came to be seen by Conte as a threat and in December 1984 was demoted to minister of education. In July 1985 he led a coup attempt against his former partner but he overestimated his support in the army and the attempt failed. He was caught and sentenced to death. It was widely believed that he had been executed, but in December 1988 he was released from jail.

450   Moussa TRAORE

Mali

Traore has ruled Mali since he came to power in a coup in 1968, although there have been a number of attempts to oust him during this period.

Born in 1936 in the Kayes Region, he joined the French army and received training in the Fréjus Military College. He returned to Mali in 1960 and became an instructor at the military college at Kati. In November 1968 he led a coup against the government of Modibo Keita and became head of state. He established the Military Committee of National Liberation, with himself as its president. Many of the original members of the Committee have since attempted to stage coups against Traore, but none has been successful.

In 1974 he announced that a referendum would be held on a plan for a partial return to civilian rule. In June the new constitution, which allowed for a five-year transitional period, was approved. This constitution was opposed by many within the army and several abortive coup attempts followed. In 1976 Traore announced the formation of a new political party, the UDPM, which was to be the sole legally permitted party. Traore has been secretary-general of the party ever since. In June 1979 elections were held and Traore, as the only candidate, was elected president. In 1985 he was re-elected for a second term. Under the UDPM the military in reality remain in power, although the change has allowed some power sharing with civilians. The latter have been included in the cabinet, but the key posts have tended to remain in military hands, with Traore himself holding the defence portfolio.

Traore has been a pragmatic, non-ideological leader. The move back to a more free enterprise economy in the 1980s was due to the impossibility of sustaining inefficient state-run enterprises rather than ideological conversion. The Malian economy remains extremely weak and dependent on outside aid and with the virtual absence of natural resources this seems unlikely to change. Traore has given the Malian political system a level of stability and continuity it might not otherwise have had and has certainly shown himself to be a skilled political survivor.

451   Andries Petrus TREURNICHT

South Africa

Treurnicht has been the leader of the far-right CP since its formation in 1982 and was previously a member of the NP government.

Born in 1921 in Piketberg in the Cape, he was educated at Stellenbosch University and Stellenbosch Theological Seminary and became a minister in the Dutch Reformed Church. In 1960 he became the editor of the church's newspaper *Die Kerkbode* which he used as a vehicle for his conservative views. He first entered parliament in 1971, winning a by-election in Waterberg, and also became chairman of the quasi-secret Afrikaner society, the Broederbond. In 1976 he joined the government as deputy minister of Bantu Administration and was subsequently elevated to minister of public works and, in 1980, minister of state administration. In 1978 his position had been enormously strengthened by his election as NP leader in the Transvaal. His support for the retention of hard line apartheid began to bring him into conflict with the, then, very minimal reformist stance of the government and in 1982 he led a group of 17 NP MPs who broke away to form the CP. In the 1987 election the CP won 22 seats to become the official opposition and in 1989 it increased its parliamentary representation to 39, winning nearly one-third of the total (white) vote. Since then Treurnicht has led opposition to the reforms undertaken by the government, especially the release of Nelson Mandela and the unbanning of the ANC, calling on the NP to hold another election or a white referendum to test support for its policies. Whilst the actual extent of white support for Treurnicht's reactionary stance is unknown, it is certainly substantial especially amongst the Afrikaner community.

452   Etienne TSHISEKEDI Wa Mulumba

Zaire

Tshisekedi was a leading figure in the government during the early Mobutu period and is now the major opposition leader in Zaire.

Born in 1933 in Kasai into the Luba ethnic group, he was educated locally before going on to university in Belgium, where he obtained a doctorate in law. In

the early 1960s he was justice minister in the Katangese secessionist government of Moise Tshombe. In 1965 he became the minister of the interior in the first Mobutu cabinet and later served as minister of justice and of planning. He was also the first national secretary in the MPR, the political party created by Mobutu in 1967. By 1975 he had lost his government posts but was still re-elected to parliament in 1977. Over the next few years he became openly critical of the government and began to campaign for the restoration of a multi-party system. He was arrested in 1981 but was soon released. In 1982 he founded the UDSP, but was subjected to a series of arrests and detentions. In 1987 he went into exile in Belgium, returning home the following year following promises of safety from the government. After arriving home he organized a peaceful opposition demonstration but was shot and then confined to a mental home. In 1990 he was first transferred to house arrest and then released completely. In the light of promises by President Mobutu to permit a return to multi-party politics, it appeared that the UDSP would be the main opposition party under Tshisekedi's leadership.

453   Moise Kapenda TSHOMBE

Zaire

Tshombe was president of the secessionist Katanga Republic from 1960 to 1963 and prime minister of Zaire (then Congo Republic) from 1964 to 1965.

Born in 1919 in Musumba, in Katanga (now Shaba) Province, into the royal family of the Lunda ethnic group, he was the son of a wealthy businessman. Although he inherited his father's business he was more interested in politics and became involved with several Lunda groupings. In 1958 he brought together a number of these groupings to form CONAKAT. He strongly supported the idea of a loose confederal state at independence but lost out to Patrice Lumumba, who favoured a unitary state. In the pre-independence elections CONAKAT was the majority party in Katanga Province and Tshombe became provincial president. Shortly after independence he declared Katanga a separate state with himself as president, a move which had the support of Belgian business interests and the tacit support of the Belgian government. This action precipitated the civil war in the country and the involvement of UN peace-keeping forces. In January 1963, Tshombe abandoned Katangese secession and went into exile, although the war continued in several parts of the country.

In July 1964, President Kasavubu invited Tshombe back to lead the government and appointed him prime minister. In 1965 the two men quarrelled and the army leader, General Mobutu, seized power and ousted both. Tshombe again went into exile. In 1967 a plane in which he was travelling was hijacked to Algiers and he was placed under house arrest. Algeria refused to extradite him and he died there of a heart attack in 1969.

454 Kojo TSIKATA

Ghana

Tsikata has been a leading figure in the PNDC regime of Jerry Rawlings and is regarded by many as its 'strong man'.

A member of the Ewe ethnic group, he was a member of Nkrumah's Young Pioneers and was sent to train the emerging MPLA in 1963. A captain in the army, he emerged on the political scene in 1975, when he was involved in a failed coup attempt and was jailed. A close friend of Rawlings, he was closely involved in both of the latter's successful coups. After the 1981 coup he became head of state security and special adviser to the PNDC government. In 1982 he was implicated in the murder of three high court judges and many feared a cover-up when he was not charged. He was later appointed PNDC member responsible for foreign affairs, the equivalent of foreign minister. He is regarded by many as the most hardline member of the Rawlings regime and its most unpopular figure.

455 Philibert TSIRANANA

Madagascar

Tsiranana was the first president of Madagascar at independence in 1960, but was ousted by the military in 1972.

Born in 1912 in Ambarikorano into a poor peasant family, he did not begin his schooling until he was 12 but later qualified and worked as a teacher. He later obtained a teaching diploma in France. In 1956 he was elected to the French National Assembly and founded the SDP. At independence in 1960 the SDP was the dominant party and he became the country's first president.

Although he claimed adherence to socialist ideology, Tsiranana followed a fairly conservative style of government. In foreign affairs he was extremely hostile to communist states and established close links with South Africa whilst maintaining very harmonious links with France. He was re-elected president in 1965 and 1972. His latter victory, in which he claimed 99.9 per cent of the votes cast, sparked off large-scale anti-government riots and demonstrations and in May 1972 he was forced to hand over power to the army. In 1975 he was charged with complicity in the assassination of Ratsimandrava, but was acquitted. He died of a heart attack in 1978.

456   William Vacanarat Shadrach TUBMAN

Liberia

Tubman was president of Liberia from 1944 until his death in 1971.

Born in 1895 in Maryland County into the Americo-Liberian elite, he qualified and practised as a lawyer before entering politics with the TWP, which had been in power since 1877. In 1922 he was elected to the senate and remained a member until he resigned in 1930, following a scandal over forced labour. In 1937 he was appointed deputy president of the Supreme Court. In 1944 he was chosen as presidential candidate of the TWP, which guaranteed his election.

As president Tubman was the first to make serious attempts to reduce the total dominance of the Americo-Liberian elite by coopting some hinterland people into positions of power within the government and expanding educational provision in the rural areas. He introduced universal adult suffrage, but a property qualification still meant that a majority of those not belonging to his own elite ethnic group were still unable to vote. In 1951 he scrapped a constitutional law which had stipulated an eight-year maximum term for the presidency and thereafter was re-elected virtually without challenge. He kept a close control of all government business and it is believed that all government expenditure over 25 dollars had to be personally approved by the president.

Because Liberia had never belonged to the European colonial empire in Africa, Tubman was able to give considerable diplomatic support to the post-war nationalist movements in other African states. Liberia was a founder-member of the United Nations. Although Tubman was an outgoing and popular figure, the long-term dominance of the TWP regime was beginning to look weaker by the time of his death. When he died in 1971 he was succeeded by his son-in-law, William Tolbert.

457   Desmond Mpilo TUTU

South Africa

Tutu is the Anglican Archbishop of Cape Town and has been a leading figure in the anti-apartheid movement.

Born in 1931 in Klerksdorp, he originally qualified as a teacher and taught for three years before training as an Anglican priest. He was ordained as a priest in 1961 and rose rapidly within the Anglican clergy, becoming Dean of Johannesburg in 1975 and Bishop of Lesotho the following year. From 1978 until 1984 he was secretary-general of the South African Council of Churches. In 1985 he became Bishop of Johannesburg and in 1986 he was appointed Archbishop of Cape Town, making him the head of the Anglican church in South

Africa. Apart from his clerical duties, he has been a leading campaigner against apartheid and although he strenuously denies any personal political ambitions he has been a leading anti-government figure and has been subject to frequent police harassment. A strong supporter of non-violent change, he has frequently demonstrated great personal courage in intervening in violent situations to protect human lives. He was awarded the Nobel Peace Prize in 1984.

U

458 Ebitu UKIWE

Nigeria

Ukiwe was the second most important figure in the Babangida administration until he was sacked in 1986.

Born in 1940 in Abiriba, Imo State, he joined the Nigerian navy after leaving school and received officer training in Britain. He reached the rank of commodore and after the 1975 coup was appointed to the ruling SMC. In 1977 he became military governor of Niger State. Following the Buhari coup at the end of 1983, he was again appointed to the new SMC. After the ousting of Buhari in 1985 he became chief of general staff under Babangida and effectively the second most powerful figure in the regime. In October 1986 he was dismissed from this position.

459 Herbert USHEWOKUNZE

Zimbabwe

Ushewokunze has been a senior, but controversial, figure in the government for most of the post-independence period.

Born in 1934 in Marondera, he was educated locally and at the University of Natal, where he qualified as a medical doctor. He was a senior member of ZANU but not a major participant in the guerrilla war. At independence in 1980 he became minister of health and then minister of home affairs (1982–4). In 1984 he was appointed minister of transport and retained this position until he was dropped from the cabinet in 1988. In 1989 he was rehabilitated politically after leading the ZANU campaign in a by-election victory over the newly-formed ZUM of Edgar Tekere. After the 1990 general election he was appointed minister of energy, water resources and development. He remains an ambivalent figure, a wealthy businessman with a heavily criticized record of non-payment of his workers who also indulges frequently in revolutionary Marxist rhetoric.

V

460 Mamman Jiya VATSA

Nigeria

Vatsa was a senior figure in the Buhari and Babangida regimes before being executed for a failed coup attempt in 1986.

Born in 1944 in Vatsa, Plateau State, he was a classmate of Babangida in secondary school. He joined the army in 1962 and received officer training in India and England. He rose rapidly in the military hierarchy and by 1976 was commander of the Brigade of Guards. An unusual extra dimension to his character was that he was an accomplished poet and published several volumes of poetry, including *A Bird that Sings for Rain* (1976). He was a major participant in the internal coup which brought Babangida to power in 1985. He served as minister for the Federal Capital Territory in both the Buhari and Babangida regimes. In December 1985, just four months after helping Babangida into power, he launched a surprise coup against him. The attempt failed and Vatsa was executed in February 1986.

461 Hendrik Frensch VERWOERD

South Africa

Verwoerd was prime minister from 1958 to 1966 and was one of the chief architects of the apartheid system.

Born in 1901 in the Netherlands, he moved to South Africa as a child. Following education in South Africa, the Netherlands and Germany, he began an academic career at Stellenbosch University, becoming the head of its sociology department. In 1937 he became the editor of *Die Transvaler*, an Afrikaner nationalist newspaper which became well known for its pro-Nazi sympathies. After the war he stood as a National Party candidate in the 1948 election, but failed to secure election. He was appointed to the Senate, which he led until 1958, when he was elected to parliament. From 1950 he served as Minister of Bantu Affairs and was responsible for the construction of the apartheid system. Following the death of Johannes Strydom in 1958, Verwoerd became prime minister. As premier he continued to construct the apartheid system. In 1960 he banned the ANC and the following year he withdrew South Africa from the Commonwealth because of the organization's increasingly multiracial character. In 1962 he launched the Bantustan scheme, under which the African population were to be given 'independent' homelands and deprived of South African citizenship. This scheme was to remain the masterplan of apartheid for many years. In 1966 Verwoerd was assassinated on the floor of parliament by a deranged Afrikaner messenger.

462 Joao Bernardo (Nino) VIEIRA

Guinea–Bissau

Vieira has been president of Guinea-Bissau since he staged a coup in 1980.

Previously he was a major guerrilla leader in the war of liberation and prime minister in the post-independence government.

Born in Bissau in 1939, he was an electrician before joining the armed struggle against Portuguese colonial rule. He became a member of the PAIGC in 1960 and, after receiving political training in Conakry and military training in China, he rapidly advanced through the ranks of the movement, holding several senior positions. By 1970 he held full national responsibility for the military operations of the War Council and in 1971 he became secretary of the PAIGC permanent secretariat. Following independence in 1974 he became commander-in-chief of the armed forces and presided over the national assembly. In 1978 he was appointed prime minister. By the end of the decade he had become disenchanted with the failings of the leadership of President Luis Cabral and in November 1980 he led a coup to oust the latter.

Following the coup the national assembly was abolished and replaced by a new revolutionary council with a predominantly military membership. The PAIGC remained in existence with Vieira as its new leader. In 1984 a new constitution was introduced which created a new national assembly whose members were to be elected by the regional councils. The assembly itself elects a council of state which is the effective government. The PAIGC remains the only legal party and Vieira leads both the party and the council of state. His personal power is further consolidated by his retention of the post of commander-in-chief of the armed forces.

The Vieira regime began by adopting some liberal measures such as the release of political prisoners, but, following a major coup attempt in 1985, it has resorted to a highly authoritarian form of rule. Vieira has introduced some liberalization of the economy and to some extent replaced ideologists with technocrats within the bureaucracy. However, with the economy still depressed and a significant exiled opposition in existence, he does not appear totally secure.

463 Balthazar Johannes (John) VORSTER

South Africa

Vorster was prime minister from 1966 to 1978 and president from 1978 to 1979, when he was forced to retire following a major scandal.

Born in 1915 in Jamestown, in the Cape, into the family of a poor sheep farmer, he was a student at Stellenbosch University, where one of his lecturers was the later prime minister Hendrik Verwoerd and with whom he formed a close alliance. After graduation he worked as a lawyer. During the second world war Vorster was detained because of his violent pro-Nazi sympathies. After the war he was a keen member of the Broederbond, the right-wing Afrikaner secret society which enjoyed enormous political influence. He was first elected to parliament as a Nationalist Party MP in 1953 and served in several minor ministerial roles. In 1961 he was promoted to minister of justice and was responsible for the drafting of most of the harsh security legislation of this period, including detention without trial. When Verwoerd was assassinated in

1966, Vorster took over as prime minister. Whilst in office he pursued a more flexible foreign policy which sought to establish friendly relationships with any willing African states, but at home he continued with the harsh suppression of all opponents of apartheid. In 1978 he stood down as prime minister, citing ill health, and took over the (then) largely ceremonial presidency. The following year he was forced to resign, following revelations of his participation in the Information Scandal. The latter, also known as 'Muldergate' due to the participation of the head of the Department of Information, Connie Mulder, involved non-accountability to parliament, embezzlement and various other financial improprieties. Vorster died in 1983 in relative political obscurity.

W

464　Jaja Anucha WACHUKWU

Nigeria

Wachukwu was a senior political figure in both the First and Second Republics.

Born in 1918 in Mbawsi Ngwa, Imo State, he was educated locally before graduating in law at Dublin University. He was elected to parliament in 1952 and, at independence in 1960, became speaker of the Federal House of Representatives. Later that year he was appointed minister for economic development and in 1962 he became foreign minister. In 1965 he was demoted to minister for aviation. During the military period he had a successful career as a lawyer and businessman. With the lifting of the ban on political parties in 1978, he joined the NPP and in 1979 was elected to the senate, where he became NPP leader. The 1983 coup ended this phase of his career.

465　Abdoulaye WADE

Senegal

Wade is the major opposition party leader in contemporary Senegal.

Born in 1927 in Kebemer, he was educated locally before going on to higher education in France, where he gained a doctorate in law. He later worked as a lawyer and became dean of the Law Faculty at Dakar University. With the liberalization of the Senegalese political system in the mid-1970s, he formed the PDS in 1974. He remains its leader and the party has become the most important opposition party in the country, a fact that was clearly demonstrated in the presidential and parliamentary elections of 1978, 1983 and 1988. Most PDS support comes from the urban areas and from the Casamance region (where a violent separatist movement also exists). Wade was detained for a short time when rioting followed the 1988 election. He went to France for seven months but returned to Senegal in 1989. He is undoubtedly the most important Senegalese politician outside the governing party.

466　Munyua WAIYAKI

Kenya

Waiyaki was one of the better educated government leaders who held a number of senior positions before being eased out in the mid-1980s.

Born in 1932 at Kikuyu, he trained as a medical doctor in Scotland before returning to work in government service and private practice in Nairobi. He was chairman of the Nairobi branch of KANU from 1960 to 1968. From 1964 to 1966 he was assistant minister of health, but resigned from the cabinet over a policy dispute. He was deputy speaker from 1969 to 1974, when he rejoined the government as foreign minister, a post which gave him considerable scope for policy making, owing to President Kenyatta's lack of interest in foreign affairs. After Moi became president he was gradually downgraded, along with other powerful Kikuyu figures. He served as minister of energy (1979–81), minister of industry (1981–2) and minister of agriculture (1982–4) before being dropped from the cabinet.

467   Idris Abdul WAKIL

Tanzania

Wakil has been a leading figure in the government and is currently second vice-president and also the president of Zanzibar.

Born in 1925 in Zanzibar, most of his early career was spent in the diplomatic service. He served as ambassador to West Germany, the Netherlands and Guinea before being appointed chief of protocol in 1977. His major power base has always been in Zanzibar and when Ali Hassan Mwinyi vacated the Zanzibari presidency to become president of the republic, Wakil succeeded him as the president of Zanzibar and, automatically, second vice-president of the republic. In the presidential election Wakil received only 61 per cent of the votes cast, even though he was the only candidate. He is known to be very unpopular on the island of Pemba. In 1988 he claimed that a coup was being plotted against him and arrested several ministers in his government. In 1989 a further coup plot was discovered. His position appears to be less than totally secure.

468   Joseph Sinde WARIOBA

Tanzania

Warioba has been the first vice-president and prime minister since 1986.

Born in 1940 he qualified as a lawyer at the University of Dar-es-Salaam.

After graduation he worked for the government as a legal adviser. In 1983 he was appointed minister of justice and attorney-general. In 1986 he was appointed by the newly-elected president, Ali Hassan Mwinyi, as first vice-president and prime minister. His appointment to what is the second most powerful position in the regime came as a surprise, as at the time he was not an elected member of parliament, nor was he on the executive of the ruling party, Chama cha Mapinduzi (CCM – Party of the Revolution), although the latter has since been rectified. He is generally regarded as a technocrat rather than a grass roots politician.

469   Thomas WEH SYEN

Liberia

Weh Syen was a leading participant in the 1980 coup and became vice-head of state before being executed for his part in an attempted coup.

Born in 1952 in Pyne Town, Sinoe County, he received some local schooling before joining the army in 1969. By the time of the 1980 coup he had been promoted to the rank of sergeant, but following it he became a major-general. He was a leading figure in the coup. He became co-chairman of the ruling People's Redemption Council and vice-head of state, and was the most important figure in the regime after Samuel Doe. However he very soon clashed with Doe, partly over policy differences and partly because of a personal power struggle. In August 1981 he led a failed coup attempt and was executed after the most perfunctory of trials.

470 Joseph Edet Akinwale WEY

Nigeria

Wey was a leading figure in the civil war and in the military government of Gowon.

Born in 1918 in Calabar, he was educated locally before joining the merchant navy as a technical apprentice in 1939. In 1957 he transferred to the Nigerian navy and by 1964 he was its head. Following the July 1966 coup he was appointed to the ruling SMC. During the civil war the navy, under his leadership, played a vital role in blockading Biafran ports and cutting the rebels' route to the sea. In the post-war government he was commissioner for establishments and for labour. In 1973 he was appointed chief of staff, Supreme Headquarters. He was forcibly retired following the 1975 coup.

471 Edgar Cuthbert WHITEHEAD

Zimbabwe

Whitehead was prime minister of Southern Rhodesia from 1958 to 1962.

Born in 1905 in Germany of British parents, he moved to Southern Rhodesia in 1928 and worked in the civil service. He was first elected to the legislative assembly in 1939 but soon left to fight with the British army in the second world war, later becoming high commissioner to London. In 1953 he was appointed as representative of the CAF in the USA. When Garfield Todd was ousted as prime minister in 1958, Whitehead was recalled from the USA to take over the premiership. In 1961 he pushed through constitutional changes to allow for some African representation in parliament. The following year he was voted out of office by the more right wing RF, a move which eventually led to UDI in 1965. Whitehead died in 1971.

472 Oumar WONE

Senegal

Wone is an opposition party leader and was a presidential candidate in 1983.

Born in 1929 in Podor, in the north of the country, he received higher education in France, where he qualified as a medical doctor. He was the leader of the Senegalese students' organization in France and on his return to Senegal he joined the communist PAI. The party was subsequently banned and he was jailed for several months. He later abandoned Marxism and set up a private medical clinic in Diourbel, an Islamic religious centre. With the total lifting of the restrictions on party formation, he founded a new party, the PPS, in 1981 and has led it ever since. He stood in the 1983 presidential election but came a bad fourth. The party did not contest the 1988 election but it continues to exist. Wone must be regarded as marginal to the real struggle for power in Senegal and yet he is also typical of the leadership of the smaller parties which proliferate in the Senegalese political system.

473 Dennis John WORRALL

South Africa

Worrall is the co-leader of the liberal opposition DP. He was previously a leading figure within the ruling NP and

228

served as ambassador to the United Kingdom.

Born in 1935 in Benoni, he was educated at universities in South Africa and the USA, gaining a doctorate in political science. He then embarked on an academic career and held senior academic posts in South Africa, the USA and Nigeria. He was MP for Cape Town-Gardens from 1977 to 1983. In 1983 he embarked on a diplomatic career and was ambassador to Australia from 1983 to 1984 and ambassador to the United Kingdom from 1984 to 1987. In the latter position he was recognized as a leading international spokesman of the South African government, for whom he projected a reformist image. By 1987 he had ceased to believe in the accuracy of the image he was projecting and resigned to participate in opposition politics at home. In the 1987 election he stood as an independent candidate but lost by a few votes. In 1988 he launched the IP, but in 1989 he merged his party with the other liberal opposition parties to form the DP and became its co-leader. In the 1989 election the DP won 33 seats and one-fifth of the votes.

Y

474   Philippe YACE

Côte d'Ivoire (Ivory Coast)

Yace has been a senior member of the Ivoirian government and ruling party for most of the period since independence and is currently president of the economic and social council.

Born in 1920 into the small Alladian ethnic group, he worked as a teacher before entering politics. He was the first secretary-general of the RDA and one of the main leaders of the PDCI from early on, serving from 1966 to 1980 as secretary-general of the party. He was also president of the national assembly from 1960 to 1980.

Although he has been close to Houphouet-Boigny for most of the period, he has always been a powerful and personally ambitious politician, which has created disharmony in his relationship with the president from time to time. For the first half of the 1980s his career appeared to be in decline, but in 1986 he became president of the economic and social council, which is the third most important post in the political system. He is regarded as a potential candidate in the eventual succession to Houphouet-Boigny.

475   Maurice YAMEOGO

Burkina Faso

The first post-independence president of his country, Yameogo survived in office until 1966, when he was overthrown by a military coup.

He was born in 1921 in Koudougou, and after leaving his Catholic mission school entered the French colonial service. In 1946 he was elected to the Territorial Assembly. In the pre-independence governments of Ouezzin Coulibaly he served in several important positions, including minister of agriculture and minister of the interior. On the death of Coulibaly in 1958, Yameogo became leader of the government. At independence in 1960 he became the country's first president. His period in office was marked by political authoritarianism as he crushed opposition to his rule. Corruption and poor management by his government led to economic decline and when this was accompanied by Yameogo's ostentatious flaunting of his own personal wealth, including a hugely expensive marriage to a young beauty queen, his regime lost most of its support. The official results of the 1965 election, which gave him 99.98 per cent of the popular vote, were not widely believed. In early 1966 a general strike and riots in the capital weakened his position even further and he was deposed by the military, led by Sangoule Lamizana. He was later tried for corruption and sentenced to five years' hard labour, but was released in 1970.

Although he enjoyed some influence with future governments he remained largely a background figure. In 1987 he became the deputy chairman of the National Union of Burkinabe Elders, a largely honorific position.

476   Shehu Musa YAR'ADUA

Nigeria

Yar'adua was the second most important figure in the Obasanjo government from 1976 to 1979.

Born in 1943 in Katsina, he was educated locally before joining the army and receiving military training at Sandhurst in England. He became a brigade commander in 1969. In 1975 he was one of the major participants in the coup which overthrew the Gowon regime. Following the coup he was appointed commissioner for transport. After the abortive Dimka coup in February 1976, when Murtala Muhammed was assassinated, Yar'adua was rapidly promoted to chief of staff Supreme Headquarters and vice-chairman of the SMC. This dramatic promotion was vitally important in restoring the regional balance within the ruling military elite by bringing in a northerner following the replacement of Muhammed (a northerner) by Obasanjo (a southerner). The appointment of Yar'adua did much to placate northern interests. He retired from the army when civilian rule was reintroduced in 1979.

477   YELMA Deressa

Ethiopia

Yelma served in most of the top ministerial roles in the government of Haile Selassie, but was executed following the 1974 coup.

Born in 1907 into the Oromo royal family, he was educated in England and for many years was Ethiopia's only trained economist. Following the ousting of the Italians in 1941, he became minister of finance and subsequently held the portfolios for commerce (1949–53), foreign affairs (1958–60), finance again (1960–9) and commerce again (1969–74). From 1953 to 1958 he was ambassador to the United States and also published books on Oromo history. He was executed after the overthrow of Haile Selassie.

478   Joachim YHOMBI-OPANGO

Congo

Yhombi-Opango was a leading military politician and Congolese head of state from 1977 to 1979.

Born in 1939 in the Fort Rousset region, he joined the army in 1957 and received officer training in France. In the late 1960s he held several important diplomatic and military posts, including military attache in Moscow, commander of the paratroop battalion and head of the gendarmerie. In 1970 he became head of the armed forces general staff. He was a supporter of President Ngouabi and joined the PCT politburo in 1973; in 1977 he became the president of the PCT's military committee. In 1975 he was also director of public works. After the assassination of Ngouabi in 1977 he became head of state.

Although, as president of a Marxist state, he was prepared to pay lip-service to Marxism–Leninism in public, in private he boasted of his total lack of knowledge of, or interest in, the writings of Marx and Lenin. His style of rule was dictatorial and incompetent and opposition to him grew within the army. He survived a coup attempt in 1978 but in 1979 he was ousted by Sassou-

Nguesso. He was then expelled from the PCT and his property was confiscated. Following a period in detention he was released in 1984. In 1988 he was again detained after an abortive rebellion in the north of the country.

479   Fulbert YOULOU

Congo

Youlou was the first post-independence president of the Congo, but was overthrown in 1963.

Born in 1917 into a Lari family in Madingou, he entered a seminary at the age of 12. Although he interrupted his education with a period in teaching he was eventually ordained as a Roman Catholic priest in 1946. He was elected mayor of Brazzaville in 1956 and in the same year he founded a political party, the UDDIA. In 1957 he became minister of agriculture in the pre-independence government. In 1958 he negotiated a coalition deal with some of the minor parties and became prime minister. In the final pre-independence elections of June 1959, the UDDIA won an overall majority and Youlou became the first president of the country.

He advocated a union of the Francophone states of central Africa but received little support. At home his popularity decreased and economic failure resulted in massive anti-government riots in the capital. In August 1963 he was forced out of office by the army and was detained. In 1965 he escaped and went into exile in Spain, where he lived until his death in 1972.

Z

480   Mohamed El Moctar Ould ZAMEL

Mauritania

Zamel was one of the senior civilian politicians in a series of military governments from 1978 to 1984.

Born in 1946 in Toungad, Adrar, he was trained as a statistician in France. Returning home in 1972, he worked as director of the Central Census Bureau and as director of planning. In 1976 he was elected to the national assembly and following the coup of 1978 he was brought into the military government as minister of planning. In 1980 he was promoted to foreign minister. In 1981 he was demoted to minister of mines and energy (an economically important post) and in 1983 he was further demoted to minister of information. In 1984 he was dropped from the government following the Taya coup.

481   Saye ZERBO

Burkina Faso

A member of several military governments, Zerbo was head of state from 1980 to 1982.

Born in 1932, he joined the French army in 1950 and served in Algeria. Rising to the rank of captain, he was minister of foreign affairs in the government of Lamizana from 1974 to 1976, but was later ousted. In 1980 he led the coup which ousted Lamizana and established himself as head of state. He organized the Military Committee for the Enhancement of National Progress, but his regime was noted for its inefficiency and corruption. In November 1982 he was ousted in a coup led by Colonel Some Yoryan and was replaced as head of state by Commander Jean Baptiste Ouedraogo. In 1984 he was tried for corruption and sentenced to eight years in jail.

482   Emile Derlin ZINSOU

Benin

A prominent political leader in the colonial period, Zinsou served in several post-independence governments and was president from 1968 to 1969.

Born in 1918 in Ouidah Zinsou, he was educated mainly in Dakar, where he qualified as a medical doctor. He was one of the founders of the first political party, the UPD. From 1955 to 1959 he was an elected senator of the French Republic and also served as minister of commerce in the pre-independence government at home from 1958 to 1959. After independence he was president of the Supreme Court and ambassador to France. From 1962 to 1963 he served as foreign minister, losing his post after the 1963 coup. Between 1965 and 1967 he was again foreign minister until a further coup intervened. In 1968 the military installed him as president. In this position he proved a strong disciplinarian and attempted to introduce more efficiency in the bureaucracy and cut down on corruption. His policies made him many powerful enemies and he was ousted by a coup in December 1969.

Zinsou went into exile in France and in 1975 was sentenced to death *in absentia* for alleged complicity in a failed coup plot. Since then he has been a prominent member of the opposition in exile to President Kerekou and his name has been linked with several attempts to overthrow the latter. In 1990 all charges were dropped and, along with other political exiles, he returned to Benin to participate in the newly liberalized political system.

483   Alexander Grey ZULU

Zambia

Zulu has been a senior figure in the government since independence and is the secretary-general of the ruling UNIP.

Born in 1924 in Chipata, in Eastern Province, he was educated locally to secondary level and later worked with the colonial administration and as a manager with the Kabwe Cooperative Society. He joined the government at independence in 1964 as minister of commerce and also served briefly as minister of transport and of mines. In 1967 he was promoted to the home affairs portfolio and in 1970 to defence. From 1973 to 1979 he was secretary-general of UNIP. From 1979 to 1985 he was secretary of state for defence and security, before returning to his party role, which he still performs. He has thus alternated top positions within the government with the second most important position within the party. He is very much a loyal supporter of President Kaunda and a leading figure of the old guard of the party. When the president reluctantly agreed to a referendum in 1990 on the possible return to a multi-party state, Zulu was appointed to lead the campaign for a retention of the single-party state.

484   Eddison Jonas Mudadirwa ZVOBGO

Zimbabwe

Zvobgo has been a senior government figure for most of the post-independence period.

Born in 1935 in Masvingo, he was educated locally and at universities in Lesotho, the USA and England, where he qualified as a lawyer. He was a founder-member of ZANU in 1963 and became its deputy secretary-general until 1977. During the period of the guerrilla struggle he was mainly abroad and acted as ZANU's legal adviser. He was a major participant at the Lancaster House Conference of 1979 which produced the independence settlement. In 1980 he organized ZANU's election campaign and at independence joined the government as minister of local government. In 1982 he moved to become minister of legal and parliamentary affairs and in 1984 the justice portfolio was added to his duties. He retained this post until he was dismissed from the government in 1988, following personality clashes. When he was out of the government he acted as a critic of President Mugabe's proposals to establish a single-party state. Following the 1990 election he was brought back into the government in the less elevated post of minister of state for public service.

485   Ambrose Phesheya ZWANE

Swaziland

Zwane has been the leading opposition figure in Swaziland since independence in 1968.

Born in 1924 in Luhlokohla Ngqulwini, he was educated locally and in South Africa, where he became the first Swazi to qualify as a medical doctor. He worked in hospitals in South Africa and Swaziland. In 1960 he was the founder and leader of the SPP, but the party suffered internal splits and he went on to found the NNLC in 1962. The NNLC became the most important of the opposition parties, but in the pre-independence elections of 1967 it failed to win any seats despite gaining 20 per cent of the vote. In the 1972 elections the NNLC won three seats and Zwane entered parliament as leader of the opposition. In 1973, however, King Sobhuza scrapped the constitution and abolished all political parties. Zwane was arrested and detained for a time. During the 1970s he was detained several times before leaving for exile in Tanzania. In 1979 he returned to Swaziland after receiving a written guarantee from the king that he would not be politically harassed. Throughout the 1980s he worked as a doctor and continued what little political opposition was possible under the severe legal restrictions existing in the country. In 1989 he was once again arrested and detained on what appeared to be fabricated charges.

Chronology of Major Events Since 1960

Angola

(Independence 1975)

1961   Start of armed struggle against colonialism

1974   Coup in Portugal heralds the end of colonialism but liberation movements are seriously divided

1975   Intervention by Cuban and South African forces in civil war. MPLA government proclaimed in Luanda

1977   Attempted coup fails

1979   Death of President Neto and succession of Jose Eduardo Dos Santos

1988   Agreement on withdrawal of all foreign troops, but civil war continues

1990   Abandonment of Marxism–Leninism and introduction of multi-party system

Benin

(Independence 1960: called Dahomey until 1975)

1972   Coup installs Kerekou regime

1974   Declaration of Marxist–Leninist state

1989   Abandonment of Marxism–Leninism

1990   Re-introduction of multi-party system

Botswana

(Independence 1966: previously Bechuanaland)

1967   Discovery of diamonds at Orapa

1980   Death of President Seretse Khama followed by orderly succession of Quett Masire

1989   BDP wins sixth successive democratic electoral victory

Burkina Faso

(Independence 1960: called Upper Volta until 1984)

1966   First coup led by Sangoule Lamizana

1978   Restoration of democratic civilian rule

1980   Civilian rule overthrown in coup led by Saye Zerbo

1983   Thomas Sankara seizes power in coup

1987   Sankara murdered and replaced by Blaise Compaore

Burundi

(Independence 1962)

1966   First coup led by Michel Micombero

1972   Widespread massacre of Hutu civilians by Tutsi soldiers

1987   Coup led by Pierre Buyoya

1988   Renewed massacre of Hutu by Tutsi

Cameroon

(*Independence 1960*)

1961 Unification of British and French Cameroon
1982 Retirement of President Ahidjo and his replacement by Paul Biya
1983 Failed coup attempt
1988 Biya re-elected president as sole candidate
1991 Opposition parties legalized

Cape Verde

(*Independence 1975*)

1974 Coup in Portugal paves the way for independence
1981 Abandonment of previous plan to unify with Guinea-Bissau
1990 Introduction of multi-party system
1991 Victory for opposition in legislative and presidential elections

Central African Republic

(*Independence 1960: formerly Ubangi-Shari: called Central African Empire from 1976 to 1979*)

1966 Bokassa seizes power in coup
1977 Bokassa crowns himself emperor
1979 Bokassa overthrown in coup
1981 Attempted return to civilian rule overturned by coup after six months.

Chad

(*Independence 1960*)

1975 Overthrow of Tombalbaye regime in a coup

1978 Escalation of internal conflict into civil war, later including Libyan and French involvement
1988 Agreement of, largely successful, cease-fire in civil war
1990 Habre regime overthrown by coup

Comoros

(*Independence 1975: formerly Comoro Islands*)

1975 President Abdallah overthrown in coup led by Ali Soilih
1978 President Soilih overthrown in coup led by Abdallah
1989 President Abdallah overthrown in mercenary-led coup (many of the same mercenaries were involved in all three coups)

Congo

(*Independence 1960*)

1968 Coup led by Marien Ngouabi
1969 Proclamation of Marxist–Leninist 'people's republic'
1977 Assassination of Ngouabi
1979 Denis Sassou-Nguesso named as president
1991 Opposition parties legalized

Côte d'Ivoire

(*Independence 1960*)

1963 Coup plots uncovered
1969 Major student disturbances
1987 Announcement of moratorium on debt repayments
1990 Opening of multi-million pound basilica at Yamoussoukro provokes considerable criticism. Multi-party system reintroduced.

Ruling PDCI wins legislative and presidential elections

Djibouti

(Independence 1977: formerly Territory of the Afars and Issas)

1981   Creation of single-party state
1986   Hosting of talks between Ethiopia and Somalia
1987   President Gouled re-elected unopposed

Equatorial Guinea

(Independence 1968: formerly Spanish Guinea)

1969   President Macias Nguema seizes emergency powers and begins reign of terror
1979   Macias Nguema overthrown and killed by his nephew, Obiang Nguema, whose rule has proved equally dictatorial

Ethiopia

(Independent apart from Italian occupation from 1935–1941: formerly Abyssinia)

1974   Overthrow of Emperor Haile Selassie by military
1977   Violent power struggle within the military. Formation of Marxist–Leninist state. Start of war with Somalia and escalation of Eritrean liberation struggle.
1984   Major famine in many parts of the country
1989   President Mengistu announces partial abandonment of Marxism–Leninism

Gabon

(Independence 1960)

1967   El Hadj Omar Bongo becomes president
1968   Declaration of one-party state
1986   Bongo re-elected unopposed for fourth seven-year term
1990   Following serious unrest, Bongo agrees to re-establishment of multi-party system. Ruling party wins elections by a narrow margin

The Gambia

(Independence 1965)

1970   Introduction of republican constitution following referendum
1975   Launch of opposition NCP
1981   Failed coup attempt
1982   Establishment of Senegambian Confederation
1987   President Jawara's PPP wins victory in fifth consecutive democratic election
1989   Break-up of Senegambian Confederation

Ghana

(Independence 1957: formerly Gold Coast)

1966   Overthrow of President Nkrumah by military coup
1969   Re-establishment of civilian rule under Kofi Busia
1972   Overthrow of Busia regime in coup led by Ignatius Acheampong
1979   First coup by Jerry Rawlings, followed by return to civilian rule

1981   Second Rawlings coup returns
        him to power

Guinea

(Independence 1958)

1970   Invasion by Guinean exiles led
        by Portuguese fails to seize
        power
1977   Violent suppression by the gov-
        ernment of demonstration by
        market women
1984   Death of President Toure fol-
        lowed by military coup led by
        Lansana Conte

Guinea–Bissau

*(Independence 1974: formerly Portu-
guese Guinea)*

1973   Nationalist leader Amilcar
        Cabral assassinated
1974   Coup in Portugal paves the way
        for independence
1980   Coup led by Joao Vieira over-
        throws PAIGC regime
1985   Further coup attempt fails

Kenya

(Independence 1963)

1969   Assassination of Tom Mboya
1978   Death of Jomo Kenyatta. Daniel
        Arap Moi becomes president
1982   Failed coup attempt by air force
1990   Mass unrest and demands for
        multi-party system

Lesotho

*(Independence 1966: formerly
Basutoland)*

1970   President Jonathan retains power

        through a coup following elec-
        tion defeat
1974   Outbreak of anti-government
        violence
1986   Jonathan overthrown in a coup
        led by Justin Lekhanya

Liberia

*(Independent since establishment of
republic in 1847)*

1971   Death of President Tubman and
        succession of William Tolbert
1979   Major anti-government riots
1980   Military coup led by Samuel
        Doe
1985   Dubious multi-party elections
        won by Doe
1990   Outbreak of civil war and killing
        of Doe by rebels

Madagascar

*(Independence 1960: called Malagasy
Republic until 1975)*

1972   President Tsiranana hands over
        power to army leader, Gabriel
        Ramanantsoa
1975   Ramanantsoa hands over power
        to Richard Ratsimandrava, who
        is assassinated six days later.
        Gilles Andriamahazo becomes
        president but is replaced by
        Didier Ratsiraka four months
        later.
1986   Famine and anti-government ri-
        ots in the south of the island

Malawi

*(Independence 1964: formerly
Nyasaland)*

1964   Two months after independence,

President Banda sacks all the radical critics in the cabinet
1966 All opposition parties banned
1967 Invasion led by opponents of Banda is defeated. Malawi becomes the first black African state to establish diplomatic ties with South Africa

Mali

(Independence 1960: formerly French Sudan)

1968 Overthrow of regime of Modibo Keita in a coup led by Moussa Traore
1979 Traore elected to the presidency unopposed under new constitution
1987 Border clashes with Mauritania.

Mauritania

(Independence 1960)

1978 Overthrow of President Moktar Ould Daddah in the first of several coups
1979 Abandonment of claims to Spanish Sahara and ending of war with POLISARIO guerrillas
1986 Outbreak of communal violence between black and Moorish Mauritanians
1990 Border clashes with Senegal

Mauritius

(Independence 1968)

1971 State of emergency following dock strikes
1982 Opposition MMM win power in election
1983 MMM lose power in further

election. Aneerood Jugnauth becomes prime minister

Mozambique

(Independence 1975)

1974 Coup in Portugal paves the way for independence
1984 Signing of Nkomati Accord with South Africa
1986 Mysterious death of President Machel in plane crash
1989 Abandonment of Marxism–Leninism as state ideology. Start of peace talks with RENAMO guerrillas
1990 Multi-party system introduced

Namibia

(Independence 1990: formerly South West Africa)

1966 Start of guerrilla campaign by SWAPO against South African occupation
1978 Announcement by South Africa that it will arrange an internal settlement
1988 Agreement on withdrawal of foreign troops
1989 Pre-independence elections. SWAPO emerge as majority party
1990 Independence, with Sam Nujoma as president

Niger

(Independence 1960)

1974 Overthrow of regime of Hamani Diori in a coup led by Seyni Kountche
1987 Death of Kountche and succes-

sion of Ali Saibou, followed by release of political prisoners

Nigeria

(Independence 1960)

1966   First and second military coups in January and July
1967   Outbreak of civil war as Eastern Region declares independence as Biafra
1970   End of civil war as Biafra surrenders
1975   Gowon regime overthrown in coup led by Murtala Muhammed
1976   Muhammed assassinated in failed counter-coup and succeeded by Obasanjo
1979   Return to multi-party civilian rule. Election of Shehu Shagari as president
1983   Overthrow of Shagari and the end of the Second Republic through coup led by Muhammadu Buhari
1985   Ibrahim Babangida overthrows Buhari in further coup
1987   Announcement of further return to civilian rule in 1992
1990   Major failed coup attempt

Rwanda

(Independence 1962)

1963   Communal violence between Hutu and Tutsi
1973   Coup led by Juvenal Habyarimana overthrows government of Gregoire Kayibanda
1979   Habyarimana elected unopposed as president under new single-party constitution

1990   Invasion by anti-government soldiers

Sao Tome and Principe

(Independence 1975)

1974   Coup in Portugal paves the way for independence
1979   Population census provokes serious rioting
1986   Liberalization of economy introduced
1990   Multi-party system introduced
1991   Opposition win legislative elections

Senegal

(Independence 1960)

1962   Alleged coup attempt
1976   Three-party system introduced
1980   President Senghor retired and is replaced by Abdou Diouf
1981   Open multi-party system re-introduced
1987   Strike by police force
1988   President Diouf returned to power in open elections

Seychelles

(Independence 1976)

1977   Government of James Mancham overthrown in coup. Albert Rene becomes president
1979   Rene returned unopposed to the presidency in single-party elections
1981   Failed coup attempt by South African mercenaries

Sierra Leone

(Independence 1961)

1967   Coup following victory of opposition APC in election

1968   Counter-coup brings APC leader Siaka Stevens to power

1971   Further coup attempt fails

1978   All opposition parties banned

1985   President Stevens retires and is succeeded by Joseph Momoh

Somalia

(Independence 1960: formerly British and Italian Somalia)

1969   Siad Barre comes to power in coup

1975   Nationalization of land

1977   Start of Ogaden war with Ethiopia

1982   Part of army mutinies

1990   Outbreak of major anti-government unrest

1991   Siad Barre regime overthrown

South Africa

(Independence 1910)

1960   Sharpeville massacre followed by banning of ANC and PAC

1961   Withdrawal from Commonwealth and declaration of republic

1964   Nelson Mandela sentenced to life imprisonment

1966   Assassination of Prime Minister Verwoerd and succession of Vorster

1969   Right wing faction in NP breaks away to form HNP

1976   Mass violence of the Soweto riots

1978   P.W. Botha becomes prime minister

1982   Further right-wing break-away from NP with the formation of the CP

1983   Whites only referendum approves creation of Coloured and Asian parliaments and new executive presidency

1984   Signing of Nkomati Accord with Mozambique

1989   F.W. de Klerk replaces Botha as NP leader and president. Election gives NP reduced majority

1990   Release of Nelson Mandela and unbanning of ANC, PAC and other anti-apartheid groups. Opening of discussions between ANC and government.

1991   Government announcement of intention to scrap most apartheid legislation

Sudan

(Independence 1956)

1969   Numeiri seizes power in coup

1972   Addis Ababa Agreement brings temporary end to civil war between north and south

1983   Civil war resumes

1985   Numeiri overthrown in coup

1986   Multi-party elections produce government led by Sadiq al Mahdi

1989   Government overthrown in coup led by Omar al-Bashir

Swaziland

(Independence 1968)

1973   King Sobhuza scraps the constitution and assumes absolute power

1982 Death of King Sobhuza
1986 Coronation of King Mswati.

Tanzania

(*Formed in 1964 from unification of Tanganyika – independent 1961 – and Zanzibar – independent 1963*)

1964 Revolution in Zanzibar
1965 Introduction of single-party state with some electoral competition
1967 Arusha Declaration establishes leadership code
1977 New CCM party replaces TANU
1979 Tanzanian army invades Uganda to depose Amin regime
1985 Nyerere retires as president and is replaced by Ali Hassan Mwinyi

Togo

(*Independence 1960: formerly Togoland*)

1963 President Olympio overthrown in military coup which installs civilian government of Grunitzky
1967 Coup brings Gnassingbe Eyadema to power
1979 New constitution introduced. Eyadema elected unopposed to presidency

Uganda

(*Independence 1962*)

1966 Army storms the Kabaka's palace. Kabaka goes into exile
1971 Government of Milton Obote overthrown in coup led by Idi Amin
1972 Mass deportation of Asians
1979 Overthrow of Amin regime by Tanzanian army
1980 Obote returned to power in contested elections
1985 Obote overthrown in further coup
1986 Yoweri Museveni and the NRA come to power

Zaire

(*Independence 1960: current name adopted in 1971: formerly Belgian Congo, Congo–Kinshasha*)

1960 Secession of Katanga and outbreak of civil war
1963 End of civil war, although unrest continues
1965 Mobutu seizes power in coup
1967 Establishment of MPR party
1977 Invasion of Shaba Province by exiled opposition defeated
1974 Mobutuism established as national ideology
1990 Mobutu promises legalization of opposition parties

Zambia

(*Independence 1964: formerly Northern Rhodesia*)

1972 Declaration of single-party state
1986 Major urban riots follow withdrawal of food subsidies
1990 President Kaunda promises referendum on multi-party state in response to popular demands for a restoration of democracy. Later restores multi-party system without recourse to referendum

Zimbabwe

(Independence 1980: formerly Southern Rhodesia)

1965 Unilateral Declaration of Independence by white settler government

1966 Start of armed struggle by African nationalists

1972 Pearce Commission finds agreement between British and Rhodesian governments unacceptable to black population

1979 Internal settlement fails to gain international recognition. Lancaster House Agreement produces acceptable constitution

1980 Elections won by Robert Mugabe and ZANU. Independence with Mugabe as prime minister

1983 Crushing of dissidents in Matabeleland

1987 Agreement between Mugabe and Nkomo to unify their parties

1989 Major corruption scandal involving government ministers

1990 Mugabe wins election in the face of a challenge from new opposition party. Plan to introduce single-party state abandoned

Geographical Index